AF559652

INDUSTRIALISATION IN TRIBAL AREAS

INDUSTRIALISATION IN TRIBAL AREAS

(TRIBAL LIFE IN INDIA—4)

Edited by

DEVENDRA THAKUR
D. Litt.
Former Professor, L.N. Mishra College of Business Management
B.B.A. Bihar University, Muzaffarpur

and

D.N. THAKUR
Ph.D.

SECOND REPRINT EDITION

DEEP & DEEP PUBLICATIONS PVT. LTD.
F-159, Rajouri Garden, New Delhi - 110027

INDUSTRIALISATION IN TRIBAL AREAS
(Tribal Life in India—4)

First Published: 1994
Second Reprint Edition: 2009

ISBN 978-81-8450-107-0 (Vol. 4)
ISBN 978-81-8450-114-8 (Set)

Typeset by THE LASER PRINTERS, 8/15, 3rd Floor, Subhash Nagar, New Delhi-110027.

Printed in India at NEW ELEGANT PRINTERS, A-49/1, Phase I, Mayapuri, New Delhi-110064.

Published by DEEP & DEEP PUBLICATIONS PVT. LTD., F-159, Rajouri Garden, New Delhi-110027. Phones: 25435369, 25440916. E-mail: ddpbooks@yahoo.co.in • ddpubs@gmail.com
Sales Showroom: 2/13, Ansari Road, Daryaganj, New Delhi-110002
Phone/Fax: 23245122

Contents

Preface

Unknown from the fact that there are rich reserves of valuable minerals under their feet, the tribal people gathered food and wandered for hunting in the forests for centuries and centuries. Even after exploration of the fact, they had to lead their lives either as silent spectators or as unskilled labourers. In the name of industrialisation, they have only their cottage industries.

Though industrialisation in the tribal belts started in the pre-Independence age, it took a dynamic turn only in the post-Independent India when heavy industries like heavy engineering plants at Ranchi, iron and steel factories at Rourkela, Bhilai, Durgapur, etc. were established in the tribal areas. In course of time, now the tribal land which was free from environmental problems, is full of industrial garbage and smoke. In spite of that the tribal people get almost nothing as a return. They are still working as unskilled labourers and have not been freed from their age-long poverty and backwardness. Moreover, sometimes, they have to alienate not only from their land, but they have also to become homeless.

The present volume is intended to study the facts and figures of industrialisation in the tribal belt. It starts with the review of tribal economy in the context of industrialisation. It further deals with large, small and cottage industries established in the backward regions of the tribal people. In addition to these, it presents the study of industrial complexes in the tribal belts. Industrial planning in the tribal areas has also been a significant part of this work. Finally, the scope of modern industry has been the subject of our observation.

We would like to extend our regards to those scholars and friends from whom we received a lot of support and sympathy and our pleasure lies in application of our ideas to tribal welfare. So, if this work is of use for the socio-economic development of the down-trodden tribes, our purpose would be served.

Muzaffarpur

DEVENDRA THAKUR
D.N. THAKUR

Introduction: Industrialisation in Tribal Areas

BHUPINDER SINGH

It may be given to very few to wrest freedom from foreign masters; it is given to a chosen generation to undertake the task of consolidation and reconstruction of the country after it has been left in shambles by the conquering race. The present generation should count itself lucky that the task has fallen to its lot. But it thrusts a heavy responsibility. National reconstruction cannot be equated to mere economic development or increase in gross national product. In a polity which cherishes progress in a democratic framework, it implies a march in unison towards the goal of harmonious development in all fields. Describing the travails of a developing society, Mandelbaum (1981) states "... the processes of establishing rooted development usually take considerable time, often involve internal conflicts, and are best conducted according to some sequence of appropriate changes, social and cultural as well as economic." We have to discover for ourselves the path to development, a progression towards maturity, bearing in mind, however, that we are committed to growth being tempered with social justice.

Years ago when the Rourkela, Bhilai and Durgapur steel

plants had already come up in the tribal areas, the Heavy Engineering Corporation had got established in the Chota Nagpur plateau of Bihar and the Bokaro Steel Plant was in the offing, social analysts came across a revivalist movement among the tribals of the region born out of frustration. The cry was to go back to primeval ways of living. A large number of tribals started attending the Karma festival, the Akharas, the ceremonial dances and the Morma Mela (fair), and at one time nearly two lakh adivasis converged from all parts to pay homage to their deities. The discontent arose largely out of alienation of adivasi lands by legal as well as fraudulent means for the gigantic public and private sector undertakings, the uprooting being made harsher by delays in payment of compensation for lands acquired and absence of suitable avenues of investment.

The parameters of a policy for industrialisation of tribal areas were spelt out by the Dhebar Commission (1961) when they averred that while it would not be fair to expect the march of industrialisation to be halted, there would be a consequential obligation to the tribals to see that the process does not sweep them off their feet. In other words, industrialisation could proceed unabated, but the tribals should be enabled to build on their own moorings. The Commission recognised that industrial development has its impact on the individual, the family, society and on the entire environment with consequent psychological, social and economic consequences. They noted with regret that the problem had not been viewed comprehensively; this needed to be done. Commenting on the problem of rehabilitation consequent on displacement they observed that the major power and irrigation projects, steel projects of Rourkela, Durgapur and Bhilai had resulted in substantial displacement of tribal people. They found that on the basis of their enquiries, 14,561 tribal families had been displaced from an area of 62,494 acres and only 3479 families had been allotted alternative land. The cash compensation had hardly been utilised for production purposes being invariably used up on daily living expenses, alternative land offered for cultivation was not irrigable and could not fetch adequate return and very few of the families had taken advantage of the agriculture facilities offered in the reclamation camps.

Reporting on the social process in industrialisation of Rourkela based on the 1961 census B.K. Roy Burman (1968) stated that in addition to compensation for immovable property to displaced tribals, the Government had agreed to provide to each family facilities for living in resettlement colonies to be set-up within a radius of 8 km of the steel plant. He characterised the new social structure as "the outcome of a series of abortive social changes", the resultant system betraying "symptoms of cultural lethargy" since the old village, caste and community ties were continuing despite their having become dysfunctional; but these traits performed the important function of reducing the harmful effect of each in isolation and constituting a prop for the new structure.

The Study Team on Tribal Development Programmes, otherwise known as the Shilu Ao Team, were forthright in their report (1969) in saying that "The expectation that the industrialisation of tribal areas would help in improving the economic condition of the tribal communities has proved to be largely illusory. Major industrial projects like the mammoth steel plants located in tribal territory, far from providing employment opportunities to the tribals, have operated to their detriment by uprooting them from their hearths and homes and offering them no satisfactory alternative to the traditional methods by which they eked out a living in their old environment .... As cash compensation is squandered on drink and tribal rituals, destitution is the price the tribals have had to pay for the establishment of industries in the areas inhabited by them."

Analysing the details of tribal ethos and socio-economic systems in interaction with the new industrial systems, Sharma (1978) has stressed the inequality of the two, resulting in the disadvantage of the former following the superimposition of the latter. He has highlighted that in a tribal area, the community regulates social life by well-established codes of conduct and does not depend on outside intervenention for its preservation, that it has no formalised instiutions and that it is sustained on oral traditions. The production system is not built on surplusage or consumerism. Contrarily, the industrial society is highly specialised, the core industrial system behaving as a "closed" system, supported by ancillary functional services. Sociologically, the industrial society represents numerous regions, communities and skills drawn from differing socio-economic strata of the nation. As a result, an internalised value-system is the only guide of an individual or a group, since the constraints of the community and even of the family may not operate. Thus, the two systems suffer from a conspicuous absence of commonality. But since the modern industrial system is the stronger, the tribal communities and individuals begin to wither in the controntation which follows. Further, members of the tribal communities cannot supply the skill and talent required for the new industrial venture and this requirements is met by immigrants. The greater the differential between the two systems, the deeper will be the tribal recession accompanied by a correspondingly stronger tide of in-migration. Thus, the members of tribal communities become dispossessed of their lands and at least the first generation is driven to near-destitution. The second generation may enter the industrial system at the bottom of the hierarchy to begin with.

The Government of India in the Ministry of Home Affairs appointed a team in 1978 to review the levels of development of tribal areas, identify their special problems, suggest a suitable approach for development of industries and allied sectors and indicate broadly the level of investment necessary for bringing tribal areas to the level of other areas within a reasonable time-frame. The team observed that economic opportunities created by the establishment of industrial and mining complexes in tribal areas and the growth of large townships around them have bypassed the tribals as they did not have the necessary skills or enterprise to exploit these opportunities. The tribal hinterlands of the industrial and mining cities have become more backward and poor.

It is, thus, clear that there is almost a unanimity of opinion that though industrialisation might be synonymous with prosperity in other areas, in tribal areas the phenomenon has not been less than a disaster for the present. The hiatus in the overall development level of tribal communities and that of an industrial society is so large that the phenomenon has meant not only distortions in tribal life but even the experience has been traumatic. In the overall objectives of national policy and modern global currents, it is futile to believe that the tide of industrialisation can be stemmed; it is not desirable either. If the map of industrial and mining complex areas of the country is superimposed on a map of tribal concentration areas, the two will be found to be coincident. The plateaux and the highlands which have been the habitat of tribals are prone to be sucked into national industrial activity. Thus, a hoary agro-forest traditional culture has been and is being confronted with a modern sophisticated industrial culture, with deleterious results for tribals. But, since we cannot arrest the avalanche of industrialisation we can at least, soften the rigours of the new, alien climate. In this context, it will be worthwhile recalling the observations of some authorities.

From the comprehensive standpoint, the Dhebar Commission made the following recommendations:

(a) A permanent machinery for study of every individual project and its impact on tribal interest should be set-up. Besides following up proper rehabilitation of tribal families, the machinery should be responsible for integrated planning, right from the inception of the project. The scheme of rehabilitation should be an integral part of the project itself. The time lag between displacement and rehabilitation should be minimised.
(b) The schemes for rehabilitation should include programmes for education, training and equipment of the displaced people.
(c) Emphasis should be laid on technical education. High priority should be attached to absorption of the tribal people in permanent employment.
(d) The displaced families should be settled in avocations relating to primary needs of the township dwellers and factory workers like production of foodgrains, vegetable milk, eggs, meat and other requirements of the people.
(e) It should be the responsibility of the project authorities to provide water supply, sanitation provision for schools, medical relief, etc., in the colonies for tribes.

While supporting the recommendations of the Dhebar Commission, the Ao Team stressed that care should be taken in the selection of trades to turn out craftsmen for whose skill there is demand. Further training programmes should be so arranged as to harness the traditional skills of the tribals. The training courses be intensive to fetch returns. Steps should be taken in advance to open conventional educational schools in the area preferably of the 'ashram' type, to enable students to take advantage of technical training facilities.

The 1978 Team took stock of the matter again and recommended as follows:

(i) The entire tribal sub-plan area should be declared as backward area and capital subsidy as well as other incentives and concessions provided to industries for backward areas should be made available. In their view, the backward areas to enlarged will have to be categorised into two, one consisting of the non-tribal areas and some comparatively advanced tribal areas which may continue to have the existing level and pattern of subsidy, concessions, tax-rebate and other incentives, while the second category should include the bulk of the tribal areas for which a higher rate of subsidy, concessions, tax-rebate and incentives may be fixed.

(ii) The policy of licencing, control and incentives may be followed so that industries based on raw materials available in tribal areas are required to be located only there.

(iii) Maximum benefits to the local community should be given while establishing projects.

(iv) Steps for upgrading the skills of tribals should be undertaken through training of suitable young men and women, on on-the-job training of members of the local community and an intensive programme of general and technical education in the hinterlands of industrial complexes.

(v) Industries in tribal areas should be required to reserve for tribals a percentage of the total posts relative to the percentage of tribal population to the total population in the area.

(vi) In order to ensure that the local tribals are able to undertake trading and business activities, a programme of entrepreneurial training should be undertaken jointly by the industrial projects and the Government.

(vii) An intensive programme of general, technical and citizen education, in the hinterland is necessary in order to inculcate general awareness, develop a modern outlook and generally strengthen the local community so that they can effectively compete with the more advanced, enterprising and clever immigrants attracted to the tribal areas. The technical education should be directly related to the skills specifically required by the industries of the area.

(viii) Programmes of development of hinterlands should be planned and implemented jointly by the Government and the industries. The cost of development should be taken into account for all purposes except for deciding location.

(ix) Since large industries requiring heavy capital, high degree of technical capability and sophisticated modern technology would not allow benefits to reach the tribal communities notwithstanding advanced preparation, industrial development for them should concentrate on development of cottage industries, handicrafts, village industries and small-scale industries.

(x) Marketing support will be essential and should provide suitable linkages with the local economy of the area, instead of depending completely or even largely on national and international markets. A conscious policy of using local materials, artifacts and other produce of cottage industries for all requirements of the Government and public sector organisations located in the area should be followed. Marketing support may be given through State Handicrafts Corporations or Tribal Development Corporations.

(xi) Extension centres should take the initiative of identifying and contacting families of craftsmen, carrying the message. They should reach the identified target group, motivate and galvanise it into action in order to benefit them and improve their economic condition.

(xii) Over 3.79 million persons were said to be engaged in the pursuit of sericulture, of whom over one million persons or 30 per cent belong to the weaker sections of the society particularly the scheduled tribes and the scheduled castes. The *per capita* income of the tribal

> families, according to a survey conducted by the Central Tasar Research Station, Ranchi, is just around Rs. 200 per annum as a result of which they are prone to be indebted. More than 12.7 million tribals are said to be living in the tropical tasar belt of whom hardly 1.04 lakh tribal families are engaged in tasar rearing. A big tasar programme needs to be mounted.

In the view of Sharma (1978), the concept of planning needs to be comprehensive for the fast-industrialising tribal areas. A delicate compromise had to be evolved with the object of progress of the industrial project along with graduation of the tribal community through the transitional period. The traditional rights of the individual and the community over the resources in the area, the traditional method of managing social system and the traditional sanctions for dealing with defiants will have to be honoured and, wherever necessary, provided the support of the new legal system itself. The problem of rehabilitation of displaced families should be viewed in a moving time-dimension so that with the development and progress of the area, the displaced community becomes a co-sharer in its prosperity. One particular suggestion, i.e., a specified number of shares in the industry or dividends in favour of a local community should be a part of a long-term arrangement, deserves to be considered seriously. In regard to the hinterland communities, he proposes that a special organisation be established with the specific task of "protecting the weaker groups and taming the process of change in these areas." According to him, a comprehensive educational programme will be the most important input for harmonising the relationship between the tribal and the industrial world. The senior management and workers in the core sector should be re-oriented for a correct appraisal of the socio-economic situation in the tribal area. At the apex, there should be a meeting point for the top management and labour leaders from the industrial sector, the top leaders from the local communities and the people's representatives; this forum should be responsible for guiding the direction of change for the entire region. Besides engendering a new sense of participation in the hinterland communities, the core industry and the hinterland can then move together in unison.

The foregoing review amply demonstrates the concern which

is being felt over the state of affairs in industrialised and industrialising tribal areas as also the measures which are contemplated to be essential for minimising the hardships of tribal communities and their long-range participation in the industrial process. Broadly speaking, two steps stand out: (i) effective rehabilitation of the displaced families, the older generation in hinterland activities like farm, dairy, animal husbandry, cottage, village and small industries hitched to the new markets, and (ii) employment of the younger and the succeeding generations in the industrial enterprise. The broad concrete suggestions in this regard are as follows:

(a) No project report of an industry should be deemed complete without inclusion therein of consideration of the future of the local communities based on a study of all related aspects like the present socio-economic status, the cultural profile and the anthropology of prospective developments by inter-disciplinary teams composed of plant technologists, administrators, economists, sociologists, etc. The project reports should spell out, firstly, positive and negative repercussion flowing from the establishment of the industry on the local communities, secondly, steps required to be taken for their active involvement in the industry; and thirdly, steps for continuation of traditional avocations, culture, etc. of those members who stay in the hinterland.

(b) Land should be acquired or purchased from tribals only when strictly necessary. Allotment of suitable land in exchange should be the general rule. If payment of cash compensation becomes necessary, not only should it be paid timely, but efforts for its prudent investment should also be made.

(c) The ability to face the harsh forces of the modern industrial age has to be built into tribals through education of the young and the old alike.

(d) Skills should be imparted in advance to enable the trial communities to avail of industrial opportunities in the new establishment. If not the first generation, individuals belonging to the second generation might absorb the skills.

(e) Plans for the development of zones of influence of industrial and mining complexes should be prepared, the idea being that investment in these areas should develop a region rather than a small localised industrial or mining complex.

(f) Traditional tribal handicrafts and products of arts and crafts should be encouraged and markets found therefor. To the extent possible, the technology of the tribal artisan may be upgraded.

(g) A substantial programme of training in entrepreneurial skills, with follow-up in helping and getting financial support, marketing outlets and supply of raw materials should be built up.

(h) Forest-based cottage, village and small industries, e.g., honey extraction, lac culture, beedi leaves processing, oil extraction, tasar culture, tamarind conversion, wood-based industries, gums and resins, broomsticks manufacture, carpet-making, etc. have good scope. A long-term perspective for the development of all items with clear targets for the Sixth Plan period should be spelt out.

(i) The entire Scheduled Area, except the industrially advanced pockets, should be treated as industrially backward.

Committees have been constituted by some industrial ministries like the Ministry of Industrial Development, the Ministry of Heavy Industry, the Ministry of Steel and Mines to scrutinise various aspects relating to tribal affairs. It is hoped that these committees will go into the matter in depth. In this connection, the experience in regard to Malajkhand Copper Project in Madhya Pradesh has not been unsatisfactory. The Committee concerned had examined various aspects and given some directions: rehabilitation of the displaced families is being looked after and some tribals have also been able to secure employment. But, evidently the matters have to be taken much farther. It should be possible to work out satisfactory arrangements in respect of two massive prospective projects having tribal hinterlands, i.e., the Vishakhapatnam Steel Plant with the Andhra Agency Area behind it and the Alumina Complex in Orissa which is located in the

Koraput heartland of tribals. I have no doubt that adequate attention will be paid. The Ministry of Home Affairs have appointed in 1980 a committee of administrators, academicians and other experts to advise on the future lines of development in the Central Indian belt, particularly in and around industrial complexes with a view to minimising adverse effects on and maximising involvement of tribals in the process of industrialisation. Its recommendations are awaited with interest. Further, a regulation under the Fifth Schedule of the Constitution for safeguarding the interests of tribal labour, particularly from malpractices employed by contractors in Scheduled Areas where industries are located, has been drafted and it is under the consideration of the State Governments.

Today, the issue is not of "isolation" *versus* "assimilation" of tribals in the mainstream; it is of integration—integration of the various segments of the society to form a composite whole to contribute to, and profit from, progress and prosperity. During these 34 years of Independence, the nation has been subject to various jolts, some external, many internal. But, wisdom and foresight lie in the recognition of the undeveloped sections of the nation. If the nation's constiuent ethnic groups march forward step-in-step the advancement will not only be orderly but also enduring. If such an advance is marked by internal upheavals, setbacks will often slow down and weaken the progress. Wisdom, therefore, lies in reconciliation of the national and sub-national interests. This is the principle which might be kept in view in the formulation of policy and implementation of industrialisation of tribal areas.

The Draft Regulation

1. This regulation has been framed for regulating industrial and related activities in Scheduled Areas in the State with a view to safeguarding the interest of members of Scheduled Tribes.

2. The Regulation will be called for Scheduled Areas (Regulation of Industrial and Related Activities) Regulation, 1978. It shall be applicable to all tracts in the country declared Scheduled Areas under the Fifth Schedule of the Constitution. It shall come into force with effect from the date of its promulgation.

3. (i) 'Contract' in this Regulation means an act whereunder human labour is utilised in the furtherance of an

agreement entered into by an individual or association of individuals named 'contractors' and another body or authority or person.

(ii) 'Scheduled Areas' will have the same connotations as in the Constitution.

4. The project report of a proposed medium and big industrial scheme shall take the organic development of its hinterland into consideration in its formulation, and make adequate provision therefore; such area planning shall be a continual process and responsibility, therefore, shall rest on a body comprising representatives of the State Government, the local authority and the Management.

5. Before launching the project, steps necessary for ensuring the participation of local tribals in the undertaking by way of education, training, etc., shall be taken by the management with a view to their gradual absorption in the undertaking keeping pace with the phases of completion of the project.

6. Cooperative framework comprising predominantly members of Scheduled Tribes will be encouraged and utilised in the execution of various jobs, works, etc. The services of professional men like contractors will be restricted as far as possible.

7. Where there is difficulty in constituting or running cooperatives, as an alternative, preference will be given to the association of Scheduled Tribes organised by their headmen. Such work parties may be recognised for handling various works.

8. Such contractors as have to allowed to operate in these areas, shall be required to register themselves with the State Government and the District Magistrate before there they can be awarded any contract by the management of public sector or private sector undertakings. Contractors with an anti-social record or who are believed to indulge in anti-social activities shall not be given clearance for the purpose of securing tenders of jobs.

9. In the event of any dispute arising between a contractor and management in this behalf, the decision of the State Government shall be final.

10. In the event of any question of interpretation of this regulation arising, a reference will be made to the State Government.

REFERENCES

Government of India: *Report of Scheduled Areas and Scheduled Tribes Commission, 1960-61.*

Government of India, Planning Commission, New Delhi: *Report of the Study Team on Tribal Development Programmes Committee on Plan Projects, 1969.*

Registrar General of India, Ministry of Home Affairs: *Census of India, 1961,* Vol. I, Monograph No. I, Part XI E, Social Processes in the Industrialisation of Rourkela with reference to Displacement and Rehabilitation of Tribals and other Backward People, 1968.

Government of India, Ministry of Home Affairs: *Report on Industries and Allied Sectors in Tribal Areas, 1978.*

Government of India, Ministry of Home Affairs: *Report of the Working Group on Tribal Development during Sixth Plan, 1980-85,* October 1980.

Maydelbaum, David G.: "*Anthropology and the Challenges of Development,*" in Ideas and Trends in World Anthropology, Concept Publishing Company, New Delhi, 1981.

Roy, Burman B.K.: *Social Science and Contemporary Challenges,* Presidential Address at the Fourth Indian Social Sciences Congress, March 22-25, 1968.

Sharma, B.D.: *Tribal Development: The Concept and the Frame,* Prachi Prakashan, New Delhi, 1978.

Singh, D.N., Tribal Backlash Against Change, *The Statesmen,* November 22 1966.

Tribal Economy and Industrialisation

Economic System

The economic system and the social system in a tribal area and indistinguishable. The former is really an extension of the latter. The community heavily depends on the forces of nature which it propitiates by a variety of rites and rituals performed individually or in groups or by the community as a whole. Religion flowers spontaneously within their social and economic life and becomes an invisible thread fully integrating the whole system. The economic life of the individual, therefore, is not governed by concepts of utility and exchange, which are now commonplace in the modern society. The community is more like a big family in which each may contribute according to his capacity; even the devient may be tolerated and supported; communal enjoyment of the fruits of labour may finally settle all their mutual 'accounts'. The 'surplus' produce with an individual may have no meaning in terms of its 'storevalue'. It may be used for throwing a big feast just to gain prestige or for some other common purpose. There are limits, both lower and upper, to personal consumption and, therefore, the deprivation and affluence do not co-exist in this system. Labour has only two functions, viz., for production for own consumption or for helping some one else in need. Production itself has limited end-use—personal consumption or helping someone else who may be in need or social consumption. The property rights may not be recognised beyond the right to cultivate the land and right to collect the fruits. Since the community must manage its affairs as a group, individual rights are not permanent and continue to be re-adjusted in the context of emerging needs. Lending is more in the form of assistance for one who needs than an economic transaction.

Social Organisation

The community is governed by its own social code which is influenced by its level of economic development. The role and responsibilities of women in the economic life are substantially higher than in advanced communities. Growing in a tribal community is a social phenomenon; the child acquires the necessary skills as a member of the group rather than as a member of the family. Bringing up of child, therefore, is neither a special responsibility nor particularly a burden. The woman is an equal partner in the economic life and, in fact, contributes a bigger share of labour input. Consequently, she is more free than an average Indian woman; in particular she is free to take her own decisions regarding matrimony; marriage bonds can be broken with comparative case.

The community regulates the social life by well established codes of conduct and does not depend on outside intervention to keep itself going. Social ostracism is the ultimate penalty, the severity of which is hardly appreciated by those who are used to individualistic social systems where even family may not represent an essential unit of an individual's life. The less severe penal provisions are in the form of a feast to the community, or minor pecuniary compensation. In a non-mentioned economy, where an individual lives at the subsistence level and does not particularly care for the morrow, even small fines are heavy since the individual must produce surplus in cash to pay up the fine. In fact, this means a much harder labour on the part of the individual over a long period than what he is generally used to.

There are no formalised institutions. The tentacles of

administration and economic institutions, by and large, may not have reached these areas and even when they reach their significance is hardly appreciated. Although the tradition of lightly administering the tribal areas of the pre-Independence days is not formally continued, still there is a hang-over of this concept. It is only gradually that these areas are coming within the effective purview of modern formalised institutional system. The tribal community has no comprehension of the new formal system. It largely depends on the word of mouth and tradition which is so well known to the entire society. The legal frame, which is the source of all formal authority, is a great mystery to the tribal.

The New System and Its Dynamics

Let us now review the basic socio-economic structure of the new industrial complexes which are established in these areas. In the first instance, we will concentrate on typical core industry and only thereafter try to understand the formal and informal extensions of this system around the core.

Industry—A Formal Institutions Par Excellence

An industry comes into existence as a result of conscious decision of a group of people within a formal frame which may be defined by numerous laws, regulations and conventions. Whatever may be its form, each industry has a given objective of specific production portfolio and schedule. Therefore, its entire activity is organised with reference to achieving the production targets. Here one finds an extreme example of programming by the final objective. It must be recalled at this stage that the over-concern of the industrial system, particularly in the earlier part of its history, with higher production at minimum cost had resulted in severe adverse implication for the poor sections of the community who provided the required labour force. With the liberal concepts gaining ground, this practice became incongruous. Gradually extensive regulations were imposed on the industrial activity itself. These constraints in due course, came to be formalised either in the form of law or convention. The outstanding examples are the regulation of the labour relations, regulation of profits and regulation of standards of product. These constraints became necessary because the premise that economic actions of all individuals in the nation will get harmonised though the natural process of interaction between different groups and balancing forces does not hold good when some of the elements acquire greater strength because of their better organisation, or when some groups acquire greater manipulative power because of their strategic position. Social intervention, therefore, becomes necessary to bring about harmony and balance, at least to the first order of approximation which could be expected to have been otherwise achieved under normal conditions. Thus, briefly, industrial complexes are creatures of high level formal decisions. They are controlled and regulated by conventions, rules, and statutes formulated in the light of experience in the more advanced areas.

A formal institution, by definition, must have all its relations formal. Each of its activity is governed by well defined rules and, in an ideal situation, there is no place for non-formal relationships. These relationships finally are translated in terms of money-exchange equations. Thus, money becomes the invisible thread permeating the entire organisational system. It may not be necessary here to go into the basis of exchange equations which get established as a result of the interplay of complex forces operating at numerous points in the economy. In this system every thing must have money-value and, therefore, is defined as such. The source of authority is the 'rule', which is the final form of a long process of formal deliberations at numerous levels in the system. The rule, therefore, becomes sacrosanct since any change in it would involve again a long chain of formal deliberations. The system, so long as a rule stands, abides by it; but it also abides by another rule with equal vigour once the old rule is replaced by a new one even though the new rule may be completely different. This essentially represents the mechanistic approach of the system. This approach not only extends to material objects and formal systems but tends to be applied with equal tenacity, to human situations as well.

The above analysis on the industrial system may appear to be harsh and may represent the model in its extreme form. It is, however, necessary to understand the central argument around which the whole system is built up so that its numerous varieties and manifestations in different forms can be better understood. The above principles are central to the system itself around which the entire industrial world and its 'eco-system' moves. Unless there is a clear perception of this central theme, it will be difficult to understand the processes which are generated in the peripheris and in the hinterlands of industrial complexes.

Industrial Community—'Community' of a Sort

We may now examine the social, economic and institutional systems of the industrial community which is superimposed on a simple tribal scene when an industry is established in a backward tribal area.

The economy of the industrial society is highly specialised. Each individual is assigned a position with reference to his role in the system. The central industrial activity is supported by ancillary functional services both as an extension of the industrial activity itself and as supporting services to the community which provides the manpower to the central industry and its ancillaries. These may include small service establishments, shops, cinema houses, etc. The core industrial system generally behaves as a 'closed' system. It may draw its sustenance either from the immediate hinterland or from distant centres, 'market' being the guiding force in either case. In a more backward area, there is little linkage between the core industrial society and the tribal society in the hinterland, particularly in the earlier phases.

The industrial society is an amalgam of different groups and individuals drawn from a large area. The community is highly structured. In fact, the composition of different sections of the community at various levels in the hierarchy may be completely different. Higher the position in the socio-economic structure, bigger is the geographical areas of possible choice for selection. Thus, members of the top management core may be drawn from anywhere in the nation or even some foreign countries. As one reaches the lower levels, the geographical area of possible choice gets narrower. Normally the local community should have substantial representation in the lower echelons. But in the tribal regions, there is a shadow zone comprising its hinterland and surrounding area, which contributes little to the central society. Sometimes, linkage may appear to be established with the nearby villages. But it is more likely that contact points here may be provided by the migrant groups, which are not a part of the social system but are only physically located within the immediate hinterland.

Thus, the core society represents numerous regions, numerous communities, numerous skills drawn from various socio-economic strata throughout the nation. They may get organised in informal groups which may be based sometimes on professional background, sometimes of language and sometimes on caste or regional considerations. Each individual or group is far away from its parent society and, therefore, has little direct outside influence on his individual or group behaviour. In this context, internalized value system is the only guide of an individual or a group. In this amalgam, individual enjoys anonymity as a member of a crowd; and here his behaviour pattern can be anything. Since the core industry itself is organised exclusively around the goal of higher production, it provides a frame for their professional behaviour only. The informal social groupings may help in providing a peer reference frame to an individual. But it is voluntary and individual can afford to keep himself completely aloof from any of these informal constraints on his social behaviour. These small groups may also act unitedly for mutual protection. They may behave as a body whenever their common accepted code is violated by one of their own members or someone else. These groups, however, may be neutral with reference to the personal and social actions of an individual if it does not strictly concern the group itself.

In brief, the core industrial society gets organised around the principle of least interference in individual affairs, so long as his behaviour pattern does not affect a section of the core community itself. It has no common accepted social code and, therefore, it cannot provide a suitable frame for behavioural pattern of each individual. The individual is free from the immediate constraint of the community of his origin and, in many cases, even from constraints of his own family. His life gets fragmented between work and social-personal activities; he himself is the sole arbiter of right or wrong in relation to his personal behaviour.

The core industrial society brings with itself the entire institutional support of the modern world like police station, law courts, etc. In fact, in a way, the core society is like an outpost of the advanced social system in a backward region. Therefore, even if institutional support system may not be established in this area for some time the community can always draw upon the support of the institutions located in the advanced areas which have formal jurisdiction over this region as well. Thus, invisible threads of authority permeate the entire geographical space. The new society takes full advantage of its knowledge of these invisible sources of power to protect itself and to advance its interests. When an institution like a police station is actually established, it is presumed to subserve the central industrial society which may have demanded for its establishment. The central industrial society, thus, draws US Authority and strength from the national 'power-grid', defined by the multitude of laws implemented through the formulised administrative and institutional infrastructure.

Emergence of Dualistic Socio-economic Situation—Contact and Conflict

We may now compare and contrast the quality of interaction at different points between the central industrial society and the hinterland tribal community. In the economic sphere, the central society is a highly organised one. In a way, the hinterland tribal community has nothing much to offer. There is a functional gap between the core industrial activity and the hinterland economy. For example, the community in the hinterland may not be able to provide ordinary services or even offer agricultural and animal products required by the organised industrial society. This gap is gradually filled by the migrant communities which become a part of the central society. The industry itself begins its operations within the formal frame as may have been defined by its Articles of Association, Project Report, etc. It is a truism to say that formal system recognises only formal rights and formal obligations. Thus, the tribal community is, all of a sudden, faced with a structure which is not 'free' to negotiate. Since the formal frame has the general approval of the power structure, its blueprint begins to unfold itself with all its rigidity and ruthlessness. The tribal community is unaware of the new processes and, faced with a strong organised structure, finds itself helpless. There may be sporadic resistance, but the from of this resistence may not be within the accepted frame of the new law and can be easily brushed aside. The contradictions may come to the notice of higher decisions-making centres only when resistance turns violent or when some sensitive elements in the system itself, may be, a people's representative, a civil servant or a union leader, appreciate the inherent injustice in the new situation where the other side has not been given even a chance to be heard because they cannot speak.

Economic Deprivation

In this process, the community which enjoyed command over local resources by tradition, stands completely dispossessed. It may get nominal compensation for some land over which it may have had a formed right. In relation to the forest resources, there has always been a vast conceptual difference in so far as the tribal community considers itself as the master of what it sees whereas the State thinks otherwise. The new articulate groups begin to compete even for usufruct of the natural resources which may have been providing bulk of the subsistence to the tribal community. Thus, the migrant may begin to hunt in the hinterland with more powerful weapons; he may even prove better in this art. The new supplemental economic activities like vegetable, cultivation, dairying, etc., which are taken up by the secondary migrants, begin to compete for the grazing grounds around and even for more valuable land. The tribal may try to adjust for some time but may recede further into the recesses of forests abandoning everything and, thus, relinquishing even his actual command over the resources in the periphery. This 'vacuum' gradually gets field by secondary migration. The central industrial community begins to have a more 'satisfying' net-work of supporting services; its teething troubles which arise because initial 'unfavourable' conditions in the hinterland, are over; it witnesses with satisfaction the extension of its own system. The new development enhances the value of lands around. The core community begins to take advantage of the unearned increment arising from the new opportunity matrix. There is visible prosperity all round. The tribal community, which has been drawing its sustenance from this region, has finally withdrawn. The region presents a gratifying and beautiful picture with none to merit its scenic grandeur.

Exchange without Appreciation

In the long drawn conflict-situation discussed above, the tribal-migrant dichotomy may not be absolute. Some contact point may get established between the industrial society and the tribal communities. On the one hand, a few individual tribals may be drawn into the core industrial system for a variety of reasons. On the other hand, the well known spread effects may also begin to work. The first manifestation of these processes is exchange of fancy goods of the modern society with 'valuable' commodities of the traditional community. The new migrant goes about with covetous eye and surveys the scene assessing what can be taken to the best of his advantage. Thus, the valuable timber and the tribal lands may be purchased for a song; on the other hand, a fancy item like transistor radio may be sold for a fortune. Whatever small surplus, the tribal economy may have gradually exchanged for spurious urban commodities which may have only fancy value. These examples have been quite common in the history of civilisation when the advanced communities came in contact with the lesser developed communities; they need no elaboration. The same very process begins with greater finish in these areas when industries are set-up for the first time.

New Power of Money

The penetration of money economy without adequate preparation continues to weaken the tribal community and provides an upper hand to the industrial society. It is well known that the cost of living in the far off industrial centres is very 'high' and liberal compensation is provided to the members of the new community as a part of the Project design itself. If the same phenomenon is viewed from the side of the tribal community, it provides a completely different picture. Here is a small 'island', where money is pouring in. In the non-mentioned economy of the tribal money is a scarce commodity and has a high value; larger sums beyond a few scores of rupees are incomprehensible. The internal equations of social and economic relationships in the tribal communities are determined without any reference to money. Monetary sanctions are the biggest deterrents. In the new context, therefore, the modern man not only carries the vast authority of the System and the dazzle of higher consumption, he also enjoys the tremendous power of money which is very cheap in his system but is extremely costly in the tribal world. The new community, therefore, begins by alluring some, purchasing some others and deceiving the rest.

Taming of the Tribal

We may now examine the way the entire system begins to operate. The wage structure is very high in the central area. It has been designed to attract better skills from outside. In the initial stages, when the Project is in a hurry it can neither afford to wait till the tribal offers himself voluntarily to the discipline of the new activity or his skills can be upgraded, even marginally, to suit the conditions of the core economic activity. The easier course, therefore, is to manipulate the wage rate so as to attract persons from the more advanced areas. This migrant aristocracy of the core sector requires supporting services, some of which may be obtained from the advanced areas but a more preferable choice would be to recruit persons locally with reference to their (tribal's) money-equations. The complete disorder, which prevails just after the first confrontation when the tribal community is in the process of withdrawing, is one of the opportune moments where some of those who may have fallen behind can be 'trapped' into the new System. In the earlier stages, when money may not prove an effective instrument for this 'capture', the core may use the services of the articulate who know the local situation better. The petty contractors may use all devices to draw the tribal in. This may include devices like giving an impression to the tribal that this is what they have been desired to do by the 'Government'. To the simple tribal, any one with 'white clothes' is a representative of the State. They may even take advantage of his weakness for liquor by offering it as an allurement. In many cases, he may be initially offered some 'unwanted' things giving him an impression that he owes something to the contractor and, thus, giving rise to an obligation to work for him.

In these transaction, conditions are always most unfavourable to the tribal, which are so manipulated that he may never be able to get out of the obligation of one who employs him. This is how they see that the tribal is 'broken in' to satisfy the need-pattern of the new system. Gradually, the tribal begins to 'crawl' into the System at its bottom filling in the vacuum. The adjustment of a member of an equilitarian social system at almost the bottom of a highly structured society is most traumatic experience and needs some explanation. There is no doubt that it is a great psychological shock initially to many, who try to escape into their own world where they can breath freely. But other processes also begin to work. In many cases, the tribal has no option after losing his land and frittering away the money-compensation. Slowly, the differential in the money value, the aura of new structure and the glitter of his new possessions begin to provide him to a new value orientation which enables him face his own community with a sense of 'achievement and pride'. He fails to appreciate the implications of the new relationship. Thus, the wheel of history moves on mercilessly.

Disorganisation of the Tribal Community

We may now examine some of the important aspects of the new social dynamics in the area. The tribal community, as an organisation, is subjected to almost a fatal blow in the new process. Since the group is not even in a position to protect it's traditional terrain, the deep seated faith of the community in its own power to guard its rights is shaken. This psychological blow is devasting. The community has had the tradition of full control on the life and the behaviour of all its individual members; the deviant had no choice. Even if a rebel were to run away in defiance from his own community to another area, he could not but find himself amidst a similar group where be may he required similarly to repent and behave. The new industrial centre breaks up this closed system, opens up the area and provides an escape route to a defiant member. The tendency to disregard the traditional social organisation increases as the contact of its individual members with the industrial centre increases. Individual rights get asserted; differentials begin to grow; the prestige of the community leadership gets compromised as it encounters more situations where it is helpless before the stronger intruding culture. Within a short time, the disorganisation is complete and the articulate industrial centres has at its feet and entire community which can be treated in any way it likes.

Weakness of the 'Flesh'

We may look at one of the well known phenomenon constantly recurring in these areas, which is loosely, mischievously and with some amount of perversity, ascribed to human weakness and described as its universal manifestations. The tribal community, as earlier alluded, recognises a better right of the woman in contracting and dissolving marriage bonds. Marriage is a loose association between two individuals within the community. As the responsibility of child rearing in the community has not as yet devolved on the family, the socio-economic situation does not call for a strong to make the family an abiding unit for bringing up the next generation as is necessary for the middle classes in advanced areas. The group, however, has a strong community bound and there is inviolable taboo against any affâir outside its own limits; any violation may be meted out with most severe consequences. The advanced communities, which have drawn in their women-folk within the protective shell of the family, are unable to appreciate the different situation where the inviolable protective line, in the case of tribal communities, is drawn not around the family but around the big community. Therefore, they (non-tribals) are prone to describe with casualness the accepted norms of social behaviour within the tribal community about sex and marital relationship. When the tribal moves are viewed by them with reference to their own narrow family-oriented frame, which is different, they may feel free to behave as they like because they may think that their behaviour does not violate the moral code of the tribal community. They may further rationalise their behaviour by imaginary arguments having little validity in the tribal context.

The tribal woman is an equal partner in the family and is a bread-winner. In the tribal communities, she moves about freely like the gentle breeze without much restriction and ventures unwittingly into the industrial centre in mixed groups which, as already described, may be allured, purchased or cheated into the new System. She finds here a completely new world, where woman is not a bread-winner but a piece of decoration in the household. The glitter of numerous fancy goods begins to appeal to her faminine curiosity and possessiveness. There are allurements all round in this new 'hungry' world. A vague feeling begins to take possession of her inner-self. The alternatives of the two systems to a young girl, as an individual, become so very striking. Her position would get completely transformed from the 'drawer of water' to a damsel in the decore. The attraction becomes irresistible; allurements starting with petty gifts, which in money-equations cost nothing to the migrant but are coveted possessions to the uninitiate, may lead her to the bed-room of the new 'aristocracy' of the central core-labour, technician, petty official, trader or a *sahib*. Even offers of toffees, a washing soap, a powder-box may be sufficient to start the affair with an innocent adolescent girl. The girl used to a higher status, independent decision-making and economic freedom steps into the new System with misplaced self-confidence little realising that her community is incapable of providing the protective shield and she cannot claim the protection of the new System as she is merely an intruder and the woman is a 'weaker sex' in this world.

The articulate may see no harm or objection in this transaction and 'transformation' if it improves the condition of the woman. If she exchanges her wretched position in the traditional society by more comfortable life, there can be no protest whatsoever. This approach and argument would be irresistible if the entire scene could be viewed as an 'operational salvage' of members of a vanquished community where disorganisation is complete. But if it accepted that the situation needs a rational corrective, there can be no solace in the above model.

The underlying presumptions in this situation will need to be spelt out. In terms of the relationship between two groups, a situation seems to emerge in the early phases at least where the new system appears to have no use for the tribal male. He is an unskilled person who can aspire for a place only in the substratum of the new structure. The industrial core, however, can 'offer' something for the tribal woman. Can this preposition be accepted in terms of a planned group dynamics in a situation of fast change? The answer is obviously 'No'.

Let us look into some other factors in this entire chain of events. What has the tribal girl opted for ? Her world-view is that of her own society where if a man and woman are living together they are accepted as husband and wife, the formal marriage may be solemnised at any time even long after the couple begets children. There is no illegitimacy and the children are full members of the community. It may be recalled that the children are more a responsibility of the community than of the individual. In the industrial area, therefore, she falls into the new trap with a different perception about marital relationship, family responsibility etc., since she has no other experience to go by. The utmost she would like the young man to do is to give a feast to her community which, according to her perception, would be a final seal on her relationship; even her parents and the community may feel satisfied. But in the modern frame these rituals have no value. Therefore, she inadvertently accepts the position of a 'keep' who has no light. And her relationship may last only till she is able to charm the man. The children in the new setting are responsibility of the family, the implications of this situation are beyond her comprehension. The full realisation of her real position may come only when the man disappears and she finds herself on the streets of the new centre without any support whatsoever.

The traditional social organisation, which in itself is in disarray in the new situation, proves to be helpless, notwithstanding the fact that it could exercise some option if it so wished, by forcing a confrontation. The extreme penalty, which it could earlier inflict for violating his girl, is unfortunately not available to the group; in the new setting the traditional group action of revenge against the guilty is not recognised by the law-Stray instinctive retaliation against misbehaviour or criminal assault against their women may bring full wrath of the new system against him through manipulation of the normal processes of law by the more articulate who know the tricks of the trade; the community soon comes to realise that retaliation does not pay. But in this process, the group is left with no option, particularly when its own authority has been questioned. Certain face-saving compromises like payment of compensation, therefore, may be sought from both sides. Here the community falls into a trap. Even moderate economic sanctions were so severe within their traditional frame that they were effective deterrent against any deviation. The community is tempted to impose the same financial sanctions as an alternative even in the new situation. It has little realisation that once this is done, the honour of the community gets priced and can be exchanged for money which has little real value in the modern society. Once the protective wall of its inviolable custom and deterrent consequence is cracked, the honour of the community can be compromised for money. The 'conquest' is complete and the morale of the local community suddenly collapses. A situation comes, when the innocent ignorant individual may feel happy if he can get any thing for the new alliance which, on the face of it, is contracted 'freely'. And the articulate takes no time to raise an accusing finger towards the 'moral deprivity'; he gets reassured about the failings of the flesh and the rationality of the behaviour of his own kind. Inability to protect the honour by the sanctions which the community could have enforced, lack of protection from the new institutional frame, non-appreciation of the worthlessness of monetary sanctions in the new situation, the element of deceit in monetary compensations, the allurement into comfortable life without any lasting obligation and the utter helplessness of the system to protect itself result in a chaotic situation which is rationalised by the articulate by ascribing it to weakness of the man and generalising it with profoundness as a universal phenomenon.

The Final Stage

The wheel of history begins to move faster as the wheels of industry rotate with ever-increasing speed. Industrialisation represents a new philosophy of life in which all emotional and human bonds are squeezed out and the Human System emulates the Great Mother Machine in all its detail. The tribal society must jump quite a few stages in the process of social evolution to adapt itself to the ruthless logic of the Machine Age. In the final analysis, the entire human society appears to be inexorable moving in the same direction and must finally be engulfed by the System. The aberrations from the final formal mechanistic frame can be treated only as transient.

The ultimate fate of the human society with industrialism engulfing it is any body's guess. There may be a strong reaction against this regimenation. A new amalgam, however, is bound to appear. In the long-run, the differences between man and man may not be on the basis of region, language, caste and community. But there can be no consolation in this ultimate analysis, as the problems of tribal areas are essentially the problems of transition. It is true that any system will have a differential between the high and the low. Some groups may still be found occupying substratum in the most egalitarian systems. Perhaps, exploitation is inherent in any system, its forms may change—even new appreciation may present the same phenomenon in a different perspective. Perhaps the problem of 'high' and 'low' is inherent in a scheme of big organisation because bigness itself implies large differences, unless a big system comprises only micro-units, all of which are co-equals. It may be a Utopian dream in the new context, yet the tribal world is perhaps closest to the Model. But these small 'words' are being sucked by the gigantic new System.

The most undesirable aspect of the tribal scene in the above analysis is that with the meeting of two systems, at a crucial point of its history, the tribal system is forced to retreat and go down. The final outcome, in the immediate context, is not equitable. A desirable possible course of development would be where the two systems may be drawn into begin a new order and the position of their members in different strata of the society is determined according to some objective criteria and not because of a fortuitous situation in the history of one of the groups where it is unaware of the new processes and is caught unwittingly in the whirl of fast change.

In the early phases of new industrial system, as the things stand, the tribal society has no alternative but to withdraw or occupy a position in the substratum of the new system. The situation does improve gradually and, perhaps, will continue to improve with the passage of time. This time perspective, however, may be anything. The complexion of the industrial core itself may gradually change. The individuals, who are drawn into the system at the lowest rung in the beginning, may begin to appreciate the basic character of the new system and assert themselves in such forms and forums as are acceptable to the System. Some of the new educated persons from the hinterland may also be gradually drawn in at comparatively higher levels in the Core economy. The economy of the immediate hinterland continues to get diversified; although in this process the tribal may continue to withdraw deeper into the processes of back-woods. A stage soon reaches when there are no apparent contradictions in the immediate neighbourhood of the Core. The members of the tribal community, who are drawn into this system in the substratum, become gradually, indistinguishable from the urban poor and become a part of the dew economic phenomenon of 'Poverty'.

The story is repeated, with lesser severity, as the core industrial activity gradually expands. Small satellite settlements may get established deep into the hinterland. Here again the same process may begin all over again. But since the core activity in the new centres may be of smaller dimension and with the passage of time the local community acquires a comparatively better understanding, the conflict is not as a severe. It has, however, to be remembered that the pace of spread effect is extremely show in the more backward areas. The conditions may remain unchanged for a pretty long time even within a few miles of the core industry. Consequently, industrial development in the more backward areas may essentially mean super-imposition of the new system, displacement of the traditional economy, a lower position to the local community and a more severe struggle for existence at the subsistence level in the surrounding region.

Whither Planning?

The basic question, therefore, before us is whether fast industrial development in the primitive areas, which is forced on them on national considerations, can be tamed. There are limits to adaptation on both the sides. The industrial process has its own logic and some of its basic elements must be implemented! Similarly, the primitive economy cannot change over-night. Having recognised these two important constraints, it will be necessary to define the areas of adaptation which may help in ensuring that industrial development need not necessarily be at the cost of the local community. With the development in the area and growth of the industrial activity, the local communities should be in a position to take benefit of the new growth. One thing is clear—in view of the extremely unequal power structure of the two systems in these areas, the process of adjustment cannot be left to the operation of free social and economic forces. Indian planning does not recognise a state of *laissez-faire* economy. But the concept of planned economy in the tribal areas cannot be limited only to well recognised boundaries evolved for the advanced areas. For defining the special features in the concept of planning is necessary for these areas, we may recapitulate the process of development in the industrially developed regions and countries and contrast it with the situation in tribal areas.

Differential Adaptation

In the long history of industrial development, economic, social and legal institutions of now developed nation-states continually got adapted to the emerging needs of the new situation. Perhaps in all the three spheres, viz., economic, social and legal, there has always been some time-lag between the level of industrial development and the desired institutional structure. In the developing countries, on the other hand, the position appears to have been somewhat different. In some of these spheres, time-lag is similar to the one experienced in the advanced industrial societies. For example, the social institutions are slow to change and, therefore, they are adjusting themselves to the emerging needs with considerable time-lag. However, the formal structures of economic institutions and legal institutions are amenable to being changed by a conscious decision of the State. Therefore, in some cases, this could be done even in anticipation of the requirements of the industrial sector. Two important cases stand out in this regard and can be good illustrations. The labour laws, which have been adopted in the developing countries in very early stages of industrial growth, are comparable to those which were accepted by the Industrial Nations at a much later stage. The other example is that of technical skills. Training of personnel, particularly in relation to higher skills, has moved far ahead of the pace of industrial growth as a result of conscious state intervention. It is, thus, clear that the growth-paths of institutional structure in developing countries has been substantially different from that in advanced industrial nations.

The tribal areas represent a sub-system within the national economy. The preparedness of a sub-system with reference to the level of industrial development may not be the same as that of the system as a whole. Here the basic differences between the socio-economic structures of the tribal communities and other communities in the country come to the fore. The simple socio-economic situation of the tribal regions was largely left undisturbed because of the comparative isolation and the tradition of 'lighter' administration in these areas during the pre-independence days. Consequently, their economic, social and legal institutions are undifferentiated and tend to be a unique amalgam of different elements. In the advanced areas, the legal institutions, as distinct from economic and social institutions, have now a tradition of more than a century. Economic institutions, as distinct from social institutions, are also now well established. Therefore, adaptation of the general system to the industrial system can take place parts with different speeds. The change does not represent complete disruption for the entire system, though it has its painful imprint on the social institutional frame. Even in relation to social institutions, industrial establishments have only a limited role to play. The society is subjected to numerous other strains caused by forces of modernization. Therefore, there is greater resilience in the system. The advanced areas are able to absorb the shock of new forces of industrialisation because, basically, the same social system prevails in the industrial core and its periphery. The new industrial centre does represent a new mix of diverse elements. But, if the entire industrial macrocosm is viewed as an aggregate of the numerous micro-worlds, each one still may have a close link with the social system in the hinterland or in a larger comparable area. The industrial system does not bring about a qualitative change but the internal forces of these micro-units play an active role in its evolution. The economic, social and legal institutions in these areas evince a continuing process of adjustment with the new situation, although the degree of adjustment may vary.

As the internal social pressures and other economic forces in the national context, are expected to balance out with some time-lag only, the concept of planning in general with reference to establishment of industries is considerably circumscribed. It extends generally to influencing their location, regulating the working condition of labour and moderating their influence on environment and ecology. In exceptional cases, pricing, use of raw material etc., are also covered. It is presumed that if these aspects are taken care of through suitable regulations, the entire process will get balanced with the operation of numerous other forces and counter-forces at different points in the socio-economic structure in a region. The same presumption is implicit when this concept of general planning is extended to the tribal areas. It is clear that this presumption is not valid. Therefore, the very concept of planning for tribal areas will need to be extended much beyond the accepted norms for the advanced regions.

Implications of Planning

Our analysis in the preceding section shows that the economic, social and legal institutional structure of the tribal society is at the other extreme compared to the structural requirements of the industrial society. Here another important factor comes into play. The institutional frame of the tribal society does not enjoy the sanction of the law of the land except in a very limited sphere of personal law relating to marriage, inheritance, etc. The new confrontation, therefore, renders the traditional structure powerless. As it loses its life force, the new institutional frame begins to extent its tentacles in almost an 'empty' space, where individual members of the tribal society seek in vain the protection of their older system. They are sucked in or thrown out by the new system purely in terms of *their utility to the System.* It is this process which has to be tamed, humanised and converted into a force of good for the community around the Core. It is difficult task since the industry itself has its own logic. However, one important fact has to be clearly appreciated. Under the shadow of the central figure of Industrialism, a number of other interest-groups also acquire reflected aura of inevitability. If these forces are isolated and only basic logic is accepted, the task may not be difficult in the final analysis. There is another facet of the present situation. The spurious logic or inevitability is demoralising; it gives rise to a feeling of purposelessness even to the serious planning effort and element of fatalism enters even in what is described as the highest form of rationalism.

It is, thus, clear that the concept of planning will have to be comprehensive, particularly in those tribal regions which are witnessing fast industrialisation. No specific aspect can be left out of the ambit of directed change because the missing element may be crucial to the entire process, particularly because the tribal system continues to be a non-differentiated and unstructured amalgam of all life-elements. Therefore, the dimensions and the precise area of planning in these regions should be clearly defined which should mean bringing in—

(i) a longer time perspective;
(ii) a much larger geographical area than occupied by the core industrial activity;
(iii) a broader spectrum of economic activity irrespective of the fact whether it formally belongs to the core, organised or unorganised sector; and
(iv) inclusion within the ambit of planning all social, economic and legal institutional aspects of the tribal system directly affected by the new economic activity in the industrial core.

When the speak of a longer time perspective, the entire socio-economic dynamic of the region comes within the ambit of purposive planning and directed change. This is particularly so because here we will have to begin at a stage of development where even agricultural economy is not well-set. Therefore, the first task in this case would be to identify those 'weak' spots of the traditional system which make it vulnerable to the onslaught of the new system. In the context of fast social change, which these communities will be witnessing, mere outside assistance or even a protective wall will not serve as they may give way, sooner or later, to bigger forces engendered in the core sector. It is essential that the community itself is enabled to respond to new challenge. Mere protection makes a community weak; successful acceptance of a challenge enables it to face the growing challenges with a greater confidence making the process self-sustaining. It may be remembered here that even very small groups have been able to assert themselves against extremely high pressure under favourable circumstances.

The most important single reason for the weakness of the traditional institutional systems is their sudden irrelevance when they are pitched against systems having the support of law. It is precisely to meet such situations that certain provisions in the Fifth Schedule to the Constitution give extensive powers to the Executive to adapt the legal frame to suit the local situations in the scheduled areas. The traditional rights of the individual and the community over the resources in the area, the traditional method of managing the social system and the traditional sanctions for dealing with the defiants will need to be honoured and, wherever necessary, provided the support of the new legal system itself. It is not necessary to consider the tribal system as immutable but, with the same token, institutional frame of the advanced areas also need not be extended to these regions as it is. A delicate compromise should be evolved with the clear objective of enabling the community to graduate successfully through the transitional period without being put to undue disadvantage simply because it had been used to a different system and cannot adapt itself to the new system without going down in the process.

The above principles are generally accepted as principles, but it appears that other forces tend to prevail in actual working situations. It is, therefore, necessary that these principles are worked out in terms of concrete action-programmes for each specific situation. There is no short-cut to this detailed exercise. At this stage, however, some common elements, which appear to hold in all the tribal areas, could be brought out so as to provide suitable guidelines for preparation of detailed action programmes.

In the suggestions which follow, there are two parallel themes which have been clearly distinguished at each stage. The first element concerns itself with the 'softer' spots of the tribal socio-economic scene. Urgent protective measures needed to attend to these spots on a priority basis have been suggested. The second element comprises certain positive action programmes which will enable the community to become a partner in the new developmental processes.

(a) Directly-affected Groups

(i) Protective

In the first instance, we focus our attention on those groups which are directly affected by the establishment of an industry and its supporting services. It is essential that the rights over the resources, which these groups have been enjoying, formally or informally, are fully recognised. No narrow legalistic view should be taken in this regard; this fact should be specifically mentioned in the Project Report itself so that there are no formal objections subsequently. A direct corollary of this approach is that the loss to the displaced tribal community should not be computed purely in money-terms. The Project should take note of the fact that these are the communities which have been drawing their full sustenance from the area under their command which they will lose with the establishment of the industry. Consequently, full rehabilitation should be a part of the project itself for which adequate financial provision should be made.

(ii) Positive

The whole concept of compensation, which is purely in static terms, will also need to be reviewed in these areas. It is likely that the full rehabilitation suggested above may be worked out with reference to the 'economic' condition of the tribal when the actual displacement took place. This would be unfair since the 'economic' condition of the local community is not amenable to be computed in money-terms because their entire pattern of life is different. Such computations in terms 'our' money-equations will always put them at a very low position in the economic hierarchy of the new system. While the value of their erstwhile property soars in money terms, they are in no position either to foresee this change or to take advantage from it. Therefore, the entire problem of their rehabilitation, etc., should be viewed in a moving time-dimension so that with the development and progress of the area, the 'displaced' community becomes a co-sharer in its prosperity. In fact, this is a well-known phenomenon in the growing urban centres where original title holders prosper with development of the city because they are articulate and can ensure that they do not lose the formal title to the property. In the case of backward tribal areas, a specified number of shares in the Industry or dividends in favour of local community could be a part of the package of a long-term arrangement.

(b) Core and its Hinterland

(i) Protective

The problem of directly displaced persons in the tribal areas is extremely limited compared to the indirect influence of the industrial activity on other groups in the hinterland. Although second stage displacements and subsequent influences in the hinterland cannot be treated *at par* with the direct displacement, yet they will also need to be accorded an equally high priority. There is a qualitative difference between these two stages of displacement. Direct displacement is in accordance with certain principles, which are consciously enunciated and accepted. The administration which is expected to take care of all aspects of development, is usually a party to this arrangement. But indirect displacement is left, to varying degrees, unregulated and is generally subjected to market forces. In the context of unequal situation in these areas, these processes have to be more rigorously regulated.

The first step for providing a protective shield to this weak spot would be to create a counter force of equal strength in favour of local community. A special organisation should be established as soon as preliminaries are started for establishment of the core Industry with the specific task of protecting the weaker groups and taming the process of change in these areas. This Organisation may have the form of a Society or a Corporation. The regulation of secondary and tertiary displacements should be under its purview. The process of second stage displacements should also be viewed in its totality as has been suggested in relation to the primary displacement. There is already a parallel to this concept as well in the metropolitan development plans though with an important difference. In metropolitan places, the entire process is looked at from the side of the metropolitan centre. The displaced are expected to adjust themselves after due compensation has been paid. In the tribal areas this concept should get completely reversed. The Organization should take care of the people while other processes should adjust themselves to the emerging needs.

(ii) Positive

This hinterland-development organisation should also have an important positive role. It should be charged with the responsibility of taking advance action with reference to the secondary and tertiary activities in the region. It should retain the local population, as far as possible, with a view to help them to adapt to the emerging needs. It should ensure that the primary, secondary and tertiary sectors in the core and hinterland do not develop as isolates but adequate linkages are established by them with the local community.

(c) Educational Perspective

(i) Protective

One of the basic weaknesses of the new situation is the non-communication at various levels between the two Systems. Therefore, a comprehensive educational programme will be the most important input for harmonising the relationship between the industrial and the tribal world. It will be necessary to evolve suitable programmes of formal and non-formal education and orientation programmes addressed to different groups in the area. The first element in this package should aim at enabling the simple tribal to understand and appreciate the role of the administrative system and the method to approach it, whenever necessary. A well-organised comprehensive citizen education programme may become a crucial element in providing the protective shield to the local community.

(ii) Positive

On the positive side, the educational package should comprise four elements:

(a) A programme for reorienting the senior management and the workers in the core sector and give them correct appraisal of the socio-economic situation in the tribal area;
(b) A comprehensive programme of formal education to prepare the next generation for the new tasks in the area;
(c) A programme of non-formal education to bring within the fold of education the tribal youth who may have missed the early opportunity and enable them to join the formal educational stream at advanced points; and
(d) To restructure the formal educational system itself keeping in view the requirements of the core sector and the task of enabling the local community to join the industrial society at various levels depending on their academic and professional attainment.

Restoration of the Social Balance

The source of authority of the traditional social system is its effective control of the affairs of the community and its power to deal with the deviant. In the new context, this may be termed as the sphere of informal authority. Sometimes, in some areas a formal base, like reorganising the tribal *panchayats*, is provided. But even when the system is formalised, the local communities are not generally trusted to adjudicate on matters in which one of the parties may be a non-tribal. This is a hang-over of the colonial tradition and has a close parallel in early attempts of the British not to subject the British citizen to the jurisdiction of Indian courts. There is no reason why the traditional social organisations, which have been regulating their own community life, cannot be trusted with affairs even when a non-tribal may be involved. Their strong sense of justice and tradition of frank and free discussion are guarantee against any partisan approach. In all fairness, the local community should have the same jurisdiction over the migrants operating and residing within their jurisdiction as they may have on the members of the tribal communities. This will give the community a sense of self-confidence in its capacity to manage the affairs of the area. This will also oblige the migrants to understand the local tradition and honour it. Thus, it will help in stimulating the process of integration. The traditional system, whenever necessary, should be brought within the ambit of law. Care, however, must be taken that it is not so much formalised that the community itself may not be able to operate it.

Traditional social organizations generally function in face-to-face situations and their jurisdiction extends to small community-groups in small geographical regions. In this context, the industrial core emerges as a big force and these small traditions, unaware even of the dimension of this force, cannot stand before its pressure. In the more backward areas, spontaneous social or community action cannot be expected because of lack of communication and non-appreciation of the position of the other side. The spontaneous retaliations in extreme situations are exceptions which have generally a very short-term impact. It is, therefore, necessary that the community is helped to appreciate the problems of the core and its hinterland in a broader context. A larger forum may be organised at the regional level comprising the leaders of smaller groups. More important problems could be remitted to this body. They could also consider problems which may have far-reaching consequences for the community as a whole and provide a direction to the smaller constituent unit for regulating their relationships with the core sector. The establishment of such an organisation will help in generating a countervailing force within the local community of dimension comparable to those in the modern sector.

One of the weakest spots in the new social situation is the position of women and the allurement of money and modern comforts. This weak spot will need to be covered by suitable legal and social actions. For example, employment of girls, as domestic servants and otherwise than in a group, could be prohibited by law both in the organised and non-organised sectors. The community itself could be better educated about this aspect of their new contact. They could be induced to exert social pressure so that the tendency to send out girls for employment in the core sector otherwise than in a group is checked. Special regulations could be made for the conduct of the employees in the organised and non-organised sectors in this regard. The matters relating to misdemeanour or undesirable treatment meted out to the tribal women should be within the exclusive jurisdiction of the traditional social organisations and a special procedure should be evolved for dealing with them. Once a deviant is liable to be brought before the traditional council, the present situation of irresponsible individualism will cease to exit.

Influencing the Industrial Process

We have referred to earlier that the industrial process has its own logic which has to be honoured. Yet we have seen that what generally goes by this logic is not immutable. It will, therefore, be necessary to isolate these areas which can be influenced, harmonising the central needs of the industrial process and the development and welfare of the tribal communities. The first step in this direction should be to induct tribal leaders at different levels in the industrial system in different capacities. They could be accorded a higher social position notwithstanding their formal lower levels in the organisation. This has a close parallel in the relationship of the industry with its labour-force. The local community in these areas should be an important third partner. The concept of regular employment itself should be suitably adapted. In certain areas, group employment could be recognised in place of individual employment. The leaders of these employee groups could be given a higher position although the money compensation to them may be nominal.

At the apex, there should be a meeting point for the top management and labour leaders from the industrial sector, the top leaders from the local communities and the people's representatives. The concept of worker's participation in the industrial sector has to be extended in this case to an area comprising the Core and its hinterland. This forum should be responsible for guiding the direction of change for the entire region. This will engender a new sense of participation in the hinterland communities. The process of change can also be influenced in a more meaningful fashion so that the Core and its hinterland move together in unison.

Large-Scale Industry

It is unfortunate that inspite of the availability of minerals like mica, bauxite, china clay, iron ore, pyrites, uranium and thorium, an adequate industrial base has not yet been built up in Bihar. Since the turn of the present century mining, mineral-based and metallurgical industries sprang up in Bihar. The industrial development started with the extractive, followed by the heavy metallurgical, industries. It was not preceded by the development of the light capital goods or consumer goods industries, as has normally happened in the process of industrialisation. While the development of the mining and metallurgical industries was beneficial to the entire country, it did not create, in the words of the authors of the Techno-Economic Survey Report, sufficient employment opportunities in Bihar, nor did it lead to the diffusion of entrepreneurial activities which the development of the diversified light consumer goods industries could have done.

The Bihar economy remains palpably dual, paradoxical and unintegrated. Side by side with the peaks of modern enterprises, employing the latest flow process techniques, are the deep troughs of many traditional industries, depending on abjectly primitive techniques of production. There has been no widespread development of the medium-scale and the small-scale industries to bridge the gap. The development of the consumer goods industries, an evidence of the initial phase of industrialisation, has been slow. Industrialisation has had little spread effect.

As said already, the plain regions of the Ganges valley are rich in agricultural resources but very densely populated and industrially backward. It is difficult to see how far agriculture-based industries alone can solve the problem of unemployment in them. Special efforts would be necessary to secure a greater inter-regional balance in growth and employment. The plateau regions are rich in mineral resources and the development of heavy industries is favourable not only for fostering ancillary, feeder and derived industries but also for accelerated growth of employment in intensive farming and commerce.

Very important nodal points for economic growth and bases for a large number of multiplier effects would be created by the development of the processing of coal, the oil refinery at Barauni and the expansion of other metallurgical, chemical and heavy engineering industries. But unless special measures are adopted to encourage and establish ancillary and derived industries, the multiplier values of the nodal points would not be realised. The State has to step in either alone or in partnership with private enterprise to start new medium and small industries where private enterprise fails to respond on its own accord.

One of the effects of the growth and modernisation of an economy is that more efficient mechanical and capital-intensive processes and products replace the traditional ones. The result is that the craftsmen in the traditional trades are squeezed out of the market and become unemployed. There are, however, two ameliorating factors. Firstly, this process of substitution is generally slow because the supply of capital is not very plentiful. Secondly, for this very reason as well as on account of welfare considerations, there is a deliberate effort to spin out this process so that there is sufficient warning for the newer generation. It may also be noted that in this stage the annual accession to the labour force is so great that this small margin of technological unemployment is hardly sensed to any appreciable extent. Moreover, we find that the weakest of the traditional handicrafts tended to be eliminated by the very first impact of foreign competition. Those handicrafts which survived this first impact in the past were able to adjust themselves to the changing conditions by taking advantage of the new external economies.

Others are deliberately fostered with the objectives of saving capital and providing relief employment.

The managerial resources of Bihar are limited. Private enterprise has been singularly lacking in this State. The efforts of the Government in persuading private enterprise to undertake certain schemes and ventures inspite of the help promised by the Government have been unsuccessful. The records of the loans advanced by the Bihar State Financial Corporation show that genuine local enterprise and willingness to invest in risk capital even when the risks have been reduced considerably by the efforts of the Government are functioning. There is always an unresolvable bias on the part of the enterprises registered outside Bihar or owned or managed by persons coming from outside this State to prefer educated candidates from other States for employment. Not many enterprisers come forward and take advantage of the loan facilities extended under the State Aid to Industries Act. It is not uncommon for would-be entrepreneurs to borrow money from the Government under this Act and to utilize it for a quick turn-over in commercial activities, which are mainly employment-absorbing rather than employment-generating. Outside capital predominates in the large-scale and the medium-scale industries, whereas local capital does so in the small-scale ones. The per capita income of an average Bihari is the lowest in the country. This restricts the size of the market. And, as we all know, the size or the market has a great deal to do with the level of technology employed in any type of industry. This level is deplorably low in the small industry of the State. Bulk of the income generated leaks out to other States.

Three important considerations are involved in the question of the general growth of the economy. In the first instance, there is the question of the set-up of the economy with its facilities of the economic overheads and external economies. In the second instance, there is the question of the removal of impediments to incentives and enterprise. In the third instance, there is the question of the deficiency in the supply of private business enterprise when appreciable facilities and incentives have been provided. The economic overheads provide the facilities external to the specific industrial units. They might belong to the class which is developed as a result of the growth of an economy, for example, the economic dimension of the market resulting from the growth of national income. Another class of external economies arise out of the aggregation of industrial townships. We know, how these external economies are sought to be created in the form of common facilities by establishing industrial estate. Then, another class of external economies or overhead facilities either grow up in response to economic growth or have got to be provided wider areas in the form of specific enterprises. To this class belongs the growth of facilities of transport and communications, of banking and credit services, of the supply of raw materials, of the supply of technical skills, of a responsible labour market and various other aspects of a developed economy. All these factors affect the cost-structure and the quality of the products. They are all mutually inter-related and one stimulates the other.

Bihar is still far from manufacturing its own producer goods to any appreciable extent. A beginning has been made with the manufacture of locomotives, diesel trucks, small mining appliances and wagons, and so forth. A real beginning would be made with the development of heavy, medium and light forges and foundries, re-rolling facilities and other facilities for the manufacture of heavy, medium and light machinery. Bihar's deficiency in the capacity for the manufacture of producer goods, e.g., manufacture of machinery, agricultural implements, general and jobbing engineering, railway workshops, etc., is brought out by the returns under the Factories Act. The weakness of the producer goods industries is further brought out by the fact that with all its metallurgical resources, the State has been singularly deficient in the possession of re-rolling mills, small forges and foundries. It is no doubt a fact that re-rolling activities depend on the supply of scraps which mostly mean the volume of machinery used up during the last 20 years or so. But re-rolling also provides facilities for shaping ingot into more appropriate shapes for further use and fabrication.

All the primary and secondary industries provide the nodal points for the proliferation of small self-employing industries as well as commercial enterprises. The direct employment value of the mining, metallurgical, chemical and other large industries limited as it is, their secondary, multiplier effects can be exploited for increasing employment indirectly only by building up the ancillary, feeder and derived industries like the root system and the branches of a tree with the numerous nodal points. We have still got to work out appropriate formulas for estimating employment potentials of different levels of enterprises, firstly, in terms of the money value of investments and, secondly, in terms of the multiplier effects of each industry and its nodal points. Finally, the employment potentials of the industrial activities in creating employment in the tertiary sector have also got to be worked out in order to estimate the wide scope of private enterprise to solve our unemployment problem. The highly capital-intensive basic and heavy industries and enterprises have got very much higher multiplier values compared to the less capital-intensive industries account of the very much larger number of nodal points from which other industries stem out or for which a larger number of ancillary or feeder industries are needed. This brings out the basic importance of heavy and key industries for employment in the long-run. For instance, the extractive industries in Bihar employ nearly 3 lakh persons and there is not much likelihood of any great increase in this number. These industries, however, form the base or the foundations on which the major part of the super-structure of the processing and manufacturing industries can be built up, tier open tier. They further create the need for building up the overheads of the transport system of all kinds. Hence, although the direct employment-creating value of the extractive, the heavy metallurgical, engineering and chemical and allied industries, and the power-generating industries is not very high, yet by necessitating the transport of raw materials and finished products in large quantities and the movement of men they engender more employment in this way. These involve a large volume of constructional activities which provide employment to a very large labour force. It is because of this that the percentage of persons occupied in the non-agricultural sector is far greater in West Bengal, Punjab, Madras and Bombay than in Bihar. The want of light engineering like re-rolling mills and small foundries and forges in Bihar has seriously affected the growth of cottage and small-scale engineering industries. While re-rolling mills are concerned with the utilization of scrap, small re-rolling units are necessary for fabricating finished steel, circulating scrap and processing scrap into shapes suitable for further processing by small engineering industries. Even the large business enterprises in the private sector look upon the provision of services and ancillary industries for relieving them of much of the distributing activity which tends to impinge on sphere of their main responsibility.

Agriculture and land use have decayed around the mining and industrial areas in Bihar. Normally, these areas with their high spending power should have stimulated agriculture, animal husbandry and horticultural activities in the surrounding villages. But lack of enterprise and response has produced very abnormal retrograde consequences. The workers from these villages have become so much satisfied with the cash income which they earn that they do not want to exert more.

There is control of the Central Government over the large-scale and the medium-scale industries, while the small-scale, cottage and village industries have its patronge and guidance.

PREDOMINANCE OF THE SMALL SECTOR

The dual character of Bihar's industrial structure will be evident from the fact that in 1951 only 3.12 per cent of the workers were engaged in the manufacturing industry, large-scale, small-scale and cottage. Then in 1956 there were in the State 300 large-scale units (i.e., 0.3 per cent of all industrial units, employing 37.2 per cent of all industrial workers), 3,900 small-scale units (i.e., 3.9 per cent of all industrial units, employing 9.6 per cent of all industrial workers), and 96,000 cottage units (i.e., 95.8 per cent of all industrial units, employing 53.2 per cent of all industrial workers). Thus, 4.2 per cent of all industrial units came under the Factories Act of 1948. The number of workers engaged in the cottage units was 2,00,000 approximately. Finally, in 1961 the percentage of workers engaged in the manufacturing industry was 7.71.

The Table 3.1 is proof of the fact that in India in almost all its States the non-factory sector, i.e., the household industrial units comprising the cottage and the small-scale units, predominate over the factory sector, i.e., the non-household industrial units comprising the large-scale units, not only in terms of absolute numbers but also in those of the proportion of total industrial employment given and the proportion of total industrial output produced. In Bihar, despite its having a number of large scale

TABLE 3.1

Numerical Strength and Relative Share in Industrial Output and Employment of Factory and Non-factory Units in Selected States of India

States	*Factory (Organised or Non-Household) Sector*			*Non-Factory (Unorganised or Household) Sector*		
	Percentage of all industrial units	*Percentage of total industrial employment given*	*Percentage of total industrial output produced*	*Percentage of all industrial units*	*Percentage of total industrial employment given*	*Percentage of total industrial output produced*
Andhra Pradesh (1956)	N.A.	14.0	28.0	N.A.	86.0	72.0
Bihar (1956)[a]	4.2	46.8	66.5	95.8	53.2	33.5
Kerala (1955-56)	N.A.	17.9	35.6	N.A.	82.1	64.4
Madras (1956)	N.A.	33.0	N.A.	N.A.	67.0	N.A.
Madhya Pradesh (1956)	N.A.	20.0	24.6	N.A.	80.0	75.4
Orissa (1955-56)	N.A.	6.6	20.0	N.A.	93.4	80.0
Punjab (1956)	1.0	18.6	48.3	99.0	81.4	51.7
Rajasthan (1959)	N.A.	6.0	12.0	N.A.	94.0	88.0

a In 1961 the number of workers employed in the manufacturing industries other than the household per one lakh of population was 917.

industrial units, the cottage and the small-scale industrial units predominate in all these respects.

For all its heavy industrial establishments, Bihar is one of the least industrialised States in India. When only registered factories are considered, Bihar has proportionately the lowest number of persons deriving their livelihood either wholly or partially from the manufacturing industry. This will appear from the Table 3.2. Table 3.2 further shows that the factories in Bihar are larger in size compared to those in other States and they employ, on an average, a large number of workers and their average capital investment is greater, presumably because they belong to the heavy industries.

The next Table 3.3, which is more detailed and comprehensive, very well substantiates our above remark.

As can be noticed from Table 3.4, the percentage of total employment in the country given by the household manufacturing units was larger in Andhra Pradesh, Madras and Uttar Pradesh than in Bihar. Similarly, the percentage of total net output in the country produced by the household manufacturing units was larger in Andhra Pradesh, Madras, Mysore, Rajasthan, West Bengal and Delhi than in Bihar. The Percentage of total employment given by the non-household manufacturing units in India was larger in Andhra Pradesh, Gujarat, Kerala, Madras, Maharashtra, Uttar Pradesh and West Bengal than in Bihar whereas the percentage of total net output in the country produced by the non-household manufacturing units was larger in Gujarat, Madras, Maharashtra, Uttar Pradesh and West Bengal than in Bihar. Lastly, the percentage of total employment given by the manufacturing industry as a whole in India was larger in Andhra Pradesh, Madras, Maharashtra, Uttar Pradesh and West Bengal whereas the percentage of total net output produced by the manufacturing industry as a whole in India was larger in Gujarat, Madras, Maharashtra, Uttar Pradesh and West Bengal than in Bihar. Thus, Madras has an advantage over Bihar in all these six respects; Uttar Pradesh in five respects; and Andhra Pradesh, Maharashtra and West Bengal in four respects.

With the bringing out of the recent Report on the Small-Scale Manufacture: Rural and Urban, the National Sample Survey (Fourteenth Round) has, for the first time, thrown light on this important sector of economic activity in respect of which very little dependable data was available up-till now. Valuable estimates,

TABLE 3.2

Number of Registered Factories and their Capital Investment in Selected States

States	*Registered Factories (covered by the Census of Manufacturing Industry, 1956)*		*Productive Capital (Rs. Crores) Per cent*		*Productive Capital per Registered Unit (Rs.)*
	Number	*Percentage*			
Bihar	350	5.0	96	12.2	27,40,000
Bombay	1258	17.8	236	29.9	18,76,000
Madras	776	11.0	59	7.5	7,60,000
West Bengal	1782	19.6	171	21.7	9,60,000
All-India	7067	100.0	788	100.0	11,15,000

TABLE 3.3

State-wise Percentage Distribution of Total Employment, Total Net Output According to Different Types of Manufacturing Industry

States	*Household*		*Non-household*	
			A. Small	
	Employment (a)	*Net Output (b)*	*Employment (a)*	*Net Output (b)*
Andhra Pradesh	74.2 (2)	34.8 (3)	13.8 (13)	20.9 (10)
Assam	72.9 (3)	24.2 (6)	4.1 (15)	5.3 (15)
Bihar	66.9 (5)	18.8 (9)	18.4 (11)	22.5 (9)
Gujarat	36.2 (13)	12.2 (12)	21.8 (9)	18.6 (12)
Jammu and Kashmir	63.3 (8)	40.3 (1)	25.6 (6)	38.2 (2)
Kerala	42.5 (12)	9.2 (15)	39.0 (1)	52.6 (1)
Madhya Pradesh	69.3 (4)	32.5 (5)	16.2 (12)	18.3 (13)
Madras	56.2 (9)	13.2 (11)	27.5 (4)	34.9 (5)
Maharashtra	35.9 (14)	11.7 (13)	25.2 (9)	16.5 (14)
Mysore	54.8 (10)	14.4 (10)	26.9 (5)	36.5 (4)
Orissa	83.3 (1)	39.5 (2)	10.5 (14)	19.7 (11)
Punjab	52.5 (11)	33.8 (4)	30.2 (3)	36.9 (3)
Rajasthan	65.2 (6)	22.6 (8)	23.0 (8)	32.7 (6)
Uttar Pradesh	64.0 (7)	22.7 (7)	21.1 (10)	29.2 (7)
West Bengal	24.8 (15)	9.8 (14)	33.2 (2)	25.2 (8)
All-States	54.5	16.9	23.6	25.8

(*Contd.*)

TABLE 3.3 *(Contd.)*

States	*Non-household*					
	B. Medium		*C. Large*		*D. Total*	
	Employment (a)	*Net Output (b)*	*Employment (a)*	*Net Output (b)*	*Employment (a)*	*Net Output (b)*
Andhra Pradesh	4.3 (5)	10.9 (4)	7.7 (14)	33.4 (12)	25.8 (14)	65.2 (13)
Assam	4.6 (4)	10.4 (6)	18.4 (4)	60.1 (3)	27.1 (13)	75.8 (10)
Bihar	1.6 (13)	3.5 (15)	13.1 (7)	55.2 (5)	33.1 (11)	81.2 (7)
Gujarat	8.2 (1)	11.2 (2)	33.8 (2)	58.0 (4)	63.1 (3)	87.8 (4)
Jammu & Kashmir	1.8 (12)	4.3 (14)	9.3 (13)	17.2 (15)	36.7 (8)	59.7 (15)
Kerala	3.3 (7)	8.3 (7)	15.2 (6)	29.9 (13)	57.5 (4)	90.8 (1)
Madhya Pradesh	2.5 (9)	4.5 (11)	12.0 (9)	44.7 (6)	30.7 (12)	67.5 (11)
Madras	4.6 (4)	10.6 (5)	11.7 (10)	41.3 (9)	43.8 (7)	86.8 (5)
Maharashtra	7.9 (2)	7.8 (8)	31.0 (3)	64.9 (1)	64.1 (2)	88.3 (3)
Mysore	2.8 (8)	6.8 (9)	15.5 (5)	42.3 (8)	45.2 (6)	86.6 (6)
Orissa	1.3 (14)	4.2 (13)	4.9 (15)	36.6 (11)	16.7 (15)	60.5 (14)
Punjab	6.1 (3)	11.1 (3)	11.2 (11)	18.2 (14)	47.5 (5)	66.2 (12)
Rajasthan	2.2 (10)	5.5 (10)	9.6 (12)	39.2 (10)	34.8 (10)	77.4 (8)
Uttar Pradesh	1.9 (11)	46.8 (1)	13.0 (8)	43.3 (7)	36.0 (9)	77.3 (9)
West Bengal	3.9 (6)	4.4 (12)	38.1 (1)	60.6 (2)	75.2 (1)	90.2 (2)
All-States	4.1	7.4	17.8	49.9	45.5	33.1

Note: Figures in brackets indicate ranks.

TABLE 3.4

Percentage Distribution of Total Employment, Total Net Output, Total Contribution to National Income of Manufacturing Industry According to Types in India among different States

State/Union Territories	*Employment*			*Net Output*		
	Household Manufacturing Industry	*Non-household Manufacturing Industry*	*All Manfacturing Industry*	*Household Manufacturing Industry*	*Non-household Manufacturing Industry*	*All Manufacturing Industry*
Andhra Pradesh	14.7 (2)	6.1 (7)	10.8 (4)	7.8 (5)	3.0 (19)	3.8 (10)
Assam	29.9 (14)	1.3 (14)	2.2 (14)	3.4 (11)	2.1 (13)	2.4 (11)
Bihar	9.3 (4)	5.5 (8)	7.5 (6)	7.0 (8)	6.2 (6)	6.3 (6)
Gujarat	3.2 (13)	6.7 (5)	4.8 (10)	6.0 (9)	8.7 (4)	8.2 (5)
Jammu & Kashmir	0.6 (15)	0.4 (16)	0.5 (16)	0.7 (16)	0.2 (16)	0.3 (13)
Kerala	4.0 (11)	6.5 (6)	5.1 (9)	2.1 (13)	4.3 (9)	3.9 (9)
Madhya Pradesh	8.1 (5)	4.3 (11)	6.4 (7)	7.5 (6)	3.2 (10)	3.9 (9)
Madras	11.7 (3)	10.9 (3)	11.3 (3)	7.1 (7)	9.4 (3)	9.1 (3)
Maharashtra	7.6 (6)	16.3 (2)	11.6 (2)	14.1 (1)	21.6 (1)	20.3 (1)
Mysore	5.4 (7)	5.4 (8)	5.4 (8)	3.8 (10)	4.6 (8)	4.5 (8)
Orissa	4.7 (8)	1.1 (15)	3.1 (12)	3.0 (12)	0.9 (15)	1.3 (13)
Punjab	4.2 (10)	4.5 (10)	4.3 (11)	12.3 (2)	4.9 (7)	6.1 (7)
Rajasthan	3.5 (13)	2.2 (12)	2.9 (13)	1.8 (14)	1.3 (14)	3.4 (12)

Uttar Pradesh	15.0 (1)	10.1 (4)	12.7 (1)	11.8 (3)	8.1 (5)	8.7 (4)
West Bengal	4.5 (9)	16.4 (1)	9.9 (5)	10.0 (4)	18.6 (2)	17.2 (2)
Delhi	0.2 (16)	2.1 (13)	1.1 (15)	0.5 (17)	2.6 (12)	2.2 (14)
Himachal Pradesh	0.2 (16)	0.1 (17)	0.2 (17)	0.8 (15)	0.2 (16)	0.3 (15)
Tripura	0.2 (16)	0.1 (18)	0.2 (17)	0.3 (16)	0.1 (17)	0.1 (16)
All States	100.0	100.0	100.0	100.0	100.0	100.0

Note: Figures in brackets indicate ranks.

based on the survey, have been prepared and can now be used for varied purposes, especially for economic planning and other policy decisions.

During the year 1958-59, there were about 135 lakhs of households engaged in the unregistered small-scale household manufacturing industry in India. Total employment in this sector was estimated to be of the order of 173 lakhs, i.e., about 4 per cent of the total population and 9 per cent of total working force. The gross value of output produced during the year was about Rs. 984 crores and the value added by manufacture was estimated at Rs. 536 crores.

The survey revealed that the manufacturing activity of the unregistered household units accounted for a sizeable proportion of the total manufacturing business in India. In fact, it engaged 173 lakhs of persons, compared with 29 lakhs employed by the large-scale industrial establishments and 7 lakhs by the small-scale registered factories. These figures, however, exaggerated the role of the household units since most of the 173 lakh workers were not whole-time employed in the manufacturing sector. A more dependable picture of the size of the manufacturing activity emerged from the value of output of the different sub-sectors.

In terms of gross value of output, the household sector, accounted for nearly 22 per cent of the total, the gross value during the year amounting to Rs. 984 crores compared to Rs. 2,691 crores worth output by the large-scale units and Rs. 715 crores output by the small-scale registered factories. In terms of net output (value added by manufacture), the household sector accounted for a larger proportion, i.e., 37.5 per cent. The value added by the household unregistered factories amounted to Rs. 537 crores compared with Rs. 759 crores for the large-scale units and Rs. 136 crores for the small-scale units. It would thus, appear that the contribution of the household manufacturing units to the national income of the country was about three-fifths as much as that of all the large-scale and the small-scale registered factories taken together.

The above data also revealed that the value added by manufacture as a proportion of gross value of output was substantially higher in the case of the household units, that proportion being 54.6 per cent, against a much lower figure of 28.2

per cent for the large-scale units and 19.0 per cent for the small-scale registered factories.

During the year under review, there were only just less than 9,000 large-scale factories and 29,000 small-scale factories. As against this, the manufacturing activities in the unregistered sector were spread over 134.6 thousand households.

Though the rural sector accounted for 82 per cent of total manufacturing households and about 75 per cent of total employment, in accounted for only 49 per cent of the total value of output and about 55 per cent of the value added by manufacture. The urban sector, on the other hand, while comprising only 18 per cent of total households and about 25 per cent of workers engaged in small-scale manufacture, contributed 51 per cent of the total value of output and about 45 per cent of the value added by manufacture.

The per household employment in these industries in the rural areas was about 1.2 workers as against 1.9 workers in the urban areas. The average per household input requirement in the urban industries was about 6 times that in the case of those in the rural areas. The gross output and value-added per household in the urban areas were likewise higher than those in the rural areas by about 5 times and 4 times respectively.

The ratios of input to output for the rural and the urban industries were 0.39 and 0.51 respectively as against the average ratio of 0.45 for all-India, which meant that to produce one rupee worth of goods, on an average, 39 paise worth of input (fuel, raw materials, auxiliary materials, cattle feed, repair and maintenance of fixed capital and other expenses) was employed by the household industries in the rural areas as against 51 paise by those in the urban areas. Considering per worker input and value added by manufacture in the two areas, the small-scale household manufacturing units in the urban areas, on an average, were obviously more viable than those in the rural areas.

The value added per worker per year amounted to Rs. 228 in the rural sector and 551 in the urban sector and averaged at Rs. 310 for both sectors taken together. This meant that after paying for raw materials, fuel, repair and maintenance of capital equipment and all other expenses, a worker earned from his household manufacturing activity Rs. 19 per month in the rural sector and Rs. 46 per month in the urban sector. The combined average for both sectors worked out at Rs. 26 per month per worker. Out of this he had to pay interest charges, if any, on funds borrowed for the business. It is to be noted here that an overwhelming majority of the workers were not employed full-time in the manufacturing activity.

The survey classified all industries into 21 industrial groups for the purpose of analysis. Households engaged in manufactures relating to fool group were the largest activity in the rural areas, constituting about 36 per cent of the total manufacturing households followed with a wide margin by textile (12 per cent), wood and cork products (8 per cent), furniture and fixtures (7 per cent), metal products (7 per cent) and leather and leather products (6 per cent). In the urban areas textiles constituted the largest single household manufacturing group (about 18 per cent), closely by activities in the food group (14 per cent) and wearing apparel and made-up textile goods (12 per cent).

The pattern of employment in the two areas closely followed the distribution of households among the various industry groups. Households and worker engaged in construction activity in the urban sector were nearly double those engaged in the rural areas.

The value of fixed capital at the end of the year was of the order of about Rs. 169 crores of which Rs. 106 crores was in the rural areas and 63 crores was in the urban areas. Unlike in the case of output, the share of the household units in fixed assets was obviously small—at slightly less than 10 per cent of the total for all manufacturing units. In respect of fixed capital formation also the share of the household manufacturing units was very small. It was only Rs. 14.2 crores, which amounted to roughly 5 per cent of the total fixed capital formation in the entire manufacturing sector in India. The components of the capital formation are given below:

TABLE 3.5

(Rs. crores)

New purchases	12.4
Construction	4.2
Improvements	1.5
Total	18.1
Less: Assets lost	2.1
Assets sold	1.8
Fixed Capital Formation	14.2

The table given below gives State-wise distribution of households engaged in manufacturing activity in the rural and the urban areas. Out of the total manufacturing households in India (134.56 lakhs), the highest percentage (about 25 per cent of households were in Uttar Pradesh followed by Madras (11 per cent) and Andhra Pradesh (10 per cent). The lowest percentage (hardly 1 per cent each) in this regard was in Jammu and Kashmir and Assam. Bihar had approximately 7 per cent of all manufacturing households.

TABLE 3.6

State-wise Distribution of Households in Manufacturing Activity—Rural and Urban

(In lakhs)

States	*Rural*	*Urban*	*Total*
Andhra Pradesh	12.00 (2)	2.04 (5)	14.04 (3)
Assam+	0.68 (14)	0.18 (14)	0.86 (14)
Bihar	8.82 (5)	0.74 (10)	9.56 (6)
Gujarat	3.90 (11)	1.66 (6)	5.56 (10)
Jammu & Kashmir	0.60 (15)	0.20 (13)	9.80 (15)
Kerala	6.05 (7)	0.68 (11)	6.73 (9)
Madhya Pradesh	8.11 (6)	1.57 (7)	9.68 (5)
Madras	11.56 (3)	3.36 (2)	14.92 (2)
Maharashtra	5.60 (8)	2.42 (3)	8.02 (7)
Mysore	5.16 (10)	2.20 (4)	7.36 (8)
Orissa	5.40 (9)	0.20 (13)	4.60 (11)
Punjab++	2.97 (12)	1.51 (8)	4.48 (12)
Rajasthan	9.19 (4)	1.47 (9)	10.66 (4)
Uttar Pradesh	29.68 (1)	4.47 (1)	34.15 (1)
West Bengal	2.62 (13)	0.52 (12)	3.14 (13)
All-India	111.34	23.22	134.56

+Includes Manipur and Tripura.
++Includes Delhi and Himachal Pradesh.
Note: Figures in brackets indicate ranks.

The next Tables 3.7 and 3.8 depict the percentage distribution of manufacturing households, classified into seven industry groups, in the rural and the urban areas respectively. The importance of various industries varied from State to State as well

TABLE 3.7

State-wise Percentage Distribution of Households Engaged in Small-Scale Manufacture (Rural)

	Industry Group	*Andhra Pradesh*	*Gujarat*	*Kerala*	*Madhya Pradesh*	*Madras*	*Maharashtra*	*Punjab**
	1	*2*	*3*	*4*	*5*	*6*	*7*	*8*
1.	Textile, Tailoring & Footwear	28.6 (3)	9.6 (13)	10.2 (12)	8.0 (15)	22.0 (5)	20.7 (7)	26.3 (4)
2.	Leather & leather products (except footwear)	12.4 (2)	7.9 (6)	—	9.0 (5)	6.8 (8)	10.1 (4)	13.7 (1)
3.	Wood, Glass, Ceramic, Building and Construction	31.2 (2)	17.2 (11)	46.1 (1)	17.1 (12)	24.8 (7)	30.0 (4)	27.7 (6)
4.	Metal and Engineering	8.1 (6)	3.4 (12)	2.4 (13)	11.1 (4)	8.2 (5)	5.8 (10)	11.2 (3)
5.	Food, drinks & Tobacco	16.1 (14)	60.5 (1)	27.8 (11)	50.2 (5)	32.7 (8)	29.9 (10)	20.7 (13)
6.	Chemical and Chemical products	0.2 (7)	0.2 (7)	2.2 (1)	0.4 (6)	0.5 (5)	0.5 (5)	—
7.	Other industries	3.4 (8)	1.2 (13)	11.3 (1)	4.2 (5)	5.0 (4)	3.0 (10)	0.4 (15)
	All Industries	100.0	100.0	100.0	100.0	100.0	100.0	100.0

(Contd.)

TABLE 3.7 (*Contd.*)

	Industry Group	*Uttar Pradesh*	*West Bengal*	*Assam@*	*Bihar*	*Jammu & Kashmir*	*Mysore*	*Orissa*	*Rajasthan*
	1	*9*	*10*	*11*	*12*	*13*	*14*	*15*	*16*
1.	Textile, Tailoring & Foodwear	11.8 (10)	17.0 (8)	74.4 (1)	21.8 (6)	31.3 (2)	15.0 (9)	9.1 (14)	10.8 (11)
2.	Leather & leather products (except footwear)	2.3 (11)	1.0 (14)	1.8 (12)	4.5 (10)	5.7 (9)	7.4 (7)	1.2 (13)	10.6 (3)
3.	Wood, Glass, Ceramic, Building and Construction	18.5 (9)	23.7 (8)	9.8 (14)	30.7 (3)	30.7 (3)	28.0 (5)	17.7 (10)	15.8 (13)
4.	Metal and Engineering	6.0 (8)	16.4 (1)	2.2 (14)	8.0 (7)	6.2 (9)	8.1 (6)	12.4 (2)	4.6 (11)
5.	Food, drinks & Tobacco	53.6 (4)	36.6 (7)	10.4 (15)	30.2 (9)	22.0 (12)	38.2 (5)	56.1 (3)	56.5 (2)
6.	Chemical and Chemical products	0.2. (7)	—	—	0.9 (2)	—	0.1 (8)	0.8 (3)	0.7 (4)
7.	Other industries	7.6 (2)	5.3 (3)	1.4 (12)	3.9 (7)	4.1 (6)	3.2 (9)	2.7 (11)	1.0 (14)
	All Industries	100.0	100.0	100.0	100.0	100.0	100.0	100.0	100.0

*Includes Delhi and Himachal Pradesh.

@ Includes Manipur and Tripura.

Note: Figures in brackets indicate ranks.

TABLE 3.8

State-wise Percentage Distribution of Households Engaged in Small-Scale Manufacture (Urban)

	Industry Group	*Andhra Pradesh*	*Gujarat*	*Kerala*	*Madhya Pradesh*	*Madras*	*Maharashtra*	*Punjab**
	1	*2*	*3*	*4*	*5*	*6*	*7*	*8*
1.	Textile, Tailoring	34.1	30.6	8.6	21.5	35.7	35.0	33.7
	and Footwear	(5)	(8)	(14)	(13)	(3)	(4)	(6)
2.	Leather and Leather							
	products (except	2.6	7.1	—	4.4	2.4	3.5	6.6
	footwear)	(12)	(3)		(8)	(13)	(10)	(4)
3.	Wood, Glass, Ceramic,							
	Building &	21.6	17.2	28.5	18.2	15.8	14.4	14.8
	Construction	(4)	(10)	(2)	(8)	(11)	(13)	(12)
4.	Metal &	11.6	9.4	11.0	13.8	9.6	9.1	11.8
	Engineering	(7)	(13)	(9)	(2)	(14)	(15)	(5)
5.	Food, Drinks &	23.9	27.4	27.3	27.0	22.3	29.7	23.3
	Tobacco	(9)	(6)	(7)	(8)	(11)	(4)	(10)
6.	Chemical &	0.6	0.5	3.0	2.8	2.4	0.6	2.7
	Chemical products	(8)	(9)	(1)	(2)	(4)	(8)	(3)
7.	Other industries	5.6	7.8	11.6	12.3	11.8	7.7	7.1
		(10)	(6)	(3)	(1)	(2)	(9)	(8)
	All Industries	100.0	100.0	100.0	100.0	100.0	100.0	100.0

(Contd.)

TABLE 3.8 (*Contd.*)

Industry Group	*Uttar Pradesh*	*West Bengal*	*Assam@*	*Bihar*	*Jammu & Kashmir*	*Mysore*	*Orissa*	*Rajasthan*
1	*9*	*10*	*11*	*12*	*13*	*14*	*15*	*16*
1. Textile, Tailoring and Footwear	25.7 (11)	30.1 (9)	59.5 (1)	24.9 (12)	49.6 (2)	31.1 (7)	6.8 (15)	26.0 (10)
2. Leather and Leather products (except footwear)	5.4 (6)	10.6 (2)	4.6 (7)	3.0 (11)	6.3 (5)	3.6 (9)	—	11.2 (1)
3. Wood, Glass, Ceramic, Building & Construction	21.5 (5)	9.6 (14)	8.2 (15)	20.4 (7)	17.8 (9)	21.2 (6)	37.1 (1)	27.5 (3)
4. Metal & Engineering	9.5 (12)	11.5 (8)	8.5 (15)	11.7 (6)	12.5 (4)	10.8 (10)	14.9 (1)	13.6 (3)
5. Food, Drinks & Tobacco	28.6 (5)	29.8 (3)	17.0 (13)	35.8 (1)	10.3 (14)	21.2 (12)	34.9 (2)	170 (13)
6. Chemical & Chemical products	1.3 (6)	0.1 (11)	—	1.1 (7)	0.3 (10)	2.0 (5)	—	0.3 (10)
7. Other Industries	8.0 (5)	8.3 (4)	2.2 (14)	3.1 (12)	3.2 (13)	0.1 (15)	6.3 (9)	4.4 (11)
All Industries	100.0	100.0	100.0	100.0	100.0	100.0	100.0	100.0

*Includes Delhi and Himachal Pradesh.

@Includes Manipur and Tripura.

Note: Figures in brackets indicate ranks.

as between the urban and the rural areas within the same State. Thus, in the rural sector, manufactures relating to food, etc., were the highest (60.5 per cent) in Gujarat followed by Rajasthan (56.5 per cent) and Orissa (56.1 per cent). The lowest percentage of the food-group industries was in Assam at 10.4 per cent, preceded by Andhra Pradesh and Punjab at 16.1 per cent and 20.7 per cent respectively. Bihar held the ninth position (30.2 per cent). Next in importance in the rural areas was the 'wood, glass, ceramic, etc.' group. It engaged 46.1 per cent of the total manufacturing households in Kerala, followed by Andhra Pradesh (31.2 per cent) and Bihar (30.7 per cent). The lowest percentage in this respect was for Assam at 9.8 per cent preceded by Madhya Pradesh at 17.1 per cent. Another industrial group of importance in the rural areas was the 'textile-group'. Assam accounted for 74.4 per cent of its manufacturing households, followed by Jammu and Kashmir (31.3 per cent) with a wide margin. The lowest percentage in this regard was for Madhya Pradesh (8.0 per cent) closely preceded by Orissa (9.1 per cent) and Gujarat (9.6 per cent).

In the urban areas of the States, the same three groups (discussed above) predominated with a different order of importance. The textile group had generally a larger percentage of households followed by the food group and the wood, glass, ceramic, etc., group. In Assam the textile group of manufactures engaged 59.5 per cent of its urban manufacturing households followed by Jammu and Kashmir (49.6 per cent) and Maharashtra (35.0 per cent). The lowest in this regard was Orissa at 6.8 per cent. The food group of manufactures in Bihar engaged 35.8 per cent of its manufacturing households, closely followed by Orissa (34.9 per cent). The lowest percentage was observed to be in Jammu and Kashmir (10.3 per cent). Wood, glass, ceramic, etc., manufactures engaged the highest percentage (37.1 per cent) of Orissa's manufacturing households, the lowest such percentage being for Assam at 8.2.

Generally speaking, textile manufactures engaged comparatively a larger percentage of households in the urban areas, while in the rural areas the food group of industries predominated. Metal and engineering works were, more or less, evenly distributed between the two areas.

THE ORGANISED SECTOR

From the standpoint of average daily employment given in factories in 1958 Bihar occupied the sixth position among the States of India as shown by the following Table 3.9. But when all the establishments coming under the Shops and Commercial Establishment Act were considered, Bihar occupied the eleventh position in respect of their number and the thirteenth position in respect of the number of persons employed in them. The next Table 3.10 shows this.

TABLE 3.9

Average Daily Employment in Factories[a]

States/Union Territories	*Average Daily Employment*
Andhra Pradesh	2,21,954 (5)
Assam	75,378 (11)
Bihar	1,83,238 (6)
Bombay	10,66,677 (1)
Kerala	1,66,182 (7)
Madhya Pradesh	1,61,059 (8)
Madras	3,26,305 (3)
Mysore (1957)	1,22,359 (9)
Orissa	25,974 (14)
Punjab	1,03,981 (10)
Rajasthan	53,075 (13)
Uttar Pradesh	2,78,178 (4)
West Bengal	6,86,428 (2)
Delhi	59,399 (12)
Himachal Pradesh	1,344 (17)
Andaman & Nicobar Islands	1,609 (16)
Manipur	136 (18)
Tripura	2,068 (15)
Total	34,12,985

a Coming under the Factories Act, 1948.
Note: Figures in brackets indicate ranks.

In 1960, too, the relative position of Bihar in this regard remained almost the same. The percentage of employment given by the organised sector (i.e., the factory sector comprising of the large-scale and the small-scale units) of the manufacturing industry in Bihar remained less than the all-India average and was less than that in other States, mentioned in the following

TABLE 3.10

Number of Establishments and Persons Employed[a]

States/Union Territories	*Number of Establishments*	*Number of Persons employed*
Andhra Pradesh	1,08,111 (5)	83,655 (5)
Assam	5,936 (12)	9,813 (10)
Bihar	7,961 (11)	6,005 (13)
Bombay[b]	4,33,643 (1)	6,52,336 (1)
Kerala	24,951 (9)	48,350 (8)
Madhya Pradesh	65,676 (7)	45,085 (9)
Madras	1,76,021 (3)	2,19,010 (3)
Mysore	71,321 (6)	80,556 (6)
Orissa	1,752 (14)	6,756 (12)
Punjab	1,39,561 (4)	75,168 (7)
Rajasthan	11,579 (10)	7,299 (11)
West Bengal	1,84,573 (2)	3,79,836 (2)
Andaman & Nicobar	219 (16)	261 (16)
Delhi	47,367 (8)	85,969 (4)
Himachal Pradesh	2,353 (13)	1,435 (15)
Tripura	1,283 (15)	2,016 (14)

a Coming under the Shops and Commercial Establishments Act.
b Bilingual.
Note: Figures in brackets indicate ranks.

Table 3.11, except Andhra Pradesh, Madhya Pradesh, Orissa and Rajasthan. Because of their very low productivity the cottage and the small-scale units (not coming under the Factories Act) contributed proportionately less to the total manufacturing output, though proportionately more to the total manufacturing employment in Bihar as they did in Assam, Gujarat, Madras, Maharashtra and West Bengal. But if the contribution made by the small-scale units (coming under the Factories Act) were included, then the sum-total of the contribution made by the cottage and all the small-scale units even in these States would far exceed that made by the large-scale ones in them. The unorganised sector of the manufacturing industry sharply overshadowed its organised counterpart so far as contribution to the total manufacturing output was concerned in Punjab, Kerala, Orissa, Rajasthan, Uttar Pradesh and Andhra Pradesh,

TABLE 3.11

Share of Organised Industry in Total Manufacturing Employment and Net Output of Different States

States	*Share of Organised Total Mfg. Output (Net)*	*Industry (Per Cent) Total Mfg. Employment*
Andhra Pradesh	44.3(12)	12.0(12)
Assam	70.5 (2)	23.0 (4)
Bihar	58.7 (5)	14.7(10)
Delhi	53.7 (6)	38.5 (3)
Gujarat	69.2 (3)	42.0 (1)
Kerala	38.2(14)	18.5 (5)
Madhya Pradesh	49.2 (9)	14.5(11)
Madras	51.9 (7)	16.3 (8)
Maharashtra	71.8 (1)	38.9 (2)
Mysore	49.1 (8)	18.3 (6)
Orissa	40.8(13)	6.2(14)
Punjab	29.3(15)	17.3 (7)
Rajasthan	44.7(11)	11.8(13)
Uttar Pradesh	48.1(10)	14.9 (9)
West Bengal	65.0 (4)	42.0 (1)
All India	57.3	21.9

Note: Figures in brackets indicate ranks.

As Table 3.12 shows, the number of factory workers per 1,000 population was less in Bihar than in Andhra Pradesh, Bombay, Madras and West Bengal. Again, it was less than the all-India average. The factories in Bombay, Madras and West Bengal provided employment to a large number of workers than those in Bihar. Agriculture and occupations allied to it as well as small industries absorbed a proportionately larger number of people in Bihar than in these States.

TABLE 3.12

Factory Employment in Selected States of India

States	*Number of Factory Workers (Million)*	*Number of Factory Workers per 1000 population*
Andhra Pradesh	0.168 (5)	4.9 (4)
Bihar	0.176 (4)	4.2 (5)
Bombay	0.998 (1)	18.8 (2)
Madhya Pradesh	0.098 (6)	3.6 (6)
Madras	0.300 (3)	9.3 (3)
Orissa	0.022 (7)	1.4 (7)
West Bengal	0.653 (2)	22.9 (1)
All-India	2.882	7.4

Note: Figures in brackets indicate ranks.

In one of its occasional papers (No. 10) the NCAER has attempted a study of the regional differences in industrial pattern in India for the year 1960. From this it appears that about 84.8 per cent of the total factory output (net) was generated in 29 groups of industries for which gross output, employment, net output and related co-efficients were estimated separately. The shares of the 'defaulting' and 'miscellaneous' groups of factories in residual employment were 37.4 per cent and 62.6 per cent respectively whereas their corresponding shares in net output were 43.6 per cent and 56.4 per cent respectively. The average value of the output-employment co-efficient for all the known industries was estimated at Rs. 3,568 and the corresponding input-output co-efficient at 74.3 per cent. Non-ferrous basic metal industries topped the list with a value of the output-employment co-efficient as high as Rs. 7,933 whereas knitting mills recorded a value of only Rs. 349, thus, occupying the lowest rung of the ladder. The input-output co-efficient differed greatly from industry to industry—the minimum value being 35.2 per cent in ship-building and repairing and the maximum value being 95.1 per cent in manufacture of textiles not elsewhere classified. The average value of the output-employment co-efficient for the entire factory sector was Rs. 3,508 which was much higher than the all-India average but slightly lower than that of Assam. The largest share (21.7 per cent) of the total employment was given by iron and steel and other basic industries, which with a reasonably high value of the output-employment co-efficient (Rs. 5,588) contributed 34.7 per cent of the total output and this was partly responsible for raising the average value of the output-employment co-efficient Bihar. In respect of the volume of employment, the next two positions were occupied by sugar factories and refineries, and manufacture of rail-road equipment which, while accounting for 10.7 per cent and 7.9 per cent of the total employment respectively, generated 8.9 per cent and 6.9 per cent of the total net output respectively. In other words, the above three industries together accounted for a little more than 40 per cent of the total employment while generating about 51 per cent of the total net output of the factory sector in Bihar. On the other hand, for industries, viz., manufacture of grain mill products, knitting mills, manufacture of textiles not elsewhere specified and manufacture of pottery, each having an output-employment co-efficient less than Rs. 1,000, together accounted for 3.1 per cent of the total employment and only 0.7 per cent of the total net output. Table 3.13 is illustrative of these points.

It can be seen from the Table 3.14, given below, that 'the net output per person engaged' in 1960 in the organised sector of the manufacturing industry in Bihar was the highest in India, with the solitary exception of Assam but about the same time that in the two sectors of the manufacturing industry, organised and unorganised, was less in the case of Bihar than in that of States like Assam, Gujarat, Maharashtra and Punjab. This may be accounted for in the following manner. The net output per person engaged in the house-hold units (composed of the cottage and the small-scale) in Bihar was so much less than that in the States just mentioned that even the relatively higher net output per person engaged in the organised sector of the manufacturing industry in Bihar was unable to narrow down that wide gap. The predominance of the small-scale factories among the non-household units in Bihar scaled down the net output per person engaged from Rs. 3,508 in the organised sector to Rs. 2,164 in the non-household sector of the manufacturing industry.

The following Tables 3.15 and 3.16 show the relative position of the States in regard to the selected structural indicators. The States in the tables have been arranged in order of their percentage contributions to the total value added by manufacture. Nearly 49

TABLE 3.13

Output-Employment Co-efficient in Respect of Manufacturing Industry in Different States

(In Rs.)

States	*Output-Employment Co-efficient**			
	Household	*Non-household*	*Organised*	*All Mfg.*
Andhra Pradesh	175 (16)	946 (16)	1,387 (15)	374 (18)
Assam	385 (7)	3,238 (1)	3,544 (1)	1,159 (7)
Bihar	248 (11)	2,164 (7)	3,508 (2)	883 (8)
Gujarat	612 (4)	2,496 (4)	2,987 (5)	1,813 (4)
Jammu and Kashmir	358 (8)	915 (17)	—	562 (14)
Kerala	175 (15)	1,280 (14)	1,671 (14)	811 (11)
Madhya Pradesh	303 (9)	1,425 (12)	2,197 (12)	647 (13)
Madras	198 (14)	1,673 (9)	2,702 (9)	843 (10)
Maharashtra	607 (5)	2,553 (3)	3,421 (3)	1,854 (2)
Mysore	229 (12)	1,657 (10)	2,349 (10)	874 (9)
Orissa	210 (13)	1,605 (11)	2,902 (6)	443 (17)
Punjab	970 (2)	2,095 (8)	2,537 (9)	1,505 (6)
Rajasthan	172 (17)	1,100 (15)	1,861 (13)	495 (16)
Uttar Pradesh	257 (10)	1,554 (12)	2,323 (11)	724 (12)
West Bengal	720 (3)	2,189 (6)	2,823 (7)	1,824 (3)
Delhi	1,025 (1)	2,410 (5)	3,190 (4)	2,288 (1)
Himachal Pradesh	1,025 (1)	3,028 (2)	—	1,524 (5)
Tripura	395 (6)	756 (18)	—	507 (15)
All States	328	1,928	2,756	1,056

*Defined as net output per person engaged.

Note: Figures in brackets indicate ranks.

TABLE 3.14

Percentage Distribution of Gross Output, Employment and Net Output and Estimates of Net and Gross Output Per Person and Input-Output Co-efficient for different Groups of Industries Covering all Factories under the Purview of the Factories Act, 1948

Sl. No.	*Industry groups*	*Gross Output per person engaged (Rs.)*	*Gross Output (Percentage)*	*Net Output per person engaged (Rs.)*	*Employ-ment (Percentage)*	*Net Output (Percentage)*	*Net Output as percentage of gross Output*	*Input as percentage of gross Output*
1	2	3	4	5	6	7	8	9
1.	205	16,187	3.3	849	2.8	0.7	5.2	94.8
2.	207	11,853	9.3	2,904	10.7	8.9	24.5	75.5
3.	209	19,971	2.3	3,285	1.6	1.0	16.5	85.5
4.	211	12,336	0.2	3,893	0.2	0.2	32.4	67.6
5.	220	10.260	1.7	4,973	2.3	3.2	48.5	51.5
6.	231	—	0.9	—	2.8	1.2	—	—
7.	232	3,733	—	349	—	—	9.3	90.7
8.	260	2,952	—	1,619	0.2	0.1	54.8	45.2
9.	239	16,257	0.2	802	0.2	—	4.9	9.51
10.	271	23,724	4.0	2,986	2.2	1.9	12.1	87.9
11.	280	5,422	0.7	1,130	1.8	0.9	33.8	66,2
12.	311	12,767	4.8	2,420	5.1	3.5	19.0	81.0

(Contd.)

TABLE 3.14 *(Contd.)*

1	2	3	4	5	6	7	8	9
13.	313 & 319	6,495	0.5	3,233	1.0	0.9	49.8	50.2
14.	329	13,848	0.8	4,004	0.8	0.9	28.9	71.1
15.	331	4,668	1.4	2,472	4.0	2.8	53.0	47.0
16.	332	5,911	—	1,610	0.1	—	27.2	72.8
17.	333	1,815	0.4	823	0.9	0.4	45.3	54.7
18.	334	24,713	3.5	5,610	1.9	3.1	22.7	77.3
19.	339	8,682	4.0	2,703	6.3	4.8	31.1	68.8
20.	341	22,073	35.1	5,588	21.7	34.7	25.3	74.7
21.	342	21,455	2.5	7,933	1.6	3.6	37.0	63.0
22.	350	4,118	0.2	1,479	0.8	0.3	35.9	64.1
23.	360	6,686	1.0	2,930	2.1	1.7	43.8	56.2
24.	370	21,243	3.4	6,025	2.2	3.8	28.4	71.6
25.	381	2,241	—	1,452	0.2	0.1	648	35.2
26.	382	4,921	2.9	3,013	7.9	6.9	61.2	38.8
27.	384	7,544	0.4	1,886	0.8	0.4	24.9	75.1
28.	385	9,590	0.2	2,352	0.2	0.2	24.5	75.5
29.	511	13,664	2.3	2,981	2.3	1.9	21.8	78.2
	Total of 1 to 29		86.2		84.8	86.2		
	Other Industries		13.8		15.2	13.8		
	Total of 30 and 31		100.0		100.0	100.0		

Note: The title all of the *industry groups* are in order: Manufacture of grain mill products; sugar factories and refineries; manufacture of miscellaneous food preparation; distilling, rectifying and blending of spirit (alcohol; tobacco manufactures; spinning, weaving and finishing of textiles; knitting mills; manufacture of textiles not elsewhere classified; manufacture of furniture and fixture of pulp, paper and paper-board; printing, publishing and allied industries; basic industrial chemicals, including fertilizers; manufacture of paints, varnishes and lacquers and miscellaneous chemical products; manufacture of miscellaneous products of petroleum and coal; manufacture of structural clay products; manufacture of glass and glass products; manufacture of pottery (china and earthenware); manufacture of cement (hydraulic); manufacture of non-metallic mineral products not elsewhere classified; iron and steel basic industries; non-ferrous basic metal industries; manufacture of metal products except machinery and transport equipment; manufacture of machinery except electrical machinery; manufacture of electrical machinery, apparatus, appliances and supplies; ship-building and repairing; manufacture of rail-road equipment; repair of motor vehicles; manufacture of motor cycles and bicycles; and electrical light and power generation, transmission and distribution of electric energy.

TABLE 3.15

Percentage Shares of States (A.S.I. Census Sector—All Industries)

States	*No. of Factories*		*Productive Capital*	
	1959	*1963*	*1959*	*1963*
1	*2*	*3*	*4*	*5*
Maharashtra	19.1 0)	20.9 (1)	23.7 (1)	19.0 (2)
West Bengal	15.6 (2)	15.6 (2)	21.7 (2)	20.3 (1)
Gujarat	8.5 (4)	9.5 (3)	7.3 (4)	7.9 (5)
Madras	8.6 (3)	8.7 (4)	4.8 (6)	6.2 (7)
Bihar	3.0 (2)	3.1 (11)	14.2 (3)	8.2 (4)
Uttar Pradesh	5.9 (7)	6.9 (5)	6.7 (5)	4.9 (8)
Mysore	5.6 (8)	4.1 (10)	3.4 (8)	3.0 (10)
Punjab	4.0 (11)	4.5 (9)	2.4 (10)	2.7 (11)
Andhra Pradesh	5.3 (9)	5.4 (6)	3.3 (9)	4.7 (9)
Madhya Pradesh	7.5 (9)	5.3 (7)	1.8 (13)	9.0 (3)
Kerala	7.3 (6)	5.4 (6)	2.1 (12)	1.5 (14)
Orissa	1.0 (15)	1.2 (14)	2.2 (11)	7.7 (6)
Assam	5.1 (10)	4.6 (8)	3.9 (7)	1.9 (12)
Rajasthan	1.2 (14)	1.9 (13)	1.2 (14)	1.2 (15)
Jammu & Kashmir	0.4 (16)	0.3 (15)	0.1 (15)	0.1 (16)
Centrally Administered Territories	1.9 (13)	2.4 (12)	1.2 (14)	1.7 (13)
Total	100.0	100.0	100.0	100.0

(Contd.)

TABLE 3.15 (*Contd.*)

States	*Employment*		*Value of Output*		*Value Added*	
	1959	*1963*	*1959*	*1963*	*1959*	*1963*
1	*6*	*7*	*8*	*9*	*10*	*11*
Maharashtra	21.1 (1)	20.3 (2)	24.9 (1)	24.9 (1)	26.6 (1)	26.7 (1)
West Bengal	23.1 (1)	22.5 (1)	22.2 (2)	21.9 (2)	23.2 (2)	22.0 (2)
Gujarat	10.3 (3)	9.2 (3)	8.8 (3)	8.5 (3)	9.8 (3)	9.2 (3)
Madras	6.9 (5)	7.6 (4)	6.2 (6)	7.7 (4)	6.5 (5)	7.8 (4)
Bihar	6.1 (6)	5.7 (5)	8.6 (4)	7.0 (5)	8.3 (4)	7.2 (5)
Uttar Pradesh	8.0 (4)	7.6 (4)	7.8 (5)	6.6 (6)	5.7 (6)	5.3 (6)
Mysore	3.6 (9)	3.8 (9)	3.0 (9)	3.3 (9)	3.2 (8)	4.2 (7)
Punjab	2.4 (11)	2.8 (10)	3.0 (9)	3.4 (8)	2.0 (11)	2.9 (8)
Andhra Pradesh	4.8 (7)	5.0 (6)	3.5 (7)	3.5 (7)	2.4 (10)	2.9 (8)
Madhya Pradesh	3.0 (10)	3.9 (8)	2.0 (2)	3.5 (7)	1.7 (13)	2.8 (9)
Kerala	4.4 (8)	4.2 (7)	2.6 (10)	2.1 (11)	2.8 (9)	2.1 (10)
Orissa	0.7 (14)	1.6 (13)	1.0 (13)	2.3 (10)	1.0 (14)	2.0 (11)
Assam	2.4 (11)	2.0 (12)	3.3 (8)	2.0 (12)	4.1 (7)	1.8 (12)
Rajasthan	1.5 (12)	1.6 (13)	0.9 (14)	1.2 (13)	0.8 (15)	1.2 (13)
Jammu & Kashmir	0.3 (15)	0.1 (14)	0.1 (15)	0.1 (14)	0.1 (16)	0.1 (14)
Centrally Administered Territories	1.4 (13)	2.1 (11)	2.1 (11)	2.0 (12)	1.8 (12)	1.8 (12)
Total	100.0	100.0	100.0	100.0	100.0	100.0

Note: Figures in brackets indicate ranks.

TABLE 3.16

Some Important Structural Relationships—State-wise: (A.S.I. Census Sector—All Industries)

States	*Productive capital per factory (Rs. Lakhs)*	*Employ-ment per factory (No.)*	*Output per factory (Rs. Lakhs)*	*Value added per factory (Rs. Lakhs)*	*Productive capital per worker (Rs.)*
1	2	3	4	5	6
Maharashtra	34.93 (5)	312 (5)	52.96 (4)	15.52 (4)	11,202 (6)
West Bengal	49.44 (4)	457 (2)	61.49 (3)	16.86 (3)	10,829 (8)
Gujarat	31.97 (7)	310 (6)	39.93 (7)	11.76 (6)	10,323 (9)
Madras	27.31 (10)	280 (10)	38.99 (8)	10.83 (7)	9,769 (11)
Bihar	98.67 (2)	574 (1)	97.87 (1)	27.36 (1)	17.191 (3)
Uttar Pradesh	26.53 (11)	344 (4)	41.11 (5)	9.08 (9)	7,702 (14)
Mysore	27.85 (9)	298 (9)	35.56 (9)	12.40 (5)	9,341 (12)
Punjab	22.11 (13)	190 (14)	32.85 (10)	7.63 (10)	11,615 (4)
Andhra Pradesh	32.99 (6)	297 (8)	28.50 (12)	6.35 (12)	11,120 (7)
Madhya Pradesh	63.68 (3)	231 (13)	28.88 (11)	6.26 (13)	27,554 (2)
Kerala	11.04 (15)	261 (12)	17.86 (15)	4.961 (14)	4,236 (14)
Orissa	240.61 (1)	405 (3)	81.25 (2)	20.03 (2)	59,440 (1)
Assam	15.98 (14)	140 (15)	19.77 (14)	4.72 (15)	11,382 (5)
Rajasthan	20.07 (10)	268 (10)	28.17 (13)	7.53 (11)	8,968 (13)
Jammu & Kashmir	5.38 (16)	79 (16)	4.83 (16)	1.23 (16)	6,851 (15)
Centrally Administered Territories	29.03 (8)	285 (9)	40.04 (5)	9.58 (8)	10,174 (10)
All India	38.16	319	44.18	12.05	11,970

(Contd.)

TABLE 3.16 *(Contd.)*

States	*Value added per worker (Rs.)*	*Value added as percent value of output*	*Ratio of Productive capital to value added*	*Ratio of Productive capital to value of output*
1	*7*	*8*	*9*	*10*
Maharashtra	4,976 (1)	29.3 (3)	2.25 (14)	0.66 (14)
West Bengal	3,693 (8)	27.4 (7)	2.93 (9)	0.80 (9)
Gujarat	3,797 (7)	29.5 (2)	2.72 (12)	0.80 (9)
Madras	3,873 (6)	27.8 (6)	2.52 (12)	0.70 (12)
Bihar	4,767 (3)	28.0 (4)	3.61 (5)	1.01 (6)
Uttar Pradesh	2,635 (13)	22.1 (14)	2.92 (10)	6.65 (1)
Mysore	4,157 (4)	34.9 (1)	2.25 (14)	0.78 (10)
Punjab	4,006 (5)	23.1 (12)	2.90 (11)	0.67 (13)
Andhra Pradesh	2,141 (14)	22.3 (13)	5.19 (3)	1.16 (4)
Madhya Pradesh	2,710 (12)	21.7 (15)	10.17 (2)	2.20 (3)
Kerala	1,901 (15)	27.8 (5)	2.23 (15)	0.62 (15)
Orissa	4,949 (2)	24.7 (10)	12.01 (1)	2.96 (2)
Assam	3,362 (9)	23.9 (11)	3.39 (6)	0.81 (8)
Rajasthan	2,804 (11)	26.7 (8)	3.20 (7)	0.85 (7)
Jammu & Kashmir	1,566 (16)	25.5 (9)	4.38 (4)	1.12 (5)
Centrally Administered Territories	3,357 (10)	23.9 (11)	3.03 (8)	0.72 (11)
All India	3,780	27.3	3.17	0.86

Note: Figures in brackets indicate ranks.

per cent of the total value added by manufacture was in the two States of Maharashtra and West Bengal. Though these two States still jointly accounted for 39.3 per cent of the total productive capital, each had recorded a relative decline in 1963 over 1959. Other States which showed decline in their percentage shares of total productive capital over the period from 1959 to 1963 were Bihar, Uttar Pradesh, Mysore, Kerala and Assam. The remaining States recorded increases in their respective shares of productive capital, the highest increase being in the case of Madhya Pradesh and Orissa. In both these States the increase was mostly due to the huge capital formation in the iron and steel industry during the latter half of the Second Plan and the first half of the Third Plan; in Madhya Pradesh productive capital employed by the iron and steel industry increased from Rs. 23 lakhs in 1959 to Rs. 206.33 crores in 1963 and in Orissa it increased from Rs. 3.52 crores in 1959 to Rs. 215.86 crores in 1963.

There were large inter-State variations as the relationships varied according to the requirements of productive capital which in their turn were determined by the nature of the industry. Thus, the comparatively higher per worker productive capital employed was in Orissa, Bihar, Madhya Pradesh and West Bengal; the capital-output ratio was high in the first two States due to the predominance of the huge capital invested here in the iron and steel industry. The average capital-output ratio and the ratio of productive capital to the value of output were less in West Bengal compared with other three States. Output per factory was also comparatively higher in the three States of Bihar, Orissa and West Bengal. In Madhya Pradesh, it was quite below the all-India average because the iron and steel industry in the State was yet to go in full production.

Employment per factory was observed to be the highest in Bihar at 574 followed by West Bengal at 457; it was the lowest in Jammu and Kashmir at 79 preceded by Assam at 140.

Though, of late, the industrial structure in every State has become much diversified due to the industrial policies of the Government, yet every State has a major industry which dominates the industrial economy of the State. The Table 3.17 gives such major industry in each State together with its percentage contribution to the gross value of industrial production in that State.

TABLE 3.17

States	*Major Industry*	*Percentage contribution to total output*
1	2	3
Andhra Pradesh	Tobacco	27
Assam	Miscellaneous food preparations	77
Bihar	Iron and Steel	35
Gujarat	Textiles	53
Kerala	Miscellaneous food preparations	31
Madhya Pradesh	Iron and Steel	35
Madras	Textiles	36
Maharashtra	Textiles	28
Mysore	Textiles	20
Orissa	Iron and Steel	51
Punjab	Textiles	21
Rajasthan	Textiles	25
Uttar Pradesh	Sugar and Gur	22
West Bengal	Textiles	24
Jammu & Kashmir	Electric light and Power	50
Delhi	Textiles	24

The following Table 3.18 gives the industry-wise ex-factory value of gross output in Bihar in 1963.

The pace of industrial development in Bihar was not perceptibly increased in the years following the Second World War or during the First Plan period. The fixed capital in mines and factories rose only by Rs. 7.1 crores between 1946 and 1950, and although approximately Rs. 21.3 crores were invested in the working capital in the industries during the same period, the number of persons employed in the registered factories rose from 93,500 to 1,11,000 approximately.

Among the large-scale industrial units in Bihar we have the Tata Iron and Steel Company, the Indian Steel and Wire Products, the Tinplate Company of India, the Indian Tube Company, the Tatanagar Foundry, the Jamshedpur Engineering Company, the Tata Engineering and Locomotive Company and the Tata Agrico (all at Jamshedpur); the Sindri Fertilizer Plant, the Heavy

TABLE 3.18

Industry-wise Ex-Factory Value of Gross Output

(Annual Survey of Industries—Census Sector)

Industry Group	*Value (In Rs. Lakhs)*
Manufacture of grain mill products	580
Sugar Factories and refineries	1,397
Manufacture of miscellaneous food preparations	345
Spinning, weaving and finishing textiles	412
Manufacture of cork and wood products not elsewhere classified	8
Manufacture of furniture and fixtures	4
Manufacture of pulp, paper and board	864
Printing, publishing and allied industries	221
Basic industrial chemicals, including fertilizers	2,063
Manufacture of miscellaneous chemical products	189
Manufacture of miscellaneous products of petroleum and coal	1,807
Manufacture of structural clay products	465
Manufacture of glass and glass products	253
Manufacture of pottery, china and earthen-ware	11
Manufacture of cement (hydraulic)	1,373
Manufacture of non-metallic mineral products not elsewhere classified	584
Iron and Steel-based industries	11,548
Non-ferrous basic metal industries	888
Manufacture of metal products except machinery and transport equipment	112
Manufacture of machinery except electrical machinery	348
Manufacture of electrical machinery, apparatus, appliances & supplies	1,178
Shipbuilding and repairing	15
Manufacture of railroad equipment	802
Repair of motor vehicles	42
Electric light and power (generation, transmission and distribution of electric energy)	1,506
Other industry-groups	5,771
Total	32,786

Chemical Unit, the Metal Corporation of India Ltd., the Radio Parts Manufacturing and Assembling Unit at Nirshachetti (all in Dhanbad); the coal washeries (in Dhanbad and Hazaribagh), the

Indian Aluminium Company's Unit at Muri, the Indian Copper Corporation's copper mines at Mosaboni and reduction plant at Ghatsila and rolling mills at Manbhandar, the Chotanagpur Engineering Company and the Agricultural Implements Company (all in Ranchi), besides the other large-scale units set-up by the Central and State Governments during recent years.

Industries based on agricultural raw materials are concentrated mostly in North and South Bihar whereas those based on metallic minerals are concentrated mostly in Chotanagpur. Some industries are dispersed in South Bihar where the over-heads of transport and power are present but most of them are composed of the small-scale units.

In 1956 North Bihar had 20.7 per cent of the organised industrial units with 20.5 per cent of the total number of workers employed in such units (which amounted to 0.19 per cent of the total working force); South Bihar (including Monghyr and Bhagalpur as well) had 43.4 per cent of them with 25.4 per cent of the workers (amounting to 0.39 per cent of the total working force); and finally, Chotanagar (including Santhal Parganas as well) had 33.9 per cent of them with 54.1 per cent of the workers (amounting to 0.89 per cent of the total working force).

North Bihar consists of six and a half districts of the State, having an area of 21,000 sq. mile and a population of over 2 crores. Its population is nearly twice as large as that of Assam (11.8 millions) and larger than that of Punjab (16 millions), Rajasthan (15.9 millions), Orissa (16 millions) and Kerala (13.5 millions). It has an average density of 1,000 per sq. mile. 96 per cent of its population is rural, 93 per cent of which is engaged in agriculture. There is no industrial town. The urban areas are inhabited by lawyers, doctors, shop-keepers and business men. All that it has to its credit, besides the Barauni Oil Refinery and the Ashok Paper Mills, is nearly two dozen sugar mills, three jute mills, two general workshops, two to three distilleries and one Morton's confectionery established in the first quarter of the present century. It has one engineering college (out of five in the State), three engineering schools (out of nine) and six industrial training institutes (out of seventeen in the State).

In 1956 persons resident in Bihar held 8 per cent of the total value of all categories of shares issued by the joint stock companies registered in Bihar and 9 per cent of the total value of all categories of shares issued by the companies registered in West Bengal but working in Bihar. A good number of the joint stock companies working solely or mainly in Bihar were registered in other States such as West Bengal, Bombay and Uttar Pradesh. The average holding of a Bihari shareholder was smaller than that of a non-Bihari shareholder in respect of both the number and the value of the shares held. In the companies registered in Bihar, the Bihari shareholders (specially the service holders) showed a marked preference in holding shares in companies concerned with the production of foodstuffs while the non-Bihari shareholders specially predominated in the field of mining and quarrying. In this manner the bulk of business investment in Bihar came from non-Bihari and hence the bulk of business income went to them. This was not at any rate made up by the incomes brought home by the Bihari earners from other States of India. A study undertaken by the Bihar Unemployment Committee (1954) confirmed this view held by the NCAER. Not only was a sizable industrial segment owned and operated by outsiders but also a considerable proportion of the urban labour force, particularly in the industrial sector, consisted of migrants from other States, their proportion rising with the degree of specialised skill. The Bihari workers were engaged mostly on the unskilled categories of jobs.

Incidence of absenteeism is markedly high in Bihar mainly because workers tend to return to their village homes during the busy agricultural seasons. This affects adversely the production efficiency of the industrial units in which they work. Further, because of slow and limited industrialisation in the State, labour pools with concentration of industrial workers have not sprung up abundantly. Hence despite the vast reservoir of employable labour, there is scarcity of skilled and semi-skilled workers and new industries are faced with the necessity of training the bulk of their labour face.

The economy of the North Bihar plain has for long achieved neither internal integration nor external integration with that of either the South Bihar plain or the Chotanagpur plateau region. The periodic recurrence of widespread floods in the Central part of the North Bihar plain has had generated a permanent sense of impending disaster leading to an attitude of passive resignation, hardly conducive to the building up of a stable economic climate for industrial activities.

IMPACT OF THE FIVE-YEAR PLANS

The amount (1.04 crores) allotted in the First Plan for developmental purposes in the large and the small industries, although not substantial, could not be spent during the plan period mainly due to the shortage of the various categories of technical personnel and the requisite stock of plant and machinery. No large new plant was established in the private sector. In the public sector the Sindri Fertilizer Factory was the only unit allotted to Bihar. In the field of the cottage and the small-scale industries only what might be called pilot schemes were attempted, being chiefly schemes of assistance to the handloom industry. As part of the Central Plan the Sindri Fertilizer Factory was the only unit allotted to Bihar and it was established during the First Plan period. In the Second Plan the Central Plan envisaged preliminary work in regard to the Hatia Heavy Machinery Plant, the Foundry Forge and the Barauni Oil Refinery and the State Plan made a modest attempt to start a Super-phosphate Factory at Sindri which began producing 5,000 tons of super-phosphate from 1958 onwards against an installed capacity of 15,000 tons per annum. In addition, a start was made with the installation of a High Tension Insulator Factory which could not be started earlier because of import difficulties. Preliminary steps for the establishment of the Spun Silk Factory at Bhagalpur, the Co-operative Spinning mill at Biharsharif, and the co-operative sugar factory at Banmankhi were taken. But the fulfilment of these targets was rendered difficult owing to the shortage of technical personnel and machinery. This was the prime reason which hindered the expansion of the capacity of the Super-phosphate factory.

During the Second Plan although the production of iron and steel, sugar, vehicles, electrical equipment, chemicals, paper and textiles expanded in the private sector, no large new plant was established in this sector except the Explosives Factory at Gomia just as had been the case during the First Plan.

It was only towards the end of the First Plan that it was possible to get a clear idea of the scope of the industrial planning possible in the State Government sector as distinguished from the Central Government sector. But during the Second Plan all the amount (Rs. 9.08 crores approximately) allotted for developmental purposes in both the large-scale and the small-scale industrial sectors could not be disbursed due mainly to the shortage of technical personnel and required machinery. In the private sectors a new distillery for the manufacture of power alcohol was established at Narkatiaganj. In the public sector the National Coal Development Corporation had begun the operation of new coal mines and had also set-up washeries during the Second Plan but, candidly speaking, nothing substantial was done during this Plan in respect to any of the State Government industrial projects and the High Tension Insulator Factory had to be re-included in the Third Plan.

In the Third Plan the Hindustan Steel Limited proposed to erect a steel plant at Bokaro with an initial production capacity of 1 million ton ingots and ultimately of 2 million tons. The Third Plan proposed to take up a large number of public sector industrial projects of special significance to the State, to set-up mixed enterprises (with 51 per cent State investment and State control) in suitable cases, where private investment was inadequate or entrepreneurs were lacking, and to expand the activities of autonomous corporations to enable them to meet larger credit requirements and to take up the management of the State-owned enterprises. It proposed to expand the Superphosphate Factory at Sindri and the High Tension Insulator Factory at Ranchi and to raise their capacity to 50,000 and 4,800 tons respectively. It further proposed to constitute a Bihar State Industrial Development Authority for looking after the industrial development of areas, such as Mokameh, Barauni, Ramgarh, Barkakana and Bokaro close to the heavy industrial units located as part of the public sector and for being in charge of the large-scale industries established by the State Government and for planning properly the growth of industrial areas with the heavy industrial units as their nuclei.

During the Third Plan period the Bihar State Industrial Development Corporation took steps to set-up a malleable cast iron foundry and an electrical equipment factory. The Barauni Oil Refinery was about to be completed. The Heavy Engineering Corporation was to complete the construction of the Heavy Machinery Plant and the Foundry Forge at Hatia during this period. The Centre was to set-up the fourth steel plant in the public sector at Bokaro.

A detailed comparison of the two Tables 3.19 and 3.20 given reveals the following:

In both periods Maharashtra stood first in the number of licences issued. Whereas in the earlier period West Bengal took the second place, in the latter period Madras occupied the second place. Gujarat stood third in the earlier period. In the latter period that position was taken over by West Bengal. The number of licences issued to Rajasthan declined heavily. The rate was extremely slow for Bihar.

An examination of the industry-wise data reveals the following:

In both periods the textile group (jute, cotton and silk) stood first. As many as 245 licences were issued in the group of iron and steel castings, forging and other products in the earlier period and in the latter period the number had declined to 22. Similarly, in the coal, lignite, etc., group also there was a fall from 195 to 37. The miscellaneous group (item 25; and drugs and Pharmaceuticals and alcohol group (item 14) more than maintained themselves. For air-conditioners and surgical appliances no licence was issued at all in the latter period, while 10 and 8 licences respectively had been issued in the earlier period. In the machinery group the fall was steep from 148 to 20.

Taking iron and steel castings including forging and other products, we find that the number of lincences issued in the earlier period was 12 in Bihar, 56 in Maharashtra, 53 in West Bengal, 19 in Gujarat, 23 in Madras, 18 in Punjab, whereas in the latter period Bihar's share (2) was even poorer in comparison to some (prospecting) States like West Bengal 6, Maharashtra 4, Punjab 4 and Uttar Pradesh 3. But the position of some States was even worse than Bihar's as no licence in the latter period was issued, as for instance in Andhra Pradesh, Assam, Kerala, Madhya Pradesh, Madras, Orissa, Jammu and Kashmir, and others. In the case of coal, lignite, etc., the geological formations are the governing and limiting factors and Bihar, understandably enough, got the largest number of licences in both the periods; so also did West Bengal, though to a lesser degree. The third group was concentrated in (48 and 8) and West Bengal (22 and 6) while in Bihar the position was 6 and nil. In the machinery group, though Maharashtra and West Bengal dominated in the earlier period, other States like Gujarat and Madras also had their shares, though

TABLE 3.19

Industry-wise Distribution of Licences Issued during January 1962 to January 1964

	Industrial Groups	*Andhra Pradesh*	*Assam*	*Bihar*	*Gujarat*	*Kerala*	*Madhya Pradesh*	*Madras*	*Maha-rashtra*
	1	*2*	*3*	*4*	*5*	*6*	*7*	*8*	*9*
1.	Iron & Steel Castings & Forgings & other Products	13	3	12	19	7	13	23	56
2.	Coal, Lignite, etc.	1	3	117	—	1	16	—	8
3.	Electrical Goods	1	2	6	7	3	4	15	49
4.	Automobiles, cycles, etc.	—	1	1	6	—	—	11	24
5.	Machinery—Mining, Textile Conveying equipment, etc.	2	—	4	19	1	4	13	52
6.	Machine Tools	2		2	8	1		4	25
7.	Earth-moving machinery	—	—	1	2	—	—	2	7
8.	Hand Tools & Small Tools	3	—	—	1	—	—	3	27
9.	Air-conditioners	—	—	—	—	—	—	—	6
10.	Surgical appliances	—	—	—	—	—	—	1	3
11.	Meter—Water, Steam, Electricity and the like	1	5	—	4	1	—	2	12
12.	Chemicals	6	—	2	20	7	8	11	66

13.	Dye stuffs	—	—	—	—	—	—	—	3
14.	Drugs, Pharmaceuticals and Alcohol	5	—	1	12	1	1	1	57
15.	Textiles—Cotton, Jute and Silk Fabrics	30	1	19	81	19	25	45	98
16.	Manufacture of Paper & Paper Products	1	—	—	5	3	4	3	1
17.	Sugar	—	—	2	—	1	—	3	1
18.	Processed foods, Flour, etc.	2	1	1	6	2	—	3	7
19.	Vegetable oils	—	—	—	7	4	4	4	9
20.	Soaps, Glycerine, etc.	1	—	—	1	2		1	2
21.	Glue and Gelatin	—	—	—	—	1	—	—	—
22.	Glass and other miscellaneous wares	1	—	1	5	—	—	1	5
23.	Ceramics	—	—	2	2	—	1	6	4
24.	Cement	1	—	1	2	—	1	1	1
25.	Others	2	1	3	6	3	3	13	25
	Total	72 (9)	17 (15)	175 (4)	213 (3)	57 (11)	84 (8)	166 (5)	548 (1)

(Contd.)

TABLE 3.19 *(Contd.)*

	Industrial Groups	*Mysore*	*Orissa*	*Punjab*	*Rajas-than*	*Utter Pradesh*	*West Bengal*	*Jammu & Kashmir*	*Other*	*Total*
	1	*10*	*11*	*12*	*13*	*14*	*15*	*16*	*17*	*18*
1.	Iron & Steel Castings & Forgings & other Products	6	4	18	4	10	53	—	4	245
2.	Coal, Lignite, etc.	—	4	—	—	—	45	—	—	195
3.	Electrical Goods	12	3	11	3	5	22		4	147
4.	Automobiles, cycles, etc.	1	1	7	2	1	13	—	3	71
5.	Machinery—Mining, Textile, Conveying equipment, etc.	3	—	7	1	9	30		3	148
6.	Machine Tools	5	1	6		3	11	—	—	68
7.	Earth-moving machinery	1	—	2	—	—	2	—	—	17
8.	Hand Tools & small Tools	—	—	4	—	4	12	—	—	54
9.	Air-conditioners	—	—	2	—	—	2	—	—	10
10.	Surgical appliances	—	—	1	—	—	3	—	—	8
11.	Meter—Water, Stream, Electricity and the like	1	—	3	2	1	1	—	—	33
12.	Chemicals	3	—	3	4	5	23	—	1	159
13.	Dye stuffs	—	—	—	—	—	—	—	—	3

14.	Drugs, Pharmaceuticals and Alcohol	—	—	1	6	8	16	—	1	110
15.	Textile—Cotton, Jute and Silk Fabrics	27	9	47	22	43	91	3	15	575
16.	Manufacture of Paper & Paper Products	—	1	2	1	2	3	—	—	26
17.	Sugar	3	—	1	—	3	—	—	—	14
18.	Processed foods, Flour, etc.	1	1	5	—	5	—	1	1	36
19.	Vegetable oils	—	—	2	—	3	4	—	3	40
20.	Soaps, Glycerine, etc.	—	—	—	—	1	5	—	—	13
21.	Glue and Gelatin	—	—	—	—	1	—	—	—	2
22.	Glass and other miscellaneous wares	1	—	—	—	—	4	—	1	19
23.	Ceramics	2	3	3	4	1	—	—	1	29
24.	Cement	—	1	1	1	—	—	—	—	10
25.	Others	3	—	8	3	2	20	—	—	92
	Total	69 (10)	28 (14)	134 (6)	53 (12)	107 (7)	360 (2)	4 (16)	37 (13)	2,124

Note: Figures in brackets indicate ranks.

TABLE 3.20

Industry-wise Distribution of Licences Issued during February 1964 to January 1965

Industrial Groups	Andhra Pradesh	Assam	Bihar	Gujarat	Kerala	Madhya Pradesh	Madras	Maha-rashtra
1	2	3	4	5	6	7	8	9
1. Iron & Steel Castings & Foreign & other Products	—	—	2	1	—	—	—	4
2. Coal, Lignite, etc.	—	—	22	—	—	1	—	1
3. Electrical Goods	—	—	—	1	—	1	3	8
4. Automobiles, Cycles, etc.	1	—	—	—	—	—	4	4
5. Machinery—Mining, Textile, Conveying equipment, etc.	—	—	2	3	—	—	1	7
6. Machine Tools	1	—	1	2	1	—	2	3
7. Earth-Moving machinery	—	—	—	—	—	—	—	—
8. Hand Tools & small Tools	—	—	—	—	—	—	—	1
9. Air-Conditioners	—	—	—	—	—	—	—	—
10. Surgical appliances	—	—	—	—	—	—	—	—
11. Meters—Water, Steam, Electricity, and the like	—	—	—	1	—	—	—	1
12. Chemicals	4	—	—	4	—	1	2	13
13. Dye stuffs	—	—	—	—	—	—	—	—

14.	Drugs, Pharmaceuticals and Alcohol	1	—	1	8	1	2	—	37
15.	Textiles—Cotton, Jute and Silk Fabrics	12	—	1	27	8	1	73	26
16.	Manufacture of Paper & Paper products	1	—	—	1	2	—	—	4
17.	Sugar	—	—	—	—	—	—	—	—
18.	Processed Foods, Flour, etc.	2	1	—	1	—	—	5	1
19.	Vegetable oils	—	—	—	1	—	1	1	2
20.	Soaps, Glycerine, etc.	1	—	—	—	—	—	—	—
21.	Glue & Gelatin	—	—	—	—	—	—	—	—
22.	Glass and other miscellaneous wares	—	—	—	1	—	—	1	—
23.	Ceramics	—	—	—	1	—	—	—	—
24.	Cement	—	—	—	2	—	—	—	—
25.	Others	5	2	2	3	6	1	12	25
	Total	28(7)	3(13)	31(6)	57(4)	8(11)	18(9)	304(2)	137(1)

(Contd.)

TABLE 3.20 (*Contd.*)

Industrial Groups	*Mysore*	*Orissa*	*Punjab*	*Rajas-than*	*Uttar Pradesh*	*West Bengal*	*Jammu & Kashmir*	*Others*	*Total*
1	*10*	*11*	*12*	*13*	*14*	*15*	*16*	*17*	*18*
1. Iron & Steel Castings & Foreign & other Products	1	—	4	1	3	6	—	—	22
2. Coal, Lignite, etc.	—	1	—	—	—	12	—	—	37
3. Electrical Goods	1	—	3	6	—	2	—	—	12
4. Automobiles, Cycles, etc.	—	—	1	—	—	2	—	—	12
5. Machinery—Mining, Textile, Conveying equipment, etc.	1	1	—	—	—	5	—	—	20
6. Machine Tools	2	—	1	—	—	1	—	—	14
7. Earth-Moving machinery	—	—	—	—	—	3	—	—	3
8. Hand Tools & Small Tools	—	—	—	—	—	2	—	—	3
9. Air-Conditioner	—	—	—	—	—	—	—	—	—
10. Surgical appliances	—	—	—	—	—	—	—	—	—
11. Meters—Water, Steam, Electricity, and the like	—	—	—	—	—	1	—	—	3
12. Chemicals	2	2	—	—	4	3	—	—	35
13. Dye stuffs	—	—	—	—	—	—	—	1	1

14.	Drugs, Pharmaceuticals and Alcohol	1	—	—	—	—	13	—	—	64
15.	Textiles—Cotton, Jute and Silk Fabrics	9	2	9	2	13	16	—	5	204
16.	Manufacture of paper & Paper products	2	2	5	—	1	4	—	—	22
17.	Sugar	2	—	—	—	—	—	—	—	2
18.	Processed Foods, Flour, etc.	—	1	1	—	—	1	—	1	14
19.	Vegetable oils	—	—	1	—	—	—	—	—	6
20.	Soaps, Glycerine, etc.	—	—	—	—	—	3	—	—	4
21.	Glue & Gelatin	—	—	—	—	—	—	—	—	—
22.	Glass and other miscellaneous wares	—	—	—	—	1	1	—	—	4
23.	Ceramics	—	—	—	—	—	—	—	—	1
24.	Cement	—	—	—	—	—	—	—	—	2
25.	Others	2	—	13	2	6	8	—	2	89
	Total	23(8)	9(10)	35(5)	5(12)	31(6)	87(3)	—	9(10)	585

Note: Figures in brackets indicate ranks.

smaller. Bihar's position was not satisfactory in comparison to West Bengal and Maharashtra. For the chemical industry too, Maharashtra got the largest number of licences (66 and 13); Bihar got only 2 and nil. In respect of the drugs', pharmaceutical and alcohol group, Maharashtra, West Bengal and Gujarat secured the largest number of licences in both the periods. In textiles too, Maharashtra, West Bengal, Gujarat, Madras and Rajasthan dominated the scene. In respect of the processed foods and flour groups, Bihar got only one in the earlier and none in the latter. Even in cement, Bihar got only one licence in the earlier and none in the latter. So far as the miscellaneous industries are concerned, Bihar got the poorest share only 3 and 2, while Maharashtra got 25 and 25, West Bengal 20 and 8, and so on. Out of total licences of 2,124 in the earlier period, Bihar got only 175 (117 in coal sector only), Maharashtra 548 (balanced in every aspect) West Bengal 360, Gujarat 213, and so on. However, Bihar's position was next to all these three. In the latter period, the position was as follows: Bihar 31 (22 coal only), Maharashtra 137, West Bengal 87, Madras 104, and so on. Leaving aside the coal sector, Bihar's share was the poorest despite its vast natural resources.

During 1962-64 the State-wise distribution of licences in the motor vehicles including motor cycles and bicycles industry was as given below:

TABLE 3.21

Maharashtra	29
West Bengal	15
Madras	15
Punjab	8
Gujarat	6
Others	3
Rajasthan	2
Assam, Bihar, Mysore, Orissa and Uttar Pradesh each	1

In 1962 the production of the chemical industry was distributed among the different States in the following manner:

TABLE 3.22

States	Ex-Factory Value (Rs. Crores)
Maharashtra	126.5
West Bengal	44.4
Gujarat	35.4
Bihar	22.5
Madras	22.3
Kerala	17.8
Madhya Pradesh	15.0
Uttar Pradesh	9.3
Punjab	8.0
Andhra Pradesh	5.4
Mysore	4.9
Delhi	1.8
Jammu and Kashmir	0.4
Rajasthan, Orissa and Others	Nil

On the whole, the position of Maharashtra in respect of production in all industries of all groups was the highest in 1962 with the maximum output valued at Rs. 990 crores. It got the maximum number of licences (685) during January 1962 to January 1965. West Bengal came next with an output valued at Rs. 847 crores in 1962 and it got the second highest number of licences (447). The next position were assumed by Gujarat, Madras, and so on.

DIFFICULTIES AND PROBLEMS

The major factors determining the selection of industrial sites were availability of raw materials, availability of transport and availability of water. Bihar's position in all these matters was very bright but still, her industrial potentiality could not be utilized to the maximum.

Shortage of water supply (as in the general engineering and aluminium industries), shortage of power supply (as in the general engineering and heavy chemical industries), high transport costs due to defective means (as in the sugar mills), high electric power rates (as in the aluminium utensils industry), transport difficulties in obtaining raw materials and coal or moving finished products (as in the jute mills, bricks and tiles, glass and glasswares, and ceramic industries), shortage of raw materials available inside the country (as in the vanaspati, general engineering and brass and bell-metal utensils industries) or imported from outside the country (as in the glass and glass-wares, radio and radiogram, and insulated cables and wires industries), predominance of inferior raw materials (as in the sugar mills), competition from producers of substitute goods (as in the brass and bell-metal utensils and country-made padlocks industries), competition in the purchase of raw materials (as in the vanaspati and oil industries), shortage of finance (as in the aluminium utensils industry, production of sales tax on raw materials (as in the oil industry) are the outstanding difficulties of the industries in Bihar.

On sober view, the industrial backwardness of Bihar is complimentary neither to our industrialists nor to our State Government. Private capital in Bihar has remained shy for centuries and only a limited number of entrepreneurs have come forward with their initiative, capital and enterprise for the development of industry. Part of the blame rests on the Government as well. For long the Government has not been imaginative enough to offer necessary facilities to the private industrialists. Admittedly, the flow of investment into the industrial projects in the private sector has not at all been commensurate with their potentialities.

The Industrial Finance Corporation of India (established on the 1st of July 1948) attaches special significance to the financial needs of the large-scale industries which are of strategic and national importance. The net financial assistance sanctioned upto the 30th June, 1965 to 53 co-operative sugar factories (of which only one came from Bihar), 4 co-operative spinning mills (of which only one came from Bihar) and 1 co-operative unit for the extraction of vegetable oil amounted to Rs. 4,044,86 lakhs (of which Rs. 114.70 lakhs went in Bihar). This represented about 18 per cent of the total net assistance sanctioned by the Corporation. The following Table 5.23 shows the State-wise and industry-wise distribution of the co-operative units financed by the Corporation.

By its encouragement of the co-operative sector the Corporation has helped in the dispersal of the sugar industry and the setting up of new units for the utilization of by-products. It

TABLE 3.23

Number of Units

(Lakhs of Rs.)

States	*Sugar*	*Cotton Spinning*	*Vegetable Oil*	*Net Sanctions*
Andhra Pradesh	5 (3)	—	—	435.00 (3)
Assam	1 (7)	—	—	60.00(11)
Bihar	1 (7)	1 (1)	—	114.70(10)
Gujarat	3 (5)		—	142.50 (8)
Kerala	2 (6)	—	—	80.00 (7)
Madras	6 (2)	—	—	443.00 (2)
Maharashtra	20 (1)	1 (1)	—	1,497.46 (1)
Mysore	4 (4)	—	1 (1)	295.25 (6)
Orissa	1 (7)	1 (1)	—	116.00 (9)
Punjab	6 (2)	—	—	421.00 (4)
Uttar Pradesh	4 (4)	1	—	339.95 (5)
Total	53	4	1	4,044.86

Note: Figures in brackets indicate ranks.

has also enabled hundreds of thousands of small agriculturists to grow ,cash crops in view of the assurance of a ready and dependable off-take and to take advantage of the improved methods of farming. Furthermore, these agriculturists have been enabled to pool their savings and put these to productive use, thus, giving a fillip to the co-operative movement in particular and to the country's economy in general.

The Table 3.24 shows the State-wise distribution of the net financial assistance sanctioned as on the 30th June 1965, after adjusting for cancellations and withdrawals. Several other States have profited a lot more than Bihar from this assistance.

The rates of power are higher in Bihar than in most other States like Andhra Pradesh, Madras, Mysore, Maharashtra, Rajasthan, and so on. This is one reason why industry is developing at a faster rate in these States but at a lower rate in our State. There is also acute scarcity of power in this State. The Sachdev Committee, which went into the causes power of the crisis in this State and in West Bengal, made certain recommendations. These recommendations deserve an urgent

TABLE 3.24

(Lakhs of Rs.)

States/Union Territories	*Number of units*	*Loans*	*Guarantees for deferred payments on machinery and for foreign loans*	*Under writings*	*Total*	*Percentage of the whole*
Andhra Pradesh	29 (4)	1,024.87 (9)	433.42 (3)	141.39 (5)	1,599.68 (4)	7.0 (4)
Assam	7 (11)	305.62 (13)	—	350.00 (1)	655.62 (13)	2.9 (13)
Bihar	23 (6)	1,395.46 (7)	236.00 (6)	68.00 (8)	1,399.46 (8)	6.2 (8)
Gujarat	29 (4)	1,342.89 (4)	63.55 (11)	115.25 (6)	1,521.69 (6)	6.8 (6)
Kerala	12 (8)	811.05 (10)	102.43 (10)	15.00 (14)	928.48 (11)	4.1 (11)
Madhya Pradesh	10 (9)	251.41 (14)	26.05 (14)	162.00 (4)	439.46 (14)	1.9 (14)
Madras	46 (2)	2,271.38 (2)	772.58 (1)	326.00 (2)	3,369.96 (2)	14.8 (2)
Maharashtra	73 (1)	3,276.42 (1)	247.25 (5)	309.70 (3)	3,833.37 (1)	16.9 (1)
Mysore	28 (5)	1,065.64 (8)	214.26 (7)	43.00 (12)	1,322.90 (9)	5.8 (9)
Orissa	13 (7)	603.94 (10)	168.13 (9)	90.00 (7)	862.07 (12)	3.8 (12)
Punjab	29 (4)	1,334.79 (5)	54.73 (13)	50.00 (11)	1,439.52 (7)	6.3 (7)
Rajasthan	8 (10)	524.48 (12)	450.00 (2)	15.50 (13)	989.98 (10)	4.3 (10)
Uttar Pradesh	31 (3)	1,290.93 (6)	209.53 (8)	56.50 (10)	1.556.96 (5)	6.9 (5)
West Bengal	46 (2)	2,122.43 (3)	373.03 (4)	59.50 (9)	2,554.96 (3)	11.3 (3)
Delhi	4 (12)	82.62 (15)	62.40 (12)	8.25 (15)	153.27 (15)	0.7 (15)
Andaman & Nicobar Islands	1 (13)	11.00 (17)	—	—	11.00 (17)	—
Pondicherry	1 (13)	52.00 (16)	5.62 (15)	—	57.62 (16)	0.3 (16)
Total	390	17,466.93	3,418.98	1,810.09	22.696.00	100.0

Note: Figures in brackets indicate ranks.

consideration and an early implementation if the growing demand for power is to be met adequately.

The policy of the Central Government regarding coal is reported to be disastrous for States like Bihar. Bihar's great advantage has been the availability of coal in abundance near at hand. This advantage has been neutralised by this coal policy. The Railways have curtailed the allotment of wagons for coal below Moghalsarai and the industries in Bihar are being forced to move coal by road transport, the cost of which much higher. Distant areas are already receiving coal on a special telescopic freight and have been given further assistance by the transportation of coal by rail-*cum*-road route at the same cost through a subsidy of the Government. By the end of 1961 the situation was such that, located as most of the industries were in the coal belt not only the advantage of low coal freight was practically lost but the availability of coal had also become more difficult.

The State Government is alleged to have encouraged a good many bogus private firms by giving them loans and permits for scarce materials and to have discouraged at the same time many entrepreneurs who wanted either to start to expand their business. According to a report in a section of the local press, only those who made heavy illegal profits agreed to share them with unscrupulous politicians and officials. An inventory of the permits and licences issued and the recommendations for them made by the officials of the Industries Department and an independent enquiry into the firms and the individuals involved in them, may bring out the reasons why there has been very little progress of industry in the private sector.

The State Government has begun participating in the capital structure of private enterprises by under-writing or purchasing shares of limited companies or giving guarantee of cash-credit. However, some time ago it was reported in the local press in the private industries in which the Bihar Government had invested its capital considerations other than the soundness of the schemes had weighed with the authorities with the result that there was very little likelihood of even normal return from that investment.

Under the set-up of the present democratic planning, the decisions of the Central Government play a major part on the development of industry. The different State Governments sponsor their case and that of their industries with the Central Government and impress upon it their requirements and views so that the industries in their States get the necessary fillip and advantage for progressive development. It is here that the Bihar Government is alleged by our industrialists to have failed to bring its weight to bear adequately on the Central Government. Either its views have not been given the hearing they deserved or it has not pleaded its case effectively. The decisions of the Central Government have not been favourable. Due to this lapse the industries in Bihar are reported to have been adversely affected. Let us illustrate this point. In December 1965 the Central Government decided to locate the sulphuric acid plant at Durgapur in the larger interests of the country and did not give the Bihar Government its permission to set-up this plant at Sindri inspite of the latter's persistent efforts. An impression had been created that the Bihar Government had not strongly placed its case before the Central Government. The Pyrites and Chemicals Development Corporation had planned a sulphuric acid plant at Sindri. From all angles of view this decision was unquestionable. Sindri is much nearer to Amjhore where pyrite deposits have been located. There is already a super-phosphate factory at Sindri which is not running at its full capacity on account of the shortage of sulphuric acid. Its daily requirement is 100 tons whereas it is able to procure not more than 25 to 30 tons. In all fairness, therefore, the sulphuric acid plant should have been set-up at Sindri. This would have broadened the base of the Sindri fertilizer complex. The Sindri Fertilizer Plant produces nitrogen. The Super-phosphate Factory produces phosphate. Potash is the only thing which remains to make Sindri a complete fertilizer complex. The Central Government's decision is unfair to Bihar in another way. It is this that Bihar will be sending raw materials to another State as if it were a colony when it can easily set-up a sulphuric acid plant itself.

But it is not to deny the fact that industrial expansion in Bihar cannot be planned by picking out the industries suitable for Bihar and developing them. It must be conceived of as part of the general growth of industry in India, depending on the locational and other conditions favourable for expansion and growth, as has been stated in the Report on the Techno-Economic Survey of Bihar. Hence attention has to be paid to the mutual and interacting effects of industrial development in Bihar and the rest of India and to the problems of regional development.

The Government of Bihar is intending to set-up five new refractory manufacturing units on the advice of a team of Russian experts. Most of the newly coming up steel plants are likely to go in for new "L.B." or "L.D." or other oxygen processes. The use of refractory in the manufacture of steel is likely to be reduced very much in the future. A good many existing refractory plants have already curtailed their output in anticipation and are lying idle for want of adequate work. Their proprietors contend that when this industry is already facing such grim situation, it would be extremely unwise to commission other refractory manufacturing plants involving heavy expenditure on foreign exchange. They have discussed this matter with the Planning Commission and pointed out to it that the foreign exchange and other capital resources required for the intended refractory units can instead be utilized to the advantage of some other industry.

Our industrial sector is on the threshold of a number of significant changes and its problems have undergone sharp changes.* Emphasis has begun to shift from construction to management, from production to productivity, from manufacture to design. Research, the elixir of industry, still does not have quite the place if ought to have but there is a growing realisation of the fact that industrialisation must have a foundation in technological development. The concept of productivity is beginning to draw due attention, though over-manning is still too easily accepted the management can often plead legitimate helplessness in the face of raw material and power shortages. Foreign collaboration and export exigencies have helped in setting certain standards, although the existence of an almost unlimited, protected domestic market has contributed greatly towards rendering a section of our industries uncompetitive in terms of cost and quality. This can be perilous if it is accepted uncritically as a concomitant of development. Balance of payments difficulties have hitherto precluded larger import allocations. But maintenance requirements have not always been judiciously estimated in licensing additional capacity and there has not been a sufficiently thorough-going attempt to assess, mobilise and harness this capacity so further developmental programmes, especially in the production of ancillaries, spares, components and sub-assemblies.

* B.G. Verghese very deftly sums them up in his book.

Better utilization of the existing capacity and its expansion to take advantage of the economies of scale should normally take precedence over the establishment of new capacity. The tendency to manufacture every individual part of the composite finished products under the same roof in lieu of sub-contracting or putting out as widely as possible is both the cause and the effect of the hesitant development of the ancillary industries. The tardy growth of these industries and the dependence on imports have also resulted in plants, whether in the public or the private sector, carrying huge inventories (raw materials, stores and spares) as insurance against shortages, import restrictions and component delays.

SOME IMPORTANT INDUSTRIES

The Sugar Industry: The extinction of the indigo industry in North Bihar in the early twenties of the present century sparked-off the development of sugar-cane cultivation and gave birth to the sugar industry in this State. The British indigo planters, having lost their interest in that industry, set-up small plants here and there for the manufacture of sugar. These units were initially very small in size and capacity. Gradually, their number rose to about 15 in 1932. Although the units continued to work for a number of years, they found it hard to exist in the face of the growing competition from imported sugar particularly from Java. These units had languished and had reached the verge of extinction when the Government of India, on the recommendation of the Tariff Board in 1932, raised a wall of protection by levying an import duty on all foreign sugar.

This tariff wall saved the Indian sugar industry from collapse and provided it with an opportunity to chalk out a plan for its expansion and improvement with a view to meeting the danger from foreign sugar. It also encouraged the Indian entrepreneurs to invest their money in this new industry. The result was that within a short span of two years, the number of sugar factories rose from 14 in 1931-32 to 33 in 1933-34 in Bihar alone. This phenomenal expansion of the industry in this State and other States was mainly due to the protection from foreign competition made possible by the tariff wall.

The increase in the number of sugar factories naturally led

to an increase in the land area under sugar-cane. While the factories managed to obtain their full supplies of sugar-cane, there was hardly any organised system or method of sugar-cane purchase. In 1937 the first Congress Government of the State took up the question of putting this industry on a sound footing by bringing the sugar-cane growers and the sugar factories closer to each other. The need for a scientific and planned development of sugar-cane cultivation and for eliminating middlemen and exploiters and providing security to the sugar-cane growers regarding the disposal of their sugar-cane came to the fore, and the Government of Bihar in full collaboration with the Government of U.P. passed the Bihar Sugar Factories Control Act in the year 1937. The Act provided, among other things, for the fixation of a fair minimum sugar-cane price, necessary safeguards to the interest of the sugar-cane growers in respect of the weightment of their sugarcane and the payment of the price thereof and the reservation of compact areas to each factory to afford scope and inducement for the development of sugar-cane cultivation on scientific lines.

While the protection helped this industry to flourish, efficiency needed to be achieved in the field of yield of sugar-cane and sugar recovery per acre to meet the competition from other sugar-producing States, particularly in the South. The yield of sugarcane per acre continued to be abnormally low, near about 350 maunds per acre, as compared to Bombay and other Southern States, which produced anything between 1,000 to 1,500 mounds per acre. Although the quantity of sugar-cane crushed showed an upward trend, the total sugar output did not increase correspondingly on account of a lower sugar recovery than before. The sugar industry in Bihar, which had survived the threats of foreign sugar due to the tariff protection, come to be faced with an equally serious competition from the other States of India; namely, Bombay, Madras and Mysore, where this industry was developing rapidly.

This industry occupies a unique position in the rural economy of this State. It provides a source of livelihood to some 4 to 5 lakh families of sugar-cane growers, 20,000 skilled and unskilled workers employed in the sugar factories and a large number of other people engaged in various ancillary branches of the industry like sugar-cane transport, etc.

The industry even now faces hard competition from some sugar-producing States of India. Bihar, which used to be the second largest sugar-producing State in the country till 1956-57 has gone down to the third place, its place having been taken over by Bombay which produced 3.19 lakh tons of sugar in 1957-58 as against Bihar's total production of 2.75 lakh tons. In 1959-60 Maharashtra produced 3.92 lakh tons as against Bihar's total production of 3.25 lakh tons.

During 1960-61 the sugar factories in this State virtually faced a major crisis due to large accumulated stocks of sugar and correspondingly lower releases, entailing curtailment of funds for clearing the sugar-cane price and other dues. Steps were taken to secure larger releases and liquidate the sugar-cane price dues of the sugar-cane growers.

The sugar industry in Bihar is legitimately proud of being the pioneer in the field. In 1932-33 it had the satisfaction of producing as much as 44.10 per cent of the total sugar produced in the country. But this satisfaction was rather short-lived. Bihar's share in the country's production decreased progressively. In 1962-63 it had come down to about 8 per cent of the total sugar production in the country. This is borne out by the following Table 3.25.

TABLE 3.25

Years	*All-India*	*Bihar*	*(Figures in '000 metric tons) Approx. percentage of Bihar's productions to All-India production*
1932-33	295	131	44
1937-38	930	229	25
1942-43	1,069	241	22
1947-48	1,092	172	15
1952-53	1,318	277	31
1957-58	2,010	279	14
1962-63*	2,160	170	8

* Estimated.

The Table 3.26 clearly reveals that the development of the sugar industry in Bihar has not kept pace with its development

TABLE 3.26

State-wise Position of the Sugar Industry in India

States	*Area under sugarcane ('000 acres)*	*Yield per acre (tons)*	*Recovery of sugar (per cent)*	*Number of sugar Factories*	*Percent of sugar-cane cru-shed by factories*	*Average working days (duration of the crushing season)*	*State's produc-tion ('000 tons)*	*Sugar cons-umption ('000 tons)*
Andhra Pradesh	176 (5)	27.88 (1)	9.71 (5)	12 (4)	31.20 (3)	149 (3)	132 (4)	73 (8)
Bihar	376 (3)	8.47 (8)	9.91 (4)	28 (2)	87.03 (1)	133 (6)	275 (3)	130 (5)
Bombay	270 (4)	27.13 (2)	11.81 (1)	21 (3)	39.01 (2)	145 (5)	320 (2)	522 (1)
Madhya Pradesh	122 (7)	10.22 (6)	9.77 (6)	5 (6)	27.84 (5)	152 (2)	34 (8)	139 (4)
Madras	121 (8)	25.65 (3)	8.72 (8)	5 (6)	25.16 (6)	200 (1)	68 (7)	118 (6)
Mysore	133 (6)	24.11 (4)	10.28 (2)	6 (5)	22.19 (7)	146 (4)	73 (6)	88 (7)
Punjab	494 (2)	13.65 (5)	9.42 (7)	6 (5)	12.96 (8)	91 (8)	82 (5)	149 (3)
Uttar Pradesh	4,017 (1)	10.12 (7)	9.93 (3)	69 (1)	30.06 (4)	124 (7)	942 (1)	257 (2)

Note: Figures in brackets indicate ranks.

in other parts of the country. Thus whereas the total sugar production in the country in between the years 1932-33 to 1962-63 increased by well over 600 per cent, having risen from 2.95 lakh tons, to 21.60 lakh tons, in Bihar the increase was very meagre being only about 30 per cent from 1.31 lakh tons to 1.70 lakh tons. The number of sugar factories in Bihar fell from 35 to 28 during the same period.

Reviewed in the background that the sugar industry has been the principal industry in Bihar after the crash of the indigo industry and on it hinges the welfare of millions of the agriculturists, its present state appears to be definitely alarming.

It is rather ironical that the States in the south, and especially Maharashtra, which came on the scene very much later, have made rapid strides and seem resolved to oust even Uttar Pradesh and Bihar out of their prominent positions. The following tables are ample testimony to this contention:

TABLE 3.27

(Figures in '000 metric tons)

Years	*Bihar*	*Uttar Pradesh*	*Maharashtra*
1939-40	327 (2)	671 (1)	70(3)
1943-44	215 (2)	738 (1)	82(3)
1947-48	172 (2)	610 (1)	91 (3)
1951-52	228 (2)	847 (1)	161 (3)

Note: Figures in brackets indicate ranks.

The above figures clearly show that whereas production in other States has increased tremendously, it has declined in Bihar. Perhaps, natural factors might have been partly responsible for the sad plight of the industry in Bihar. Sugar-cane cultivation has been found more suitable for the tropical belt comprising of Maharashtra, Hyderabad, Mysore, Madras and Andhra Pradesh. In South India and Maharashtra the yield of sugar-cane is higher, one reason for this being that there are twenty to thirty waterings there as against three in Bihar. In 1956-57 over 90 per cent of the acreage under sugar-cane was irrigated in Andhra-Pradesh, Madras, and Maharashtra as against 17 per cent in Bihar. Even such areas as were irrigated in Bihar received a far lower intensity of irrigation than the areas elsewhere. The result of all this has

TABLE 3.28

State-wise Production of Sugar

Stales	*(In 1000 tons)* *1955-56*[a]	*(In 1000 tons)* *1960-61*	*(tons)* *1961-62*	*(tons)* *1962-63*
Andhra Pradesh	76 (4)	180 (4)	1,87,663 (4)	1,72,192 (3)
Assam	N.A.	6 (14)	5,428 (14)	4,272 (14)
Bihar	319 (2)	379 (3)	3,58,677 (3)	1,69,926 (4)
Gujarat	N.A.	27 (9)	33,861 (8)	36,983 (8)
Kerala	N.A.	10 (13)	10,769 (12)	12,011 (11)
Madhya Pradesh	N.A.	35 (8)	30,948 (9)	34,250 (9)
Madras[a]	51 (5)	129 (5)	1,16,264 (6)	1,12,569 (6)
Maharashtra[a]	202 (3)	515 (2)	5,07,419 (2)	5,29,629 (2)
Mysore[a]	48 (6)	118 (7)	1,37,753 (5)	1,39.127 (5)
Orissa	4 (10)	3 (15)	4,242 (15)	3,533 (15)
Pondicherry	N.A.	19 (10)	10,269 (13)	9,744 (13)
Punjab[a]	26 (7)	121 (6)	90,592 (7)	62,445 (7)
Rajasthan	13 (8)	18 (11)	15,551 (11)	13,714 (10)
Uttar Pradesh	987 (1)	1,404 (1)	12,03,531 (1)	8,49,433 (1)
West Bengal	10 (9)	16 (12)	16,081 (10)	10,733 (12)
All-India	1,855	2,980	27,29,045	21,60,561

a Indicates the figures before the re-organisation of the States and applicable to only 1955-56.

Note: Figures in brackets indicate ranks.

been that while Bihar was only three decades ago the premier sugar-producing State in the country, it has gradually lost its place first to Uttar Pradesh and then to Maharashtra. In 1960-61 and 1961-62 Uttar Pradesh held the first place, Maharashtra the second and Bihar the third. By 1962-63 Andhra Pradesh too had stolen a march over Bihar. In that year Bihar occupied the fourth place.

In the context of the need for increasing sugar production the general downward trend in the country in the 1962-63 season, when production showed a steep fall from 27.29 lakh tons to 21.60 lakh tons, has caused much concern. The fall was more in the case of Bihar where production fell from 3.59 lakh tones 1961-62 to about 1.70 lakh tons in 1962-63 even when the Government had withdrawn the statutory cut in production imposed during 1961-62.

A study of the reasons responsible for the sad plight of the sugar industry in Bihar brings out that there has been no improvement in the sucrose content of sugar-cane, rather there is some evidence of its going down. The recovery of 10.92 per cent obtained in 1942-43 has not since been regained. In fact, the recovery percentage, which was well above 10 upto 1955-56 declined progressively. The diminishing availability of sugar-cane to the sugar factories in Bihar has shortend the duration of the crushing season. The duration in 1962-63 averaged to approximately 70 days which was very uneconomic. The recovery of sugar and the duration of crushing season, the two important factors in the determination of cost of production, are low in Bihar and account for the deteriorating position of its sugar industry. The sugar industry in the country is one of the most rigidity controlled major industries. It has to bear the heavy burden of excise duty at the rate of Rs. 10.70 per maund. In addition to this is the sugar-cane cess at the rate of Rs. 0.19 per maund levied by the price paid for sugar-cane are controlled. The following table, giving the break-down of the price of sugar, shows that the industry has no control over about 82 per cent of its cost of production.

This rigidity in the cost-structure, however, operates only in the northern region where alone the controls are imposed and Bihar has had to bear the brunt of this rigid control much more severely.

TABLE 3.29

	Heads	Rs.	As percentage of total cost of production
1.	Sugar-cane cost including commission to Co-operative Societies	17.73	70.4
2.	Salary and wages including bonus and gratuity	2.77	11.0
3.	Manufacturing expenses including overheads	3.86	15.3
4.	Gross margin for income tax, reserves and dividends	0.84	3.3
	Cost of Production	25.20	100.0
	Taxes: (a) Central Excise	10.70	
	(b) Sugar-cane Cess	1.95	
		12.65	
	Ex-Factory control price	37.85	

The average daily crushing capacity of a sugar factory in Bihar today is approximately 1,100 tons, which is low and hence uneconomic and it engenders the problem of disposal of surplus sugar-cane whenever there is a bumper crop; the factories have to prolong their crushing in the summer months because, the crushing capacity being low, all sugar-cane cannot be consumed in the period of optimum recovery which in Bihar is from mid-November to mid-April.

It is, therefore, necessary to enhance the daily crushing capacity of the factories from 1,100 to 1,500 or even 2,000 tons daily. But since the working of the factories has not been economical and investment not sufficiently rewarding, the factories have not, therefore, been able to attract fresh capital. It is at the same time desirable to take appropriate measures to improve their profitability. The main aim should be to lower costs and thereby ensure higher returns on investment. This has been the secret of the rapid growth of the industry in Maharashtra and in South India in late years. In these regions there is no dearth of fresh capital.

In 1960-61 as a result of the increase in the price of sugar-cane, the Government decided to raise the ex-factory controlled price of sugar from Rs. 36 to 37.85 per maund in Uttar Pradesh and North Bihar and from Rs. 36.50 to Rs. 38.35 per maund in Punjab. This revised price came into force from October 25, 1959 in the case of all factories. The policy of incentives was continued and incentives in terms of 50 per cent rebate in excise duty on production achieved in excess of the average of the last two years were given. The Government announced a revision in the sugar-cane cess at the rate of 6 paise per maund of sugar-cane crushed in excess of the last seasons' crush, provided the factories started their operations for the season on or before November 1960.

The Government of India under the Defence of India Rules promulgated on the 17th of April 1963 the Sugar Control Order, 1963. This order empowered the Government to regulate production by the sugar factories, distribution of sugar in the markets, and its prices for various sub-regions. The ex-factory prices of sugar for the different sugar-producing areas in the country were fixed as under:

TABLE 3.30

States	*Rs.*
Uttar Pradesh and North Bihar	108.95
South Bihar, Punjab, Rajasthan, Madhya Pradesh, Maharashtra and Andhra Pradesh	109.85
Orissa	110.50
Madras, Mysore, West Bengal, Kerala & Pondicherry	112.20
Gujarat	112.50
Assam	113.85

These prices were subsequently revised and were finally fixed as shown in Table 3.31. In fixing them the cost of production of factories as given in the Tariff Commission Cost Schedule was kept in view but this does not seem to have satisfied the factories.

The profitability of the sugar industry in Bihar is claimed to have been very low and the 12 per cent return on capital allowed by the Tariff Commission has not been accruing to the factories as has been the case in Maharashtra. It is contended that under the currently enforced price-structure the factories in Bihar have been compelled to incur perpetual losses. The wide disparity in

TABLE 3.31

States	(Per Ton)
East Uttar Pradesh	Rs. 111.20
West Uttar Pradesh	Rs. 108.50
Bihar: North Bihar	Rs. 111.20
South Bihar	Rs. 112.50
Punjab	Rs. 109.85
West Bengal	Rs. 112.20
Assam	Rs. 113.85
Orissa	Rs. 110.50
Rajasthan	Rs. 109.85
Madhya Pradesh	Rs. 109.85
Maharashtra	Rs. 109.85
Gujarat	Rs. 112.50
Andhra Pradesh	Rs. 109.85
Madras	Rs. 112.20
Mysore	Rs. 112.20
Kerala	Rs. 111.20
Pondicherry	Rs. 111.20

the profit margins obtaining in the different regions will be evident from the following table:

TABLE 3.32

States	Cost as per Tariff Commission (per ton)	Price fixed (per ton)
	Rs. P.	Rs. P.
Bihar: North Bihar	118.22	111.20
South Bihar	129.36	112.50
Maharashtra	103.60	109.85
Andhra Pradesh	106.70	109.85
Madras and Mysore	106.70	111.20
Kerala	106.70	111.20

The above figures betray a sad story. Whereas other States have been allowed a fair or more than fair margin of profit, the prices fixed for North Bihar and South Bihar reportedly do not even cover the cost. In the case of North Bihar the price is lower by Rs. 7.02; more so in the case of South Bihar, where the price is lower by as much a Rs. 16.86.

In fixing the above prices the Government considered the prices prevailing during the period January 1965 to March 1965. Now, the prices prevailing in Bihar during this period were lower than those during the same period in Maharashtra and South India being the combined effect of the excessive releases made by the Government and of the factories having in stock old sugar, partly wet or otherwise damaged, a factor that should have been taken into account.

The need for higher prices for Bihar was greater during the 1962-63 season, the duration having declined to 73 days in North Bihar and to barely 45 days in South Bihar. The Tariff Commission had not visualised any such contingency and while preparing its cost-schedule, it had not provided cost-schedules for durations below 90 days. It bears no mention of the fact how costs increase inversely with fall in the duration of the crushing season. For example, costs including the return on capital increase by only Re. 0.14 when the duration goes down from 180 to 170 days and by Re. 0.58 when the duration goes down from 100 to 90 days. The extent of the rise in costs for a shorter duration of 73 and 43 days can well be guessed from this.

The Bihar Government has recently set-up a Sugar-cane and Sugar Industry Advisory Board to regenerate this most important agro-industry of the State. The plants of the sugar factories are old and obsolete and are badly in need of rehabilitation, modernisation and expansion but the factories do not have adequate finance for this and for improving the quality of sugar-cane. Whereas the Government of India has realised the need for the rehabilitation of the cotton and the jute industries and arranged for finances to them on easy terms for this National Industrial Development Corporation, the case of the sugar industry has not been entertained for the same object. This is in addition to the already narrated problems of high cost of production due to the heavy excise duty and the unremunerative price of sugar as fixed by the Government. But the story does not end here. It is alleged by the sugar factories that the Union Government was not fair to Bihar in the matter of subsidised sugar export. Bihar had participated in this programme. But when there was a favourable market and the sugar factories had a fair chance of market handsome profit, the Union Government called for tenders and required sugar to be delivered on docks at the lowest rate. Naturally, the sugar factories near the ports got an advantage over those which were situated farther away from them.

Bihar's tottering sugar industry can be resusciated and made to pay by combining better sugar-cane farming with improved sugar technology and rational utilization of the by-products in viable and valuable agro-industries.

The Cement Industry—Originally starting around 1914 the cement industry in India grew fairly rapidly since then and by 1923 there were seven or eight factories in production, having together an installed capacity of 3.86 lakh tons. This rapid growth led soon to a state of temporary saturation of demand and consequently to a suicidal price war. With the formation of the India Cement Manufacturers' Association this competition within the industry was eliminated by mutual agreement. A common price was fixed for sales; a quota system was evolved and selling and distribution arrangements of producers were coordinated.

In 1936 a group of factories formed a cartel, the Associated Cement Manufacturing Co. Ltd. (popularly known by the initials A.C.C.), combining four main groups of producers owing 10 out of 11 existing factories at that time. Further expansion during the next decade brought in more factories belonging to this cartel. About this time another group, the Dalmia Jain, came into existence, owing five factories. By 1947 there were 18 cement factories in the Indian Union with a total installed capacity of 21.15 lakh tons. With independence the industry expanded rapidly again so that by 1949 there were 21 units with a rated capacity of 28.15 lakh tons.

When we analyse the development of the cement industry in Bihar during the last fifteen years, we find that it has lagged behind that in other States.

In 1951 Bihar accounted for 31 per cent of the all-India production capacity of cement. This percentage had come down to 20 per cent by 1961. The cement industry in Bihar increased its capacity for cement production by 40 per cent in 1956 as against 200 per cent in Rajasthan and Gujarat, 100 per cent in Punjab and 60 per cent in Mysore. During 1956-61 against 400 per cent increase in the capacity of the cement industry in Andhra Pradesh,

TABLE 3.33

The Cement Industry

States	*Number of Units*			*Production (Rated capacity) ('000 tons)*		
	1950-51[a]	*1955-56*[a]	*1960-61*	*1950-51*[a]	*1955-56*[a]	*1960-61*
Andhra Pradesh	N.A.	N.A.	5 (2)	N.A.	N.A	
Bihar	5 (1)	6 (1)	7 (1)	921 (1)	1,160 (1)	
Gujarat	—	2[b] (3)	5 (2)	—	300[b] (5)	
Kerala	N.A.	N.A.	1 (6)	N.A.	N.A.	
Madhya Pradesh	1 (2)	1 (4)	3 (4)	350 (3)	350 (4)	
Madras	5 (1)	5 (2)	4 (3)	769 (2)	882 (2)	
Maysore	1 (2)	1 (4)	3 (4)	86 (5)	90 (8)	
Orissa	1 (4)	1 (6)	—	165 (7)		
Punjab	N.A.	N.A.	2 (5)	N.A.	N.A.	
Rajasthan	1 (2)	2 (3)	2 (5)	223 (4)	525 (3)	
Uttar Pradesh	1 (4)	1 (6)	—	200 (6)		
All-India	21	27	34	3,280	5,006	9,200

a Indicates figures before the re-organisation of the States.
b Including Maharashtra.
Note: Figures in brackets indicate ranks.

80 per cent increase in Rajasthan and Madras, 60 per cent increase in Mysore and 50 per cent increase in Punjab, the increase registered in Bihar was only of the order of 35 per cent. The number of licences issued for the development of the cement industry during the Third Plan in indication of nothing but a declining trend.

On the 31st October 1961, the Government of India announced its decisions on the recommendations of the Tariff Commission in respect of the fair prices payable to producers of cement. The Government made two major departures from the recommendations of the Commission. They were: (1) It rejected the Commission's suggestion for continuance of the system of differential ex-works prices and instead preferred a uniform ex-works price of Rs. 69.50 per ton for naked cement with certain minor adjustments to cover the varying cost of some units. (2) It raised the ex-factory price by less than what the Commission had recommended by Rs. 13 per ton, including selling and distribution charges of Rs. 3 per ton, as against Rs. 16 per ton recommended by the Commission.

In the Government resolution it was stated that the prices then fixed would be in force till March 31, 1966, subject to adjustments, whenever called for, for variations consequent on government action, including escalation for fuel and power.

Since then there have been increases in the cost of coal, power and lime-stone and railway freight on raw materials. After the declaration of emergency, the cement industry was also brought under the emergency risk insurance scheme.

The Government, on a representation by the cement industry, examined the incidence of these increases on the cost of production of cement and decided that with effect from June 1, 1963, the ex-works price to be paid to the industry should generally be increased by Rs. 2.75 per ton.

It has been stated that besides the ex-works cost, the distribution cost of cement has also risen on account of the increase in railway freight since November, 1961. With a view to minimising the increase payable by the consumer, the Government restricted the increase on this account and also advised the State Trading Corporation to effect all possible economy in the movement and distribution of cement by the Corporation and the selling agents. Consequently, the selling price was raised by Rs. 3.75 per ton.

The supplies of indigenous and imported cement are pooled and its distribution has been taken over by the State Trading Corporation in order to provide for substantial import of cement in the interests of consumers and to rationalise properly and regulate the use of cement when its demand has gone up so high.

The excise duty on cement was raised from Rs. 20 to Rs. 24 per ton with effect from the 1st March 1958.

The decision taken by the Central Government in 1961 on the recommendation of the Tariff Commission was criticised by the industrialists as most extra-ordinary and definitely prejudicial to the several units of the cement industry in Bihar. The Government had made an arbitrary reduction in the price of cement. It had explained that the cement price fixed by it was lower than that recommended by the Tariff Commission. On the other hand, the price of cement for the consumer had in actual fact increased by Re. 0.45 per ton over the calculation of the Tariff Commission. The

Tariff Commission had recommended that the State Trading Corporation should have a remuneration of Re. 0.60 per ton whereas the Central Government had given it a remuneration of Rs. 2.60 per ton. Another sum of Rs. 2 per ton was given by increasing Re. 0.45 in the price for the consumer and by Rs. 1.55 average reduction in the price to the manufacturers. The reduction in the case of the cement industry in Bihar worked out to nearly Rs. 2, on the average, against the all-India average of Rs. 1.55. In the case of several individual units, this comparative disadvantage went up to even Rs. 1.75 per ton. On the one hand, the recommendation of the Tariff Commission was disregarded and on the other, under the pretext of safeguarding the consumer, the price was revised resulting in an increased burden on the industry and the consumer, on the one side and an addition to the profit of the State Trading Corporation, on the other.

Cement is an essential commodity and its development has to be ensured. The essential pre-requisites for the development of the cement industry are limestone, coal and power. In Bihar limestone has to be transported from long distances to the site of the cement factories and heavy freight has to be incurred on this. In the above price fixation policy the freight on limestone was left out of consideration. This has acted as a disadvantage to the cement industry in Bihar and is an important reason of its slack development.

The Paper Industry—In respect of the paper industry too Bihar stands to lose its position when we consider the rapid development that is taking place in all other States. Bihar has been the second largest producer of paper and paper boards in India. But the increase in its capacity during the last ten years has not kept pace with that in other States. While its production capacity in Bihar increased by 80 per cent during 1956-61, that in Uttar Pradesh increased by 140 per cent, in Maharashtra by 160 percent and in Mysore by 130 per cent. West Bengal maintained its position as the largest producer with nearly 79,000 tons per year as against nearly 60,000 tons per year in Bihar. The number of licences issued for the establishment of paper mills during the Third Plan period is indicative of the fact that other States are going faster in this field too. Table 3.34 given below is illustrative of this.

Although Bihar has very suitable soil for large-scale bamboo

TABLE 3.34

State-wise Distribution of Paper and Paper Board Industry

No.		*Andhra Pradesh*	*Bihar*	*Gujarat*	*Kerala*	*Madhya Pradesh*	*Madras*
1		2	3	4	5	6	7
I.	**Number of Units**						
	February, 1951a	N.A.	1 (4)	N.A.	N.A.	N.A.	2 (3)
	April, 1956[a]	1 (4)	1 (4)	N.A.	N.A.	1 (4)	1 (4)
	1960	2 (2)	1 (3)	N.A.	1 (3)	—	—
	March, 1964	2 (5)	2 (5)	5 (3)	1 (6)	1 (6)	1 (6)
II.	**Annual Installed Capacity** (tons)						
	February, 1951[a]	N.A.	11,000 (3)	N.A.	N.A.	N.A	2,600 (6)
	April 1956[a]	2,000 (8)	29,000 (3)	N.A.	N.A.	8,000 (7)	600 (9)
	1960	20,000 (6)	48,000 (3)	N.A.	7,000 (9)	—	—
	March 1964	43.000 (7)	63,000 (3)	15,050 (10)	8,640 (11)	8.000 02)	20,000 (9)

(Contd.)

TABLE 3.34 *(Contd.)*

No.		*Maha-rashtra*	*Mysore*	*Orissa*	*Punjab*	*Uttar Pradesh*	*West Bengal*	*Total (All-India)*
	1	*8*	*9*	*10*	*11*	*12*	*13*	*14*
I.	**Number of Units**							
	February, 1951[a]	36 (2)	1 (4)	1 (4)	N.A.	2 (3)	4 (1)	17
	April, 1956[a]	46 (2)	2 (3)	1 (4)	N.A.	2 (3)	4 (1)	20
	1960	66 (1)	2 (2)	2 (2)	2 (2)	2 (2)	6 (1)	24
	March, 1964	11 (1)	5 (2)	3 (5)	4 (3)	2 (5)	5 (2)	42
II.	**Annual Installed Capacity** (tons)							
	February, 1951[a]	5,1006	4,000	31,500	N.A.	6,400	58,5000	1,36,000
		(5)	(6)	(2)		(4)	(1)	
	April, 1956[a]	11,900[b]	11,000	36,000	N.A.	9,500	66,100	2,10,000
		(4)	(5)	(2)		(6)	(1)	
	1960	30,0006	26,000	62,000	19,200	10,500	88,200	3,10,900
		(4)	(5)	(2)	(7)	(8)	(1)	
	March, 1964	48,310	53,640	98,300	45,760	31.200	1,14,550	5,49,130
		(5)	(4)	(2)	(4)	(8)	(1)	

a Indicates the figures before the reorganisation of the States.
b Including the figures for Gujarat.
Note: Figures in brackets indicate ranks.

plantation, bamboo is not available in sufficient quantity in Bihar, and hence any expansion of our paper industry will have inevitably to depend on bagasse, which is at present used by the sugar factories as fuel. It is argued that the sugar factories should use coal instead. The cost of transporting coal as an alternate fuel to the sugar factories in North Bihar will not be much. Their bagasse-fired boilers should be replaced by coal-fired ones. For this the railway freight on bagasse should be reduced so as to come to par with that on bamboo. Furnace oil is a second alternate fuel. Bamboo plantation can be a long-term solution and as such it cannot meet the immediate needs of our paper mills.

A chain of bagasse-based pulp and paper units in North Bihar would give a fillip to the development of its backward districts. Thought is also being given to the establishment of a number of modern and efficient khandsari units in this region in the hope that they might become nuclei of rural power-based industry and workshops or tractor stations in the process of agricultural mechanisation.

In 1962 the distribution of total production of paper and paper products in the different States of India was shown under:

TABLE 3.35

States	*Ex-factory value (Rs. Crores)*
Andhra Pradesh	4.2 (7)
Bihar	11.2 (2)
Gujarat	2.5 (10)
Madhya Pradesh	3.8 (9)
Maharashtra	10.2 (3)
Mysore	5.3 (6)
Orissa	10.1 (4)
Punjab	6.8 (5)
Uttar Pradesh	4.0 (8)
West Bengal	19.2 (1)

Note: Figures in brackets indicate ranks.

At present only the paper mill at Dalmianagar is using bamboo obtained from forests leased to it and from outside contractors. Approximately 1,60,000 tons of bone-dry bamboo are available in Bihar, of which about 1,25,000 tons are used by the paper mills in the State and outside it. The rest are used locally for various other purposes. By scientific methods of afforestation, the bamboo yield can be improved considerably and thereby the existing output can be stepped up by at least another 55,000 tons. It is expected that another 15 to 20 thousand tons of bamboo would be made available after 1968 from the plantations. .

A paper mill producing 100 tons of paper per day has been considered to be the most economically feasible one at present. Such a mill can be located near a sugar mill or a group of sugar mills, having a daily crushing capacity of 5,300 tons and working for about 110 days in a year. On this basis it is calculated that four paper mills can possibly be established in Bihar—two in Champaran (on each at Narkatiaganj and Motihari), one in Saran (at Hathua) and one in Darbhanga (at Samastipur) districts. The total capital investment required for an integrated pulp and paper mill of 100 tons per day capacity based on 75 per cent bamboo pulp is estimated at about Rs. 10 crores. In addition, the working capital requirement will amount to at least Rs. 1 crore, especially because a huge quantity of bagasse will have to be stored. The total production cost including depreciation and interest works out to approximately Rs. 1,100 per ton, thus yielding a net return of about 20 per cent on the invested capital. These four paper mills, when established, will produce about 1,32.000 tons of paper annually and provide additional employment, directly and indirectly, to at least 25 to 30 thousand people of this State.

The Governments of Assam, Madhya Pradesh and Orissa have refused to meet the needs of the paper industry in Bihar for bamboo and grant leases at lower rates of royalty to those industrialists who establish the paper mills inside their States.

Before the paper mills are started, it should be the duty of the Government to see that the existing mills are not denied the opportunity of expanding and modernising themselves for this would be a more economical and effective way of achieving greater production.

The Cotton Mill Industry: The number of spinning and composite mills at the end of the Second Plan is given separately below:

TABLE 3.36

States	*Spinning Mills*	*Composite Mills*	*Total*
Andhra Pradesh	11 (2)	3 (7)	14 (5)
Bihar	—	3 (7)	3 (10)
Delhi	—	4 (6)	4 (9)
Kerala	8 (2)	5 (5)	13 (6)
Madhya Pradesh	1 (7)	17 (3)	18 (3)
Mysore	7 (4)	10 (3)	17 (4)
Orissa	2 (6)	1 (8)	3 (10)
Punjab	4 (5)	4 (6)	8 (8)
Pondicherry	—	3 (7)	3 (10)
Rajasthan	2 (6)	8 (4)	10 (7)
Uttar Pradesh	8 (3)	17 (2)	25 (2)
West Bengal	14 (1)	18 (1)	32 (1)

Note: Figures in brackets indicate ranks.

The distribution of loomage in India as between the different States is shown in Table 3.37.

The two cotton mills at Patna and Gaya hardly meet 5 per cent of the total demand for cloth of the people of Bihar, estimated at about 500 million yards per year. No doubt, there is lack of raw materials for this industry in Bihar but the labour required by it is cheaper here than in Bombay, Ahmedabad or Kanpur. Besides, distribution cost is lower because of local production.

The State Government had decided to set-up a Textile Corporation to go into the question of the establishment of textile mills in this State.

The Glass Industry: In 1961 Bihar occupied the fifth positions among Part-A States in respect of the number of factories in the glass industry and the third position in respect of the annual capacity of these factories. This is indicated by the Table 3.38 given on next page.

The Iron and Steel Industry: The Tata Iron and Steel Company (TISCO): The history of the Tata Iron and Steel Company is the history of the iron and steel industry in Bihar; nay, the credit for the production of steel in India goes to the pioneering spirit, enterprise and foresight of Jamshetji Nasharwanji Tata. His career is said to have formed a true example of industrial romance. He

TABLE 3.37

Installed Weaving Capacity in Cotton Mills as on January 1

States	*1956*		*1962*	
	Composite Mills	*Looms*	*Composite Mills*	*Looms*
1	2	3	4	5
Andhra Pradesh	3 (9)	1,457 (11)	2 (11)	1,228 (13)
Bihar	2 (10)	745 (15)	3 (10)	822 (15)
Delhi	3 (9)	3,442 (9)	4 (9)	3,806 (8)
Gujarat	94 (1)	56,369 (2)	87 (1)	56,341 (2)
(Ahmedabad)	(63)	(41,642)	(61)	(42,278)
Kerala	4 (8)	1,224 (13)	5 (8)	1,397 (12)
Madhya Pradesh	18 (4)	12,911 (4)	17 (5)	12,365 (4)
Madras	24 (3)	8,016 (6)	25 (3)	7,570 (6)
Maharashtra	83 (2)	83,710 (1)	80 (2)	80,465 (1)
(Bombay City)	(58)	(65,183)	(56)	(62,478)
Mysore	10 (6)	4,529 (7)	10 (6)	4,823 (7)
Orissa	1 (11)	864 (14)	1 (12)	864 (14)
Pondicherry	3(9)	2,089 (10)	3 (10)	2,116 (10)
Punjab	3(9)	1,383 (12)	4 (9)	2,016 (11)
Rajasthan	9 (7)	3,457 (8)	8 (7)	2,563 (9)
Uttar Pradesh	17(5)	13,590 (3)	17 (5)	13,535 (3)
West Bengal	17 (5)	9,115 (5)	19 (4)	9,516 (5)
Total	291	2,02,901	285	1,99,427

Notes 1. Figures in brackets indicate ranks.
2. The above figures exclude tape looms and looms installed in spinning mills.

conceived of the idea of a steel industry in collaboration with Burjorji Padshah, Professor of Ethics and Philosophy at a Karachi College. He had set about surveying in Bengal and Bihar with the help of American and European experts with the end of setting up the industry on a large scale, utilizing the latest scientific methods, in view. Unfortunately, he died in 1904. His sons, Dorabji Tata and Ratanji Tata, advised by Professor Padshah, got the Tata Iron and Steel Company registered in 1907. Bengal helped them with capital. The foundation stone was laid at Sakchi in Singhbhum district, to be renamed Jamshedpur after the great pioneer. An American engineer of the name of Charles Page Perin

TABLE 3.38

The Glass Industry

States	*1951*		*1956*		*1961*	
	Number of units	*Annual capacity (tons)*	*Number of units*	*Annual capacity (tons)*	*Number of units*	*Annual capacity (tons)*
Andhra Pradesh	2[a] (7)	3,960[a] (8)	2[a] (8)	4,800[a] (7)	1 (7)	1,800 (11)
Bihar	8 (4)	16,380 (4)	8 (5)	39,600 (4)	4 (5)	60,700 (3)
Delhi	2 (9)	1,200	3 (7)	4,400 (8)	2 (6)	1,800 (11)
Gujarat	—	—	—	—	2 (6)	27,900 (5)
Kerala	—	N.A.	—	—	1 (7)	3,600 (10)
Madhya Pradesh	5 (5)	4,220 (6)	5 (6)	3,660 (9)	1 (7)	700 (12)
Madras	8 (4)	6,850 (5)	9 (4)	10,800 (5)	6 (4)	11,100 (7)
Maharashtra	22[b] (2)	43,560[b] (2)	186 (3)	49,1006 (3)	22 (3)	57,900 (4)
Mysore	1 (8)	360 (10)	2 (8)	1,160 (11)	1 (7)	500 (13)
Orissa	1 (8)	36 (11)	—	—	2 (6)	13,200 (6)
Punjab	4[c] (6)	4,140 (7)	3 (7)	9,300 (6)	2 (6)	5,800 (8)
Rajasthan	2 (6)	900 (9)	2 (8)	2,700 (10)	1 (7)	4,800 (9)
Uttar Pradesh	21 (3)	36,960 (3)	24 (2)	63,900 (2)	26 (1)	83.000 (2)
West Bengal	30 (1)	63,600 (1)	28 (1)	90,800 (1)	24 (2)	1,10,400 (1)
Total	109	1,88,850	109	2,91,020	97	3,83,200

a Including Hyderabad. *b* Including Gujarat. *c*. Including PEPSU.

Note: Figures in brackets indicate ranks.

was instrumental in the selection of the site at the junction of the Suwarnrekha and Khokai, with coal, lime and iron ores at a distance of 100 miles from there. One Bengali geologist called Promotha Nath Bose hade assured Perin of the supply of iron ores at that place. There occurred during 1905-1910 a great boom in the cotton textile industry in Bombay mainly in the wake of the Swadeshi Movement, leading to large profit, part of which flowed into the Tata venture. Dorabji Tata and B.J. Padshah had tried in vain to obtain most of the finance for their scheme in London, because from the degree of control desired by the English investors for their representatives of the management it had appeared that they wanted to sweep the Tata firm aside. But the response of the Indian public to the appeal of the Tatas for finance was splendid. In a lecture delivered to the Staffordshire Iron and Steel Institute in 1912 Mr. A. Sahlin, a partner of Messers. J. Kennedly, Sahlin and Co., Engineers, Pittsburg, gave a graphic description of this response in the following words: From early morning till late at night the Tata offices in Bombay were besieged by an eager crowd of native investors. Old and young, rich and poor, men and women, they came offering their mites; and at the end of three weeks, the entire capital required for the construction requirements £16,30,000 was secured, every penny contributed by some eight thousand native Indians. And, when later an issue of debentures was decided upon to provide working capital, the entire issue of £ 4,00,000 was subscribed for by one Indian magnate, the Maharaja Scindia of Gwalior. The event proved beyond doubt that ware a sound industrial scheme, sponsored by persons in whose ability and integrity the public had confidence placed before the people, probably it would not be difficult to obtain finance entirely from indigenous sources.

The project was implemented in various stages. In 1911 the blast furnaces were fired. Pig iron rolled out of the works. By the year 1913 the steel plant was in full blast. Steel ingots were produced a year later. The Company had been started with a capital of approximately Rs. 232 lakhs, two 200-ton blast furnances, four 40-ton open heat furnances and 180 copper coke ovens. The original capacity of the plant was nearly 1,80,000 tons of pig iron; 1,00,000 tons of steel and 70,000 tons of rails, beams, channels, angles, fishplates and bars. From the very beginning it was obvious that, in view of the tendencies in the industry all over the world, not only was the size of the various units too small, but the manufacturing operations as a whole had been started on too small a scale. Thus the economics of large-scale production could not be realised to the same extent at Jamshedpur as at any of the leading steel works in Europe and America against whose products the Jamshedpur steel had to compete. When this is considered and when it is remembered that the manufacture of standardised steel in a new locality and out of untried materials involves a number of technical difficulties, we cannot but come to the conclusion that the Tatas had to face an uphill task in competing with the steel manufacturers of Europe and America which had generations of experience behind them. Thus, in normal circumstances the Company would have been totally routed without some kind of protection, by luckily the First World War broke out a few months after the starting of manufacturing operations and gave the Company as effective a protection as it could have desired.

As a result of the war, while the supplies of foreign steel and steel products gradually declined to the vanishing point, the requirements of the then Government of India in the matter of rails and structural materials for use in the near Eastern and other theatres of the war increased to an enormous extent. The Tatas sacrificed a part of their profit to serve the Government in its hour of need. But so great was the demand for steel at the time and so limited were the supplies that the Company reaped a rich harvest of profit during the war and in order to meet the demand in the country greatly enlarged the existing furnaces and entered upon a programme of enormous extensions. These extensions aimed at increasing the productive capacity of the plant to nearly 10,00,000 tons of pig iron and 6,00,000 tons of steel.

During the war it supplied the Government 1,500 miles of rails and nearly 3,00,000 tons of steel material. This turned out to be a great asset in the victory of the allied powers in Mesopotamia. Following the war the Company embarked upon extension programmes, which were accomplished in various stages. As a large part of these extensions was undertaken during the years immediately following the war when prices had reached unheard of levels with the result that cost the Company more than twice of what they would have cost had the Tatas waited till the return of normal conditions.

After the war with the return of normal conditions, the profits gradually gave place to losses. The Company approached the Government for protection, pointing out that its difficulties were due to foreign dumping, depreciation of the European currencies against whose products it had to compete and its own lack of experience as well as various sacrifices which it had made during the case was referred for enquiry to the Tariff Board in 1923, war, which after seemingly exhaustive enquiries came to the conclusion that the steel industry satisfied all the conditions for protection laid down by the Fiscal Commission, that the difficulties of the Company were due mainly to higher labour cost which had been operative at Jamshedpur owing to the necessity of training extra hands in anticipation of the starting of new units under the scheme for the extension of works and of employing highly-paid foreign skilled workmen, and that all these handicaps would gradually disappear after the costs had been adjusted to production and the higher staff had been Indianised,

> "That the Company had been juggling with figures (of their own making) to prove their case for protection was evident from the fact that the advantage of nearly 50 per cent on the cost of materials over foreign countries could not have been entirely swallowed up by the higher cost of skilled labour and superintendence. The truth was that the difficulties of Jamshedpur were entirely due to mismanagement which the Tariff Board, composed as it was of laymen, was either too incompetent to detect or had no desire to detect. It was a suggestive fact that the Board refused to soil their hands with the evidence offered by Mr. Homi (a former employee of the Tatas) on the ground that it had been obtained by him without the consent of his employers ! That the company relied too much upon Government's good will and charity and too little upon its own efforts was shown by the fact that up till 1924 it had done little towards displacing expensive foreign technicians (who were drawing anything between 200 and 400 per cent more at Jamshedpur than in their own countries) by Indian staff. Further, the difficulties of the Company had been, were still, due to the fact that the cost of the plant was unnecessarily piled up by undertaking the extension programmes at a time when prices were more than 100 per cent higher than the normal."

But notwithstanding these mistakes, which were to a certain extent unavoidable in the case of a great pioneer concern, the Tatas deserved protection from foreign competition; for otherwise this important key industry would have been destroyed, and the closing down of the Company would have dealt a death blow to industrial progress in India. The loss of Rs. 15 crores invested in it would have had its repercussions on the fortunes of industrial and commercial activity in the country with disastrous consequences, apart from the fact that the various important subsidiary industries would have never been established, and all possibilities of establishing the engineering industries in the country would have been completely snapped. The Report of the Tariff Board was, in fact, based on these sentiments, though the Board tried to justify to conclusions by a crude jugglery with some sort of facts and figures, of which the Tatas themselves were the authors. A mixed system of bounties and protection was recommended and incorporated in a bill, which became the Steel Industry Protection Act of 1924. By this Act, protective duties ranging between Rs. 14 and Rs. 40 per ton were imposed on certain varieties of steels and steel products which competed with the products of the Company. At the same time these bounties were to be given to steel rails and fish-plates for three years, the rates being fixed at Rs. 32 per ton for the first year, Rs. 26 for the second year and Rs. 20 for the third year. These arrangements were to remain in operation for only three years as it was thought that during this period the productive capacity of the works would be fostered to the maximum and the European currencies would be stabilised. The imposition of these protective duties would have in any case increased the cost of steel to a corresponding extent and thus, adversely affected the various steel-using industries. As these industries (of which the engineering, tin plate, wagon, agricultural implement and steel wire industries were the most important) would have never been able to compete with the foreigners in the Indian market on account of the increase in the cost of steel, they were suitably protected by the grant of bounties or protective duties according to their requirements.

But contrary to the expectations of the Tariff Board, the European currencies continued to depreciate while the exchange value of the Indian rupee moved in the opposite direction. Thus, the price of the European steel as measured in terms of the Indian currency began to fall so that the effects of protective duties began to be nullified to a corresponding extent. The matter was again referred to the Tariff Board, which expressed the opinion that a case for further protection had been established and recommended the enhancement of import duties. The Government, on the other hand, in order to avoid a rise in the price of steel and steel products in the country, proposed further bounties. The proposals of the Government were put before the Legislature in 1925, and a bounty of Rs. 20 per ton was granted on 70 per cent of the steel produced in Indian between October 1, 1924 and September 30, 1925, provide that steel was convertible into articles already protected by the Act of 1924. After another examination in 1926 the Board recommended that the protective duties should continue in a modified form for a period of seven years but that bounties should be discontinued. The bill embodying these recommendations (placed before the Legislature in 1927) was designed to introduce imperial preference through the backdoor. It proposed the imposition of basic and additional duties on steel and steel products entering India. The former was to be imposed on all steel, both British and non-British, while the non-British products were to be subject to the latter as well. Although popular opinion was against this principle of differentiation in the fiscal treatment of the goods of British origin, yet this was in vain and the bill was passed in its original form, except that an illusory safeguard was inserted whereby the Government was enabled to increased the duty on the British steel manufactures in cases of emergency in order to make protection more effective.

The Board was again commissioned in 1933 to enquire into the conditions of the steel industry. It found that the industry was no more in need of protection against the British steel but as the European steel was still being sold at uneconomic prices, the Indian steel industry needed some protection from its unfair competition. It, therefore, recommended the adoption of free trade in relation to the British steel, while in relation to the European steel it suggested the retention of import duties in a modified form. A bill based on these recommendations was submitted to the Assembly in 1934 and was duly passed into law. An excise duty of Rs. 4 per ton was levied on all steel ingots produced in British India and in order that the Indian steel industry might not suffer unduly in consequence of the operation of the duty, it was provided that all the steel products imported from abroad should be subjected to a countervailing customs duty equivalent to the excise duty on steel ingots. The untested Tata steel was subjected to the same fiscal burden as the tested British steel regardless of a Rs. 10 price differential. The Tatas had to resort to the cutting down of the price of their untested steel with a view to finding a market for it. The British steel industry was helped at the expense of the Tatas.

By 1935 the output of finished steel of the Company had risen to 6,46,000 tons a year. When the Second World War began, the Company had a production capacity of a little under 7,57,000 tons of saleable steel. This war too proved to be a boon in disguise for this industry. In 1943 the production of the company had shot upto 7,92,000 tons.

The protective duties, which were to expire on March 31,1941, continued from time to time by the Continuation Acts, the last extension being for a period of one year till March 31, 1947. The Government froze steel prices at the level prevailing on October 1, 1939 subject only to actual increase in costs. After the war, the Government did not decontrol steel prices but in place of the pre-war system of protective duties adopted a system of statutory fixing of prices from time to time after enquiry by the Board. The basis adopted for fixing prices was to allow fair manufacturing costs plus depreciation and other facilities, plus a return at rate of 8 per cent on the gross block.

The scheme of protection to the industry was discontinued from April 1, 1947 as it had become redundant. However, protective duties continued as revenue duties.

The Tata Iron and Steel Company undertook programme of expansion and modernisation in 1951 with increasing its capacity to 9.3 lakh tons of saleable steel products. Another programme of expansion of the company related to further addition to its plant for a capacity of 2 million tons of ingots and 1.5 million tons of finished and semi-finished steel. It set out on this project in 1955 and entered into a $ 130 million agreement with Kaiser Engineers of the U.S.A. The Government also guaranteed two loans of $ 75 millions and $ 32.5 millions each from the World Bank. It also received a special advance of Rs. 10 crores from the Price Equalisation Fund operated by the Government. The new blast furnace marking the final phase of the Company's programme was commissioned in October 1958. The project embraced every aspect of steel production from the extraction and processing of ore to the rolling of finished steel at a cost of Rs. 118 crores including ancillary schemes. Apart from the special advance from the fund and the Bank loans, the Company raised equity capital of the order of Rs. 13.5 crores. In addition, a development fund was also created through a special element included in the retention price of steel for assisting the units in the private sector. Finances for the expansion projects of the Company were made available through an interest-bearing loan from the Government of the order of Rs. 7.9 crores, a special loan of Rs. 10 crores from the Fund and two loans each of $ 30.02 millions and $ 20 millions from the Bank. Additional resources were found through fresh equity capital and the development rebate allowed by the Tariff Commission in the retention price of steel produced by the Company.

The very fact that for rupee resources the Company had to rely on special interest-bearing advances from the Fund indicates that it was not able to meet its financial requirements from other sources to the full extent of its needs. Although part of the resources was met out of fresh equity capital, yet it could not attract more funds from the potential investors chiefly because of the low percentage of dividend (about 4 per cent) that it was offering in the past so many years.

The Table 3.39 gives the production figures for the Plan period.

During 1964-65 the Company was asked by the Government of India to consider an expansion of about 2 million ingot tons in the Fourth Plan period, though full production would not be achieved until the Fifth Plan period. But a project for doubling once again the capacity of the Jamshedpur Plan obviously poses technical, financial and other problems of tremendous magnitude and complexity, the solution of which is still fraught with many uncertainties. The Company is willing to undertake this provided the problem of finance is solved on a basis which would ensure its continued financial stability and the maintenance of existing dividends on the present capital and would offer prospects of a fair reward to the share-holders, and provided further that all requirements of raw materials, rail transport and power are

TABLE 3.39

Year	*Total Saleable Steel (In '000 Tons)*
1951-52	812
1952-53	803
1953-54	793
1954-55	796
1955-56	812
1956-57	812
1957-58	799
1958-59	899
1959-60	1,237
1960-61	1,263
1961-62	1,318
1962-63	1,413
1963-64	1,507
1964-65	1,568

assured. The Company feels that a further expansion up to a total capacity of 3.8 million tons to 4 million tons of ingot steel per annum based on the installation of new plant and equipment of the most modern and productive kind and permitting the shutting down of the old and obsolete units would ensure it a degree of efficiency, productivity and earning power which would obviously be of the greatest long-term advantage to the shareholders. The scheme is to be made viable financially technically and economically first. The whole project, if it fructifies, will depend on the financial support and approval of the World Bank, which also will want to satisfy itself in regard to its viability, availability of rupee finance, market demand and other factors.

Mr. J.R.D. Tata, on being consulted by the Planning Commission in 1959 with regard to the Third Plan targets questioned the need, in the context of our over-all economic development, for placing so much emphasis on and allocating such a large proportion of our resources to the development of the basic steel industry and pointed out at that time that in other countries the ratio of steel consumed to the total production of manufactured goods was much lower than planned for our country; that while it was essential to meet in full the needs of the manufacturing industries consuming steel and particularly costly special steels, there was no justification for committing so much of our scarce resources in money and foreign exchange to ensure complete self-sufficiency in steels used for non-essential purposes; and that it was wasteful to invest vast sums in steel capacity without making sure of a simultaneous expansion of raw materials, transport, power, technical and managerial skills, without which partly the new capacity would remain idle or take an unduly long time to reach full utilization. As it turned out, the expansion of steel capacity undertaken in the Third Plan period suffered greatly for a time from delays, shortages and deficiencies in raw materials and transport, and the bulk of the special steels required by the steel processing industries had to be imported. Ten years after starting the manufacture of commercial vehicles the TELCO has still to import almost every kilo of the special steel incorporated in its products even today but because of the foreign exchange crisis these imports have been curtailed and so it has been compelled to curtail production. The steel industry is the most capital intensive of all engineering industries and the one which provides for about the lowest employment potential. For every rupee spent in creating new steel capacity, products worth only half a rupee per year are created, whereas the ratio is at least 1 : 1 in more advanced industries manufacturing products made of iron and steel, while their employment potential is several times higher. In a developing economy like ours where shortages and imbalances prevail throughout and will continue for many years, we have to weigh up the pros and cons of giving a higher priority to steel for non-essential purposes than to fertilizers, road transport, electric power, education, medical care, and so on, in all of which there will be persisting shortages even after the Fourth Plan. A rigorous assessment of the relative essentiality of demand as between steel and other products in short supply is urgently called for.

The distribution of the units of other industries between the different States of India is given in Table 3.40.

1. *The Cotton Textile Industry:* It is the oldest and the biggest industry in India, contributing 28.7 per cent of the total productive capital. 41.5 per cent of the total employment and 32.8 per cent of the total value added in the 29 industries covered by the CMI in 1957. In 1948 more than 60 per cent of the cotton textile mills were localised in the Bombay State. Of the remaining 39.3 per cent,

TABLE 3.40

Showing Distribution of Units of Other Industries in Different States

(Number of Units)

Sl. No.	Industry	Andhra Pradesh	Assam	Bihar	Bombay	Delhi	Gujarat	Himachal Pradesh	Jammu & Kashmir	Karala
1	2	3	4	5	6	7	8	9	10	11
1.	Jute (1963)	4	—	3	—	—	—	—	—	—
2.	Cotton Hosiery (1956)									
	(a) Large-Scale Sector	1	—	—	5	—	—	—	—	—
	(b) Small-Scale Sector	3	2	8	70	80	—	—	—	19
3.	Soap Industry (1960-61)									
	Small-Scale Sector	14	9	68	45	29	—	—	17	31
4.	Tanning Industry (1961)	1	—	1	3	—	2	—	—	—
5.	Leather Foodwear Industry (1961)	—	—	1	1	—	—	—	—	—
6.	Wooden Toys (1959)	9	3	1	2	—	—	—	6	6
7.	Non-traditional Toys (1959)	—	—	—	1	7	—	—	—	—
8.	Coal Mining and Oil Mining Machinery & Equipment (1961)	—	—	2	—	—	—	—	—	—

(Contd.)

TABLE 3.40 (*Contd.*)

1	2	3	4	5	6	7	8	9	10	11
9.	Miscellaneous Material Handling Equipment (1960)	—	—	1	5	—	—	—	—	—
10.	Boiling House equipment (1962)	1	—	1	4	—	—	—	—	—
11.	Oil Mill Machines (1962)	1	—	3	5	—	—	—	—	—
12.	Cement Machinery (1960-61)	—	—	2	—	—	—	—	—	—
13.	Paper and Printing Machinery (1962)	—	—	3	6	—	1	—	—	—
14.	Miscellaneous Earth Moving Equipment (1962)	—	—	1	2	—	—	—	—	—
15.	Agricultural Implements (1961)	4	—	3	12	3	2	1	—	2
16.	Power Driven Pumps (1960): Small-Scale Sector	—	—	1	8	1	5	—	—	1
17.	Machine Tools (1958): Small-Scale Sector	5	—	2	5	11	30	—	—	2
18.	Hand Tools (1956-57): Small-Scale Sector	—	—	4	1	5	9	—	—	—

19. Ball Bearings (1962)	—	—	1	3	—	—	—	—	—
20. Bolts, Nuts and Rivets:									
(a) Large-Scale Sector (1962)	—	—	2	8	1	—	—	—	—
(b) Small-Scale Sector (1957)	1	4	2	18	15	1	—	—	7
21. Wood Screws (1956-57): Small-Scale Sector	—	—	1	2	1	—	—	—	2
22. Bicycle (1956): Organised Sector	—	—	1	1	1	—	—	—	—
23. Locomotives (1956)	—	—	1	—	—	—	—	—	—
24. Scientific and Surveying Instruments (1958): Small-Scale Sector	5	—	2	16	6	—	—	—	1
25. Surgical Instruments and Medical Appliances (1956)	—	—	1	4	5	—	—	—	1
26. Hurricane Lanterns (1961)	—	1	2	2	—	—	—	—	—
27. Oil Pressure Lamps (1961)	—	—	1	4	—	—	—	—	—
28. Metal Containers (1961)	—	1	1	1	2	5	—	—	2
29. Steel Wire and Wire Products (1961)	—	—	1	2	1	—	—	—	—
30. Cast Iron Pipes (1961)	—	—	1	3	—	2	—	—	—

(Contd.)

TABLE 3.40 (*Contd.*)

1	*2*	*3*	*4*	*5*	*6*	*7*	*8*	*9*	*10*	*11*
31.	Brass, Copper and Bell-Metal Domestic Utensils (1955-56): Cottage and Small-Scale Sector	21	445	376	36	33	8	—	—	6
32.	Brass, Bell-Metal Utensils (1956-57): Large-Scale Sector	—	—	—	10	—	1	—	—	—
33.	Aluminium Utensils (1956-57): Small-Scale Sector	28	—	1	9	5	—	—	—	—
34.	Electric Lamps (1961)	—	—	1	3	—	—	—	—	—
35.	Radio Receivers (1961)	—	—	1	7	1	—	—	—	—
36.	Bare Copper Conductors (1960)	—	—	1	2	—	—	—	—	—
37.	Paper Insulated Power Cables (1960)	—	—	1	1	—	—	—	—	—
38.	Winding Wires (1960-61)	—	—	1	4	—	—	—	—	—
39.	Sulphuric Acid Manufacture (1961)	3	1	7	12	1	—	—	—	3
40.	Chlorine and Bleaching Powder (1956)	—	—	1	3	1	2	—	—	1

41. Sodium Sulphate (1961)	—	—	1	7	1	2	—	—	1
42. Power Alcohol and Industrial Alcohol (1956)	1	—	2	2	—	1	—	—	—
43. Ceramics (1962)	3	—	1	8	9	13	—	—	5
44. Pottery Craft Centres (1962)	4	4	15	5	1	3	1	—	1
45. Village Pottery Manufacturing Units (1961-62)	6	14	24	19	—	18	—	—	37
46. Glass and Glass Wares (1961)	1	—	1	3	—	—	—	—	—
47. Sheet Glass (1962)	—	—	2	—	—	—	—	—	—
48. Refractories (1960-61)	—	—	12	3	1	4	—	—	1

(Contd.)

TABLE 3.40 (*Contd.*)

Sl. No.	*Industry*	*Madhya Pradesh*	*Madras*	*Mysore*	*Orissa*	*Punjab*	*Rajas-than*	*Tripura*	*Uttar Pradesh*	*West Bengal*	*Total*
1	*2*	*12*	*13*	*14*	*15*	*16*	*17*	*18*	*19*	*20*	*21*
1.	Jute (1963)	1	—	—	—	—	—	—	3	81	92
2.	Cotton Hosiery (1956)										
	(a) Large-Scale Sector	1	5	2	—	—	—	—	6	12	32
	(b) Small-Scale Sector	40	232	150	4	215	8	—	245	837	1,903
3.	Soap Industry (1960-61)										
	Small-Scale Sector	28	66	20	18	75	21	—	24	50	515
4.	Tanning Industry (1961)	1	5	1	1	1	—	—	14	2	32
5.	Leather Footwear Industry (1961)	1	1	1	—	1	—	—	5	1	12
6.	Wooden Toys (1959)	34	110	12	—	14	131	—	632	21	981
7.	Non-traditional Toys (1959)	1	1	1	—	—	—	—	—	—	11
8.	Coal Mining and Oil Mining Machinery & Equipment (1961)	—	—	—	—	—	—	—	—	3	5
9.	Miscellaneous Material Handling Equipment (1960)	—	1	—	—	—	—	—	—	8	15
10.	Boiling House equipment (1962)	1	1	—	—	1	—	—	5	3	17

11. Oil Mill Machines (1962)	—	3	1	—	2	—	—	4	1	21
12. Cement Machinery (1960-61)	—	1	—	1	1	—	—	—	—	5
13. Paper and Printing Machinery (1962)	—	2	—	1	2	1	—	—	7	23
14. Miscellaneous Earth Moving Equipment (1962)	—	—	—	—	—	—	—	1	1	5
15. Agricultural Implements (1961)	—	4	2	—	6	—	—	10	11	60
16. Power Driven Pumps (1960):										
Small-Scale Sector	1	22	—	—	—	—	—	2	7	48
17. Machines Tools (1958):										
Small-Scale Sector	6	5	4	—	246	—	—	—	28	344
18. Hand Tools (1956-57):										
Small-Scale Sector	—	5	—	—	—	—	—	2	—	26
19. Ball Bearings (1962)	—	—	—	—	—	—	—	—	—	4
20. Bolts, Nuts and Rivets:										
(a) Large-Scale Sector (1962)	—	1	1	—	9	—	—	—	13	35
(b) Small-Seals Sector (1957)	—	12	—	—	76	—	—	21	43	200

(Contd.)

TABLE 3.40 (*Contd.*)

1	*2*	*12*	*13*	*14*	*15*	*16*	*17*	*18*	*19*	*20*	*21*
21.	Wood Screws (1956-57):										
	Small-Scale Sector	—	1	—	—	14	—	—	2	4	27
22.	Bicycles (1956):										
	Organised Sector	—	1	—	—	4	—	—	3	3	14
23.	Locomotives (1956)	—	—	—	—	—	—	—	—	1	2
24.	Scientific and Surveying Instruments (1958):										
	Small-Scale Sector	4	1	6	—	68	—	—	89	15	213
25.	Surgical Instruments and Medical Appliances (1956)	—	6	—	—	37	—	—	—	9	63
26.	Hurricane Lanterns (1961)	—	—	—	—	—	—	—	3	3	11
27.	Oil Pressure Lamps (1961)	—	—	—	—	—	—	—	—	3	8
28.	Metal Containers (1961)	—	5	—	—	1	—	—	2	3	23
29.	Steel Wire and Wire Products (1961)	—	1	—	—	1	—	—	—	4	10
30.	Cast Iron Pipes (1961)	—	—	1	2	—	—	—	—	4	13
31.	Brass, Copper and Bell Metal Domestic Utensils (1955-56): Cottage and										
	Small-Scale Sector	3	39	—	1,098	85	5	—	179	3,016	5,350
32.	Brass, Bell-Metal Utensils (1956-57):										
	Large-Scale Sector	1	7	—	—	—	1	—	2	—	22

33. Aluminium Utensils (1956-57): Small-Scale Sector	—	17	—	3	4	—	—	—	22	89
34. Electric Lamps (1961)	—	—	1	—	1	—	—	4	7	17
35. Radio Receivers (1961)	—	2	1	—	3	—	—	—	5	20
36. Bare Copper Conductors (1960)	—	—	—	—	—	1	—	—	1	5
37. Paper Insulated Power Cables (1960)	—	—	—	—	1	—	—	—	—	2
38. Winding Wires (1960-61)	—	—	—	—	1	—	—	—	2	8
39. Sulphuric Acid Manufacture (1961)	2	2	1	—	1	—	—	4	6	43
40. Chlorine and Bleaching Powder (1956)	—	1	—	1	—	—	—	—	2	12
41. Sodium Sulphate (1961)	—	2	—	—	1	—	—	—	2	17
42. Power Alcohol and Industrial Alcohol (1956)	—	—	1	—	1	—	—	12	—	19
43. Ceramics (1962)	5	5	2	2	1	—	—	2	10	66
44. Pottery Craft Centres (1962)	7	35	5	1	4	3	3	6	8	106
45. Village Pottery Manufacturing Units (1961-62)	4	25	12	7	16	7	—	15	26	230
46. Glass and Glass Wares (1961)	—	1	1	1	—	—	—	7	3	17
47. Sheet Glass (1962)	—	—	—	—	—	—	—	—	1	14
48. Refractories (1960-61)	6	5	3	3	1	1	—	—	6	46

Madras had 14.8 per cent, Uttar Pradesh 6.5 per cent, West Bengal 5.4 per cent, Punjab 4.8 per cent, Madhya Pradesh 3.5 per cent, Delhi 1.9 per cent and all other States 2.4 per Cent. Bombay's share in the industry's aggregate capital, employment and net output was even greater, viz., 65.8 per cent, 64.7 per cent and 70.7 per cent respectively. Bombay's share in the total number of cotton textile factories had declined by 19.1 per cent by 1957. The shares of Uttar Pradesh, Punjab, Madhya Pradesh and Delhi had also fallen slightly. Madras including Andhra Pradesh had gained 9.7 per cent, West Bengal 3.6 per cent and other States over 10.1 per cent. Likewise, Bombay's share in the industry's aggregate capital, employment and net output had declined by 11.6 per cent, 8.9 per cent and 10.4 per cent respectively. Thus, there occurred a fair degree of dispersal in the cotton textile industry during the period 1948-57. Until recently the localisation of the Indian Cotton Textile industry had obscured the tendency towards dispersal. Table 3.41 is indicative of this.

2. *The General Engineering and Electrical Engineering Industry:* It is the second biggest industry of India both in terms of employment and net output. During 1948-57, this industry made phenomenal progress; the number of production units increased from 1,473 to 2,111, capital rose from Rs. 36 crores to Rs. 116 crores, employment grew from 1,39,888 to 2,05,579 and net output shot up from Rs. 20.6 crores to Rs. 58 crores. Broadly, the expansion was three times.

In 1958, 61.6 per cent of the total number of engineering factories were located in West Bengal (35.0 per cent) and Bombay (26.6 per cent). The remaining 38.4 per cent were distributed in Madras (10.1 per cent), Punjab (9.2 per cent), Uttar Pradesh (5.8 per cent), Delhi (5.4 per cent), Bihar (5.2 per cent) and other States (2.7 per cent). The shares of West Bengal and Bombay in the industry's aggregate capital, employment and net output were even greater, i.e. 76.2 per cent, 68.2 per cent and 76.1 per cent respectively. By 1957 there was a shift in the relative position of the States; the shares of certain States in the total number of engineering factories had declined e.g., West Bengal 10.1 per cent, Bombay 1.9 per cent, Madras 0.8 per cent, Bihar 1.4 per cent and Madhya Pradesh 0.4 per cent, whereas it had increased in Delhi 4.4 per cent, Uttar Pradesh 2.8 per cent, Punjab 2.6 per cent, Assam 0.3 per cent, Orissa 0.3 per cent and other States 4.3 per cent. The

TABLE 3.41

Cotton Textile Industry

States	*Number of factories (as percentage of total)*			*Productive capital (as percentage of total)*		
	1948	*1957*	*Percent Change*	*1948*	*1957*	*Percent Change*
Andhra Pradesh, Madras	14.8	24.5	9.7	12.6	18.2	5.6
Bombay	60.7	41.6	—19.1	65.8	54.2	—11.6
Delhi	1.9	1.6	— 0.3	2.3	2.4	0.1
Madhya Pradesh	3.5	3.4	— 0.1	4.3	3.9	— 0.4
Punjab	4.8	2.5	— 2.3	0.5	0.9	0.4
Uttar Pradesh	6.5	4.9	— 1.6	8.0	7.0	— 1.0
West Bengal	5.4	9.0	3.6	3.9	5.6	1.7
Other States (Including Union Territories)	2.4	12.5	10.1	2.6	7.8	5.2
Total	100.0	100.0	—	100.0	100.0	—

(Contd.)

TABLE 3.41 *(Contd.)*

States	*Employment (as percentage of total)*			*Value added (as percentage of total)*		
	1948	*1957*	*Percent Change*	*1948*	*1957*	*Percent Change*
Andhra Pradesh, Madras	12.4	15.8	3.4	11.2	15.0	3.8
Bombay	64.7	55.8	— 8.9	70.7	60.3	—10.4
Delhi	2.0	2.2	0.2	2.6	3.3	0.7
Madhya Pradesh	4.5	4.5	0.0	2.7	4.3	1.6
Punjab	0.6	0.4	0.3	0.3	0.9	0.6
Uttar Pradesh	8.6	7.3	— 1.3	7.6	6.6	— 1.0
West Bengal	4.7	6.0	1.3	3.7	4.3	0.6
Other States (Including Union Territories	2.5	7.5	5.0	1.2	5.3	4.1
Total	100.0	100.0	—	100.0	100.0	—

increases in other States' relative shares in the industry's aggregate capital, employment and net output by 1957 were appreciable, being 15.7 per cent, 9.4 per cent and 10.8 per cent respectively. The declines were mainly in West Bengal and Bihar in capital—3.3 per cent and 5.9 per cent respectively, in employment—7.2 per cent and 3.4 per cent respectively and in net output—8.2 and 5.3 per cent respectively. Changes in the position of other States were not significant as will be seen from the relevant data shown in Table 3.42. While a shift in the locational position of the industry was clearly discernible, there was still a high degree of concentration, especially in Bombay where the position remained practically stationary during the decade 1948-57. The equalisation of the prices of iron and steel for all rail heads in the country some time in 1956 was intended to help the growth of the industry in underdeveloped areas such as Rajasthan, Himachal Pradesh, Orissa, etc. A similar policy in respect of fuel and electricity might lead to the same object.

3. *The Iron and Steel Industry:* It ranked third in order of importance. It accounted for 10.5 per cent of the total productive capital, 4.8 per cent of the total employment and 11 per cent of the total value added. It consisted of a few primary producers which formed the core of the industry and a large number of re-rolling mills called secondary producers. Most of these re-rolling mills were localised in Uttar Pradesh and Punjab, the primary producers being West Bengal, Bihar, and Mysore (excluding State plants). Between 1948 and 1957 there was a shift in the relative importance of the States so far as the number of units in the iron and steel industry was concerned, the relative share of Uttar Pradesh declined by 30 per cent and that of Punjab rose by 24.7 per cent. The share of West Bengal increased by 4.5 per cent and of other States by 8 per cent. West Bengal and Bihar which had primary producers accounted for the 94.3 per cent of the total capital (34.8 per cent and 59.5 per cent respectively), 91.0 per cent of the total employment (40.5 per cent and 50 per cent respectively) and 96.3 per cent of the total value added (24.5 per cent and 71.8 per cent respectively) in 1948. These percentages declined in 1957 by 4.1 per cent, 13.4 per cent and 3.8 per cent respectively. It is interesting to observe that while the share of West Bengal in total capital and employment declined, its share in value added increased. In the case of Bihar even with a slight increase

TABLE 3.42

The General Engineering and Electrical Engineering Industry

States	*Number of factories (as percentage of total)*			*Productive capital (as percentage of total)*		
	1948	*1957*	*Percent Change*	*1948*	*1957*	*Percent Change*
Andhra Pradesh, Madras	10.1	9.3	—0.8	8.2	9.0	0.8
Assam	0.6	0.9	0.3	0.4	0.4	0.0
Bombay	26.6	24.7	— 1.9	34.0	26.7	— 7.3
Bihar	5.2	3.8	— 1.4	10.9	5.0	— 5.9
Delhi	5.4	9.8	4.4	1.7	1.8	0.1
Madhya Pradesh	1.3	0.9	0.4	2.1	1.9	— 0.2
Orissa	0.3	0.5	0.2	0.0	0.4	0.4
Punjab	9.2	11.8	2.6	2.9	3.1	0.2
Uttar Pradesh	5.8	8.6	2.8	3.3	3.1	—0.2
West Bengal	35.0	24.9	—10.9	36.2	32.9	— 3.3
Other States (including Union Territories)	0.5	4.8	4.3	0.3	15.7	15.4
Total	100.0	100.0	—	100.0	100.0	—

(*Contd.*)

TABLE 3.42 (*Contd.*)

States	*Employment (an percentage of total)*			*Value added (as percentage of total)*		
	1948	*1957*	*Percent Change*	*1948*	*1957*	*Percent Change*
Andhra Pradesh, Madras	10.9	9.4	— 1.5	6.8	7.4	0.6
Assam	0.7	0.6	— 0.1	0.5	0.3	— 0.2
Bombay	27.2	25.6	— 1.6	32.3	32.5	0.2
Bihar	8.9	5.8	— 3.4	9.7	4.4	— 5.3
Delhi	2.0	3.2	1.2	1.3	2.8	1.5
Madhya Pradesh	2.0	4.6	2.6	1.3	0.5	— 0.8
Orissa	0.3	0.8	0.5	0.0	0.3	— 0.3
Punjab	3.3	1.6	-- 1.7	2.2	2.8	0.6
Uttar Pradesh	3.3	5.1	1.8	1.9	2.4	0.5
West Bengal	41.0	33.8	— 7.2	43.8	35.6	— 8.2
Other States (including Union Territories)	0.4	9.8	9.4	0.2	11.0	10.8
Total	100.0	100.0	—	100.0	100.0	—

TABLE 3.43

The Iron and Steel Industry

States	*Number of factories (as percentage of total)*			*Productive capital (as percentage of total)*		
	1948	*1957*	*Percent Change*	*1948*	*1957*	*Percent Change*
Bihar	4.3	3.4	—0.9	59.5	60.2	0.7
Bombay	9.6	9.5	—0.1	1.4	1.6	0.2
Delhi	9.6	3.4	6.2	0.2	0.1	—0.1
Punjab	11.3	36.0	24.7	0.3	1.1	0.8
Uttar Pradesh	47.0	17.0	—30.9	3.0	1.6	—1.4
West Bengal	13.9	18.4	4.5	34.8	30.0	—4.8
Other States (including Union Territories)	4.3	12.3	8.0	0.8	5.4	4.6
Total	100.0	100.0	—	100.0	100.0	—

(*Contd.*)

TABLE 3.43 (*Contd.*)

States	*Employment (as percentage of total)*			*Value added (as percentage of total)*		
	1948	*1957*	*Percent Change*	*1948*	*1957*	*Percent Change*
Bihar	50.5	43.4	—8.1	71.8	57.1	—14.7
Bombay	2.0	3.8	1.6	0.8	2.0	1.2
Delhi	0.5	0.5	—	0.2	0.2	—
Punjab	0.5	2.8	2.3	0.1	0.7	0.6
Uttar Pradesh	5.1	4.2	—4.2	2.2	1.5	—0.7
West Bengal	40.5	35.2	—5.3	24.5	35.4	10.9
Other States (including Union Territories)	0.9	11.3	10.4	0.4	3.1	2.7
Total	100.0	100.0	—	100.0	100.0	—

in the share of capital, the shares in employment and value added declined by 8.1 per cent and 14.7 per cent respectively (see Table 3.43). With the setting up of State steel plants in Madhya Pradesh, Orissa and West Bengal in later years, a certain measure decentralisation had been achieved.

4. *The Jute Textile Industry:* The jute textile industry is by far the most important source of foreign exchange for India. Although the jute mills were only a little over 100 in number, they accounted for 7.8 per cent of the total productive capital, 13.2 per cent of the total employment, and 7.9 per cent of the total value added. The jute textile industry was ready the monopoly of West Bengal—over 90 per cent of the jute mills accounted for over 95 per cent of the industry's capital and over 91 per cent of the employment and over 92 per cent of the value added. The existence of jute mills in other States was really of no great economic moment. The unusual concentration of the industry in a very limited area in the Hoogly riverine was largely due to: (a) the export-oriented nature of the industry which required proximity to ports, (b) availability of raw jute fibres in bulk, and (c) the communication and cheap water transport facilities. The result was that instead of any movement as in the case of other industries, the concentrated locational positions of the jute industry was only getting accentuated as time passed on and it seemed unlikely that the monopolistic position of the Hoogly area would ever be seriously threatened. Table 3.44 is illustrative of this.

5. *The Sugar Industry:* The next important industry of India is the sugar industry with its share of 11 per cent in the total productive capital, 7.4 per cent in the total employment and 7.6 per cent in the total value added. It continued to be the industry of two States, viz., Uttar Pradesh and Bihar. In 1948 these two States together accounted for 78.5 per cent of the total sugar mills in India (55.8 per cent and 22.7 per cent respectively), 85 per cent of the total capital (65.2 per cent and 19.8 per cent respectively), 83.4 per cent of the total employment (53.9 per cent and 29.5 per cent respectively) and 70.0 per cent of the total value added (55.6 per cent and 14.4 per cent respectively). By 1957 the predominant position of Uttar Pradesh and Bihar in this industry underwent a change; the relative share of these two States in the total number of sugar factories declined by 10 per cent, in capital by 31.7 per cent, in employment by 11.7 per cent and in value added by 12

TABLE 3.44

The Jute Textile Industry

States	*Number of factories (as percentage of total)*			*Productive capital (as percentage of total)*		
	1948	*1957*	*Percent Change*	*1948*	*1957*	*Percent Change*
Andhra Pradesh, Madras	4.1	3.6	—0.5	3.0	1.8	1.2
Bihar	3.0	2.7	—0.3	3.2	0.8	—0.9
Madhya Pradesh	—	0.8	0.8	—	0.3	0.3
Uttar Pradesh	3.0	2.7	—0.3	—	1.5	—
West Bengal	89.9	90.2	0.3	93.8	95.6	1.8
Other States (including Union Territories)	—	—	—	—	—	—
Total	100.00	100.00	—	100.00	100.00	—

(*Contd.*)

TABLE 3.44 *(Contd.)*

States	*Employment* (as percentage of total)			*Value added* (as percentage of total)		
	1948	1957	Percent Change	1948	1957	Percent Change
Andhra Pradesh, Madras	2.1	2.9	0.8	1.6	2.8	1.2
Bihar	3.4	2.6	1.8	2.9	2.0	1.5
Madhya Pradesh	—	0.3	0.3	—	0.3	0.3
Uttar Pradesh	—	2.6	—	—	2.4	—
West Bengal	94.5	91.6	—2.9	95.5	92.5	—3.0
Other States (including Union Territories)	—	—	—	—	—	—
Total	100.0	109.0	—	100.0	100.0	—

per cent. Bombay and Madras (including Andhra Pradesh), which were the only two order States, recorded an increase of over 8 per cent in the number of factories, 10.1 per cent in capital, 6.9. per cent in employment and 8.9 per cent in value added (see Table 3.45).

Although in the years under survey the importance of South India had increased, North India still produced 75 per cent of the total output. In North India (largely Uttar Pradesh and Bihar) factory operations were limited to about 110-120 days per year while in the Central and Southern States (Bombay, Madras, Hyderabad and Andhra Pradesh) sugar production continued from 150 to 200 days because of a longer cane-growing season.

6. *The Chemical Industry:* The chemical industry in India made a phenomenal progress during the years under review. In 1948 the industry's share in the total productive capital in the 29 manufacturing industries was only 3.6 per cent, in the total employment only 1.9 per cent and in the total value added only 2.8 per cent. In 1957 these shares increased to 7.8 per cent, 3.1 per cent and 7.4 per cent respectively. In other words, the industry's expansion was between 2 to 3 times. As many as 66.5 per cent of the total chemical factories in India were concentrated in 1948 in West Bengal and Bombay (35.0 per cent and 31.5 per cent respectively), accounting for 75.2 per cent of the industry's total productive capital (29.5 per cent and 45.7 per cent respectively), 75.8 per cent of the employment (42.2 per cent and 35.6 per cent respectively) and 80.6 per cent of the value added (41.9 per cent and 39.6 per cent respectively). By 1957 the relative share of West Bengal had declined by 7.4 per cent in the total number of factories (Bombay's corresponding share had increased by 5.4 per cent), by 14.0 per cent in the total productive capital (Bombay's corresponding share had also fallen by 6.3 per cent), by 14.5 per cent in the total employment (Bombay's corresponding share had increased by 0.3 per cent) and by 21.1 per cent in the total value added (Bombay's corresponding share had increased by 9.3 per cent). Evidently, the degree of concentration in Bombay had increased further during the period 1948-57. There was some gain in the relative position of Bihar, Delhi and other States but the relative share of Uttar Pradesh and Madras had decreased (see Table 3.46).

Insofar as chemical industries are typically joint cost

TABLE 3.45

The Sugar Industry

States	*Number of factories (as percentage of total)*			*Productive capital (as percentage of total)*		
	1948	*1957*	*Percentage Change*	*1948*	*1957*	*Percentage Change*
Andhra Pradesh, Madras	9.20	0.03	—1.17	4.72	15.06	9.34
Bihar	22.69	16.04	—6.65	19.86	12.42	—7.44
Bombay	6.74	11.22	4.48	4.15	20.62	12.47
Orissa	1.86	0.53	—1.33	0.45	0.46	—0.19
Uttar Pradesh	35.82	52.43	—3.40	65.19	40.86	—24.40
Other States (including Union Territories)	3.69	11.76	8.07	1.63	11.75	10.12
Total	100.0	100.0	—	100.0	100.0	—

(Contd.)

TABLE 3.45 (*Contd.*)

States	*Employment (as percentage of total)*			*Value added (as percentage of total)*		
	1948	*1957*	*Percentage Change*	*1948*	*1957*	*Percentage Change*
Andhra Pradesh, Madras	6.92	9.34	2.43	18.58	14.28	5 70
Bihar	29.50	19.69	-9.81	14.35	14.89	0 54
Bombay	6.47	2.82	2.35	18.63	16.69	—2.03
Orissa	0.38	0.32	—0.06	1.08	0.18	0.19
Uttar Pradesh	53.92	52.03	—1.89	53.62	43.33	—12.29
Other States (including Union Territories)	2.01	0.80	6.99	1.74	10.72	8.98
Total	100.0	100.0	—	100.0	100.0	—

industries, frequently they develop through attempts to utilize byproducts and they always involve problems of waste and possible salvage. In them there has throughout been a marked tendency towards both a vertical and a horizontal integration.

7. *The Aluminium, Copper and Brass Industry*: It is yet another industry of growing national importance, although it accounted for only 2.1 per cent of the total productive capital, 1.2 per cent of the total employment and 2.3 per cent of the total value added in 1957. This industry was somewhat widely scattered. The largest concentration was, however, in Bombay. In 1948, 37.6 per cent of the total number of factories were located in Bombay, contributing 22.6 per cent of the total productive capital, 34.3 per cent of the total employment and 31.8 per cent of the total value added. The factories in West Bengal, being only 14.8 per cent of the total but of a bigger size, accounted for the largest share in capital, employment and value added (56.5 per cent, 35.9 per cent and 39.7 per cent respectively). Factories in Madras (including Andhra Pradesh), Uttar Pradesh, Punjab and Delhi, although constituting 44.6 per cent of the total accounted for only 11.1 per cent of the total capital, 21.4 per cent of the total employment and 11.4 per cent of the total value added. Between 1948 and 1957 there was some shift in the position of this industry. The share of West Bengal fell by 5.4 per cent in the total number of factories, 22.3 per cent in the total productive capital, 9.8 per cent in the total employment and 13.6 per cent in the total value added, the corresponding declines in Bombay being 5.1 per cent, 6.4 per cent, 11.1 per cent and 16.4 per cent respectively. The relative shares of Uttar Pradesh and Madras also declined. The shares of other States increased in the total number of factories by 6 per cent, in the total employment by 32.1 per cent and in the total value added by 33.2 per cent. In other words, the aluminium, copper and brass industry showed during the period 1948-57 an appreciable shift in its locational position from the States of heavy concentration to the States of relative under-development. Table 3.47 is illustrative of this.

The above account of the locational trends in the Indian industries during the decade 1948-57, confined as it is to certain selected industries, is adequate to give a cross-section view of the pattern of recent industrial growth in India. All the seven selected industries occupied a key position in India's national economy.

TABLE 3.46

The Chemical Industry

States	*Number of factories (as percentage of total)*			*Productive capital (as percentage of total)*		
	1948	*1957*	*Percent. Change*	*1948*	*1957*	*Percent. Change*
Andhra Pradesh, Madras	9.9	13.4	3.5	7.0	4.8	— 2.2
Bihar	7.9	3.3	—4.6	4.5	27.9	23.4
Bombay	31.5	36.9	5.4	45.7	39.4	— 6.3
Delhi	2.9	5.2	2.3	2.5	2.1	— 0.4
Uttar Pradesh	8.9	7.1	—1.8	9.7	3.4	—6.3
West Bengal	35.0	27.6	—7.4	29.5	15.5	—14.4
Other States (Including Union Territories	3.9	6.5	2.6	1.1	6.9	— 5.8
Total	100.0	100.0	—	100.0	100.0	—

(*Contd.*)

TABLE 3.46 *(Contd.)*

States	*Employment (as percentage of total)*			*Value added (as percentage of total)*		
	1948	*1957*	*Percent. Change*	*1948*	*1957*	*Percent. Change*
Andhra Pradesh, Madras	7.2	8.3	1.1	6.6	6.2	—0.4
Bihar	6.4	16.6	10.2	4.2	13.8	6-6
Bombay	35.6	35.9	0.3	39.6	49.9	9.3
Delhi	2.4	3.0	0.6	0.6	3.1	2.5
Uttar Pradesh	6.9	4.7	—2.2	7.1	3.7	—3.4
West Bengal	40.2	25.7	—14.5	41.0	19.9	—21.1
Other States (including Union Territories)	1.3	5.8	4.5	0.9	4.4	3.5
Total	100.0	100.0	—	100.0	100.0	—

TABLE 3.47

The Aluminium, Copper and Brass Industry

States	*Number of factories (as percentage of total)*			*Productive capital (as percentage of total)*		
	1948	*1957*	*Percent. Change*	*1948*	*1957*	*Percent. Change*
Andhra Pradesh, Madras	12.9	15.8	2.9	5.7	3.6	— 2.1
Bombay	37.6	32.5	—5.1	22.0	16.2	— 6.4
Delhi	2.0	6.8	4.8	0.5	0.3	— 0.2
Punjab	15.3	17.1	1.8	2.9	2.6	— 0.3
Uttar Pradesh	14.4	9.4	—5.0	2.0	1.2	— 0.8
West Bengal	14.8	9.4	—5.4	56.5	34.2	—22.3
Other States (Including Union Territories)	3.0	9.0	6.0	9.8	41.9	32.1
Total	100.0	100.0	—	100.0	100.0	—

(*Contd.*)

TABLE 3.47 (*Contd.*)

	Employment (as percentage of total)			*Value added (as percentage of total)*		
	1948	*1957*	*Percent. Change*	*1948*	*1957*	*Percent. Change*
Andhra Pradesh, Madras	10.0	10.7	0.7	5.1	3.5	— 1.6
Bombay	34.3	23.2	—11.1	31.3	15.4	—16.4
Delhi	0.6	1.8	1.2	0.1	0.5	0.4
Punjab	5.8	7.1	1.3	3.3	2.9	—0.4
Uttar Pradesh	5.0	3.0	— 1.1	2.9	1.3	— 1.6
West Bengal	35.9	26.1	— 9.8	39.7	26.1	—13.6
Other States (Including Union Territories)	8.4	27.2	18.8	17.1	50.3	33.2
Total	100.0	100.0	—	100.0	100.0	—

Together they accounted for 78.0 per cent of the total productive capital, 82.2 per cent of the total employment and 81.4 per cent of the total value added in the 29 manufacturing industries covered by the Annual CMI.

During the decade 1948-57 an assessment of the over-all position of the manufacturing industry in India shows broadly a 10 per cent dispersal of industries from the highly concentrated States of West Bengal and Bombay to the other States of lesser importance. An analysis of certain individual industries, as discussed above, confirms the dispersal tendency on the part of five out of the seven industries, during the aforesaid period. Only in the case of jute textiles and chemicals the position of concentration in and around Howrah and Bombay respectively seems to have got accentuated.

THE PROBLEM IN RETROSPECT

A discussion of the locational trends of various industries in India beginning from 1913-14 to 1961-62 will show that the intra-regional and the inter-regional tendencies of dispersal have led to a very wide dispersal of industries in almost all the regions of the country. With the development of facilities like transport and power the industries have been continuously spreading to all those regions of the country where unutilised potential resources in the form of raw materials, minerals, etc., were available for exploitation. The extent of this dispersal during the course of the last three to four decades is given in Table 3.48.

The above percentages concern those regions where a particular industry had remained heavily concentrated in the early stages of its development. Along with its growth, it has gradually moved to other regions. These four industries have now reached almost all the important regions in the country. To realise the full implications and the extent of this dispersal the decreasing percentages have to be viewed in the light of rapidly increasing all-India total production, which has now become a multiple of what it was in 1920, 1925 or 1930. The percentage share of the regions of heavy concentration has been declining rapidly simply on account of the rapid development of the industry in the less developed regions. Other industries like chemicals and engineering are also following the same pattern.

TABLE 3.48

Percentage of All-India Products

States	*Year*	*Product*	
		Cotton Textile	
Bombay (New Maharashtra and Gujarat)		Yarn	Woven goods
	1921-22	71.0	80.9
	1960	47.9	66.1
		Sugar	
Uttar Pradesh and Bihar	Average of 1931-32 to 1934-35	90.8	
	1960-61	59.9	
		Cement	
Bihar and Madhya Pradesh	1925	38.8	
	1960-61	29.0	
West Bengal	1925	84.0	**Paper**
	1961-62	23.3	

These stark facts may offer some food for cool thinking to those impatient people who are extremely critical of the Government and the Planning Commission on the score of the removal or regional imbalance in industrial development. Most of these critics are not adequately informed of the dispersal of the industries and perhaps they have not themselves given enough thought to the economic implications of placing the industries in the regions where adequate facilities of transport, power and raw materials are not available or where they are very poor in comparison to some other regions of the country. The first and the most primary pre-requisite of the establishment of industries in a particular region is the development of adequate transport and power supply facilities. Where facilities of a sound infra-structure exist of are being developed, the industries will get automatically attracted.

At the present time on account of political and other pressures industries are assigned to unsuitable areas and sometimes in the anxiety to make the industries more widespread the total target capacity is licensed in small units which are not likely to work so efficiently and economically as the units of a suitable size are apt to do. The implications of such practices are that we are forcing the unit of investment in a form and in a place in which its marginal social net product is unlikely to be maximised. Continuous skirmishes between the Centre and the States constitute a danger to the survival of unified and coherent economic planning in the country and to the concept of India as a nation. The quest for regional balance should proceed not on the basis of sharing out of imperfectly known resources but by accelerating developmental work to open up new economic opportunities. Concerted measures to remove regional economic disparities are necessary counterparts of national integration on the emotional plane. It is idle to pretend that a large integrated steel plant could be feasibly located outside the present steel-belt. This does not mean, however, that technological possibilities opened up by low-shaft furnaces using non-coking coal or lignite should not be pursued. Similar technological adaptations may be devised to overcome regional disadvantages and limitations. Atomic energy could be developed as an alternative source of power in areas distant from coal. More intensive exploration of minerals may unfold undreamt-of economic opportunities such as had happened within the last few years in relation to petroleum in Gujarat. New products, such as synthetic rubber from power alcohol, for which a plant had been set-up in Western Uttar Pradesh, provides another useful line of development. Benefits from the location of large central projects are often exaggerated. Such projects can remain completely isolated islands within vast occeans of backwardness, unless conscious efforts are made to diversify the industrial base through supplementary schemes. This has been done admirably at Durgapur by providing all the essential services and facilities necessary for new industrial units to come into being. Aspirations for regional growth should be tempered with economic common-sense. Regional and national developments are two facets of a common objective. Anything that weakened the sense of national purpose would delay the advance of the country as well. In substance, it can be said that the removal of regional disparities is essential but in the accomplishment of that task we should proceed with care and caution so that the limited and scarce resources are utilized to the best advantage of the regions as well as of the country as a whole.*

In 1939 there were 11,114 registered companies in India, which were distributed in different Provinces as shown in Table 3.49.

TABLE 3.49

(Rs. in lakh)

Provinces or States	*Number of companies*	*Provinces or States*	*Paid-up capital of companies*
Bengal	4,631 (1)	Bombay	18,805 (1)
Madras	1,581 (2)	Bengal	11,854 (2)
Bombay	1,400 (3)	Madras	1,929 (3)
Punjab	1,042 (4)	Uttar Pradesh	1,117 (3)
Travancore	478 (5)	Bihar and Orissa	584 (5)
Uttar Pradesh	465 (6)	Punjab	499 (6)
Delhi	249 (7)	Travancore	263 (7)
Assam	215 (8)	Mysore	247 (8)
Cochin	201 (9)	Delhi	244 (9)
Bihar and Orissa	196 (10)	Hyderabad	214 (10)
Mysore	190 (11)	Assam	113 (11)
Central Provinces and Berar	94 (12)	Central Provinces and Berar	105 (12)
Hyderabad	55 (13)	Cochin	50 (13)
Others	317 (14)	Others	1,015 (14)
Total	11,114	Total	29,039

Note: Figures in brackets indicate ranks.

This table shows that Bihar and Orissa was tenth among the Provinces and the States in respect of the number of companies but fifth in respect of the amount of paid-up capital. The next table shows that whereas other States have retained their relative positions in respect of the number of companies during 1958-61, Bihar and Madhya Pradesh have failed to do so and have definitely gone down. On the contrary, three States, namely, Andhra Pradesh, Rajasthan and Assam have gone up.

To recapitulate, since the beginning of the Second World War a noticeable feature has been the decentralised development and

* Based on Sir J. Ghandy's speech.

TABLE 3.50

State-wise Distribution of Companies at Work During 1958-61

States	*1958-59*	*1959-60*	*1960-61*
1	2	3	4
West Bengal	11,881 (1)	11,581 (1)	10,490 (1)
Maharashtra, Gujarat	5,371 (2)	5,629 (2)	4,920 (2)
Madras	2,254 (3)	2,396 (3)	2,596 (3)
Delhi	1,483 (4)	1,523 (4)	1,619 (4)
Uttar Pradesh	1,285 (5)	1,163 (5)	1,082 (5)
Kerala	1,147 (6)	1,050 (6)	1,014 (6)
Punjab	789 (7)	790 (7)	812 (7)
Mysore	658 (8)	629 (8)	631 (8)
Andhra Pradesh	461 (9)	456 (9)	456 (9)
Rajasthan	446 (11)	437 (10)	533 (10)
Assam	351 (13)	350 (12)	348 (11)
Bihar	483 (9)	372 (11)	347 (12)
Madhya Pradesh	380 (12)	315 (13)	312 (13)
Orissa	188 (14)	206 (14)	208 (14)
Others	26 (15)	24 (15)	25 (15)
Total	27,403	26,921	26108

Note: Figures in brackets indicate ranks.

dispersal of industry in India. The development of companies in the industrially backward States like Rajasthan, Bihar, Orissa, Madhya Pradesh, etc., is noteworthy. Uttar Pradesh, Assam, Mysore and Kerala have also shown a significant growth of companies. The three Provinces of Bengal, Bombay and Madras between themselves accounted for 86 per cent of the total paid-up capital of all companies at the turn of the century, but their share was reduced to 73 percent only in 1955 and further to 65.8 per cent in 1957-58. The share of cotton mills was 41 per cent in 1913-14 in the total paid-up capital of all companies in the State of Bombay. This went down to 22 per cent in 1938-39 and to 18 per cent in 1953-54. Similarly, in Madhya Pradesh the importance of cotton textiles decreased from 44 per cent in 1913-14 to 23 per cent in 1938-39 and to 6 per cent in 1953-54. The percentage share of tea industry in Assam went down from 69 in 1938-39 to 52 in 1953-54. Similarly, the share of jute mills in Bengal was reduced from 17 per cent in 1938-39 to 9 per cent only in 1953-54. The following percentages may be of interest in this connection.

TABLE 3.51

State-wise Distribution of Companies in Certain Years

States	*1913-14*	*1938-39*	*1947-48*	*1960-61*
West Bengal	973 (1)	4,631 (1)	8,514 (1)	10,490 (1)
Bombay	613 (2)	1,400 (3)	4,130 (2)	5,735 (2)
Madras	425 (3)	1,581 (2)	3,209 (3)	2,596 (3)
Uttar Pradesh	185 (4)	465 (6)	1,241 (6)	1,082 (5)
Bihar	55 (9)	196 (10)	143 (12)	347 (12)
Orissa	—	—	97 (13)	208 (14)
Delhi	—	249 (8)	905 (8)	1,619 (4)
Rajasthan	—	—	—	433 (10)
Madhya Pradesh	27 (10)	94 (12)	319 (11)	312 (13)
Punjab	167 (5)	1,042 (4)	1,607 (4)	812 (7)
Assam	71 (7)	215 (9)	401 (9)	348 (11)
Mysore	63 (8)	190 (11)	374 (10)	631 (8)
Kerala	—	679 (5)	989 (7)	1,014 (6)
Other States	164 (6)	372 (7)	1,476 (5)	481 (9)
Total	2,744	11,114	22,675	21,108

Note: Figures in brackets indicate ranks.

TABLE 3.52

Percentage Share of Important Industries in the Total Paid-up Capital of All Companies

Industry	*States*	*1913-14*	*1938-39*	*1953-54*
Tea	Assam	—	69	52
	West Bengal	—	9	6
Cotton Mills	Bombay	41	22	18
	Uttar Pradesh	23	16	16
	Madhya Pradesh	44	23	6
Jute	West Bengal	26	17	9
Sugar	Bihar	—	21	14
	Uttar Pradesh	—	36	16
	Orissa	—	38	3
Coal	Bihar	—	6	4
	Madhya Pradesh	—	12	—

In the decade covered by the first two Plans some success was achieved in the dispersal of industry. The selection of the locations for the three new steel plants (Bhilai, Rourkela and Durgapur), the Heavy Machinery Plant (Ranchi) and the Heavy Electrical Project (Bhopal) and the decision to exploit the lignite deposits and Neiveli in Madras, justified as these all were on purely economic grounds, have also had the effect of creating new centres of industry in areas of the country hitherto untouched by it. But preference has not always been given to the location of public sector projects in the relatively backward areas without significant prejudice to technical and economic considerations. In the licensing of the private sector projects the claims of the under-developed regions have generally been kept in view to the extent possible.

LOCATIONAL QUOTIENTS OF SOME INDUSTRIES

The locational quotient (which is a measure of the degree of concentration of an industry in a particular geographical area or region) is extremely high in respect of the rice milling, refractory, fertilizer and mining machinery manufacturing industries in the State of Bihar, whereas it is extremely low in respect of drug and pharmaceutical, and wooden furniture manufacturing industries. The sugar; distillery; steel castings and forgings; iron and steel pipes; agricultural implements; and sugar machinery manufacturing industries have fairly high locational quotients. Only in two cases, viz., drugs and Pharmaceuticals, and wooden furniture industries are the co-efficients of localisation for the country in excess of the locational quotients for this State. As we have shown at the outset, industrial activity in Bihar (except for the agro-based and animal-based ones) is concentrated in Chotanagpur division and parts of Patna division. Table 3.53 will be informative in this connection.

In Table 3.54 an attempt has been made to analyse the cost-structure of 44 industries in the State of Bihar in 1960 on the basis of the data contained in the *Annual Survey of Industries*. It would be useful to pinpoint the weaknesses of our computations.* In the

* We are thankful to the Department of Statistics of the Central Statistical Organisation (Industrial Statistics Wing), Calcutta for its comments on this.

TABLE 3.53

Locational Quotients and Coefficients of Localisation (1960)*

Sl. No.	*Name of Industry*	*Locational Quotient for Bihar*	*Coefficient of Localisation for India*
I.	**Agro-based**		
1.	Rice Milling	11.28	0.75
2.	Flour Milling	0.92	0.31
3.	Edible oil (other than hydrogenated oils)	0.44	0.33
4.	Sugar	3.56	0.55
5.	Distillery	1.30	0.49
II.	**Mineral and Metal-based**		
6.	Iron and Steel	8.06	0.53
7.	Steel Castings and Forgings	2.50	0.49
8.	Iron and Steel Pipes	3.48	0.56
9.	Cement	2.74	0.55
10.	Fire-brick	0.54	0.50
11.	Refractory	11.68	0.80
12.	Glass Hollow-ware	1.70	0.45
13.	Motor Cycles and Bicycles	0.54	0.33
14.	Agricultural Implements	2.08	0.52
15.	Railway Rolling Stock	0.56	0.39
16.	Sugar Machinery	2.86	0.33
17.	Mining Machinery	8.60	0.86
III.	**Chemical-based**		
18.	Inorganic Fertilizer	12.52	0.65
19.	Heavy Chemicals (Inorganic)	0.54	0.32
20.	Drugs and Pharmaceuticals	0.22	0.29
IV.	**Miscellaneous**		
21.	Press, Printing, Lithography and Book-binding	0.74	0.25
22.	Wooden Furniture	0.32	0.66

*Worked out by Mr. S.K. Sinha, a research student of ours.

first instance, the cost components as given in this table in respect of which percentages to the gross value of output have been computed by us do not represent the entire cost of production. Important components in the shape of services purchased from outside organisations including non-industrial services, repair,

TABLE 3.54

Cost-Structure of Industries in Bihar in 1960*

Sl. No.	*Industry*	*Main Cost Components As Percentage of Gross Value of Output*				
		Salaries & Wages	*Fuel & Power*	*Materials*	*Depreciation*	*Their Total*
	1	2	3	4	5	6
1.	Rice Milling	2.9	0.6	92.8	0.4	96.7
2.	Flour Milling	2.1	1.8	91.0	0.4	95.3
3.	Edible Oil (other than hydro-genated oils)	3.6	2.4	98.5	0.2	104.7
4.	Vanaspati (hydrogenated oil)	2.6	1.5	84.3	1.5	89.9
5.	Sugar	6.6	4.4	72.0	1.8	84.8
6.	Milk & Other Milk Products	2.5	0.9	86.1	2.8	92.3
7.	Distilling, Rectifying & Blending of Spirits (Alcohol)	10.8	18.1	40.1	3.1	72.1
8.	Cotton Textile	21.1	3.4	56.8	1.6	82.9
9.	Jute Textile	21.5	3.9	76.4	1.8	103.6
10.	Woollen Textile	6.9	2.5	79.8	1.5	90.7
11.	Silk Textile	11.8	15.0	28.0	3.0	57.8
12.	Clothing & Tailoring	17.3	3.1	67.1	1.5	89.0
13.	Cigarette	12.4	0.7	54.2	1.0	68.3

(Contd.)

TABLE 3.54 (*Contd.*)

	1	2	3	4	5	6
14.	Wooden Furniture & Fixtures	31.1	0.7	39.7	1.9	73.4
15.	Wood Pulp & Paper	12.9	15.4	49.4	8.2	85.9
16.	Tanneries & Leather Finishing Plants	9.8	0.8	84.2	2.0	96.8
17.	Footwear	18.9	0.5	74.8	1.3	95.5
18.	Cement Hydraulic	8.4	20.3	46.5	5.9	81.1
19.	Hume Pipes & Other Cement & Concrete Products	19.5	3.3	40.1	9.0	71.9
20.	Refractories	38.4	11.7	26.7	4.1	80.9
21.	Fire-bricks	33.6	18.4	25.3	5.7	83.0
22.	China-ware & Pottery	35.2	30.1	21.7	5.9	92.9
23.	Sheet & Plate Glass	16.6	12.8	56.9	2.2	87.5
24.	Glass Hollow-ware	35.8	12.6	49.8	0.8	98.0
25.	Iron & Steel	18.9	15.8	33.1	9.3	77.1
26.	Iron & Steel Structurals	29.2	4.9	46.7	6.8	87.6
27.	Iron & Steel Castings & Forgings	44.1	9.2	24.9	4.7	82.9
28.	Iron & Steel Pipes	6.4	3.9	80.4	6.9	97.6
29.	Agricultural Implements	19.1	1.8	38.6	0.4	59.9
30.	Sugar Machinery	33.1	4.3	43.5	3.1	84.0
31.	Textile Machinery	22.2	2.1	65.0	2.2	91.5
32.	Mining Machinery	39.9	3.2	32.7	6.2	82.0
33.	Nuts, Bolts, Screws, Springs, Chains, etc.	15.4	4.4	77.2	1.7	98.7

34.	Railway Locomotives	35.7	3.4	29.2	2.8	71.1
35.	Railway Rolling Stock	28.1	3.5	78.3	3.8	113.7
36.	Motor Cycles & Bicycles	11.6	1.9	66.4	6.0	85.9
37.	Other Auto-Vehicles	151	1.7	67.8	5.9	90.5
38.	Press, Printing & Book-binding	25.7	1.2	59.3	2.5	88.7
39.	Electric Lamps	10.3	1.8	59.0	1.0	72.1
40.	Radio Receivers	14.6	1.5	64.5	4.0	84.6
41.	Electrical Machinery, Apparatus, Appliances & Supplies, etc.	23.1	0.9	62.9	3.2	90.1
42.	Inorganic Fertilizer	18.0	9.2	47.2	26.6	101.0
43.	Heavy Chemicals (Inorganic)	13.5	20.2	26.0	3.8	63.5
44.	Drugs & Pharmaceuticals	5.3	0.4	52.5	0.7	58.9

* Prepared by Mr. S.K. Sinha, a research student of ours from the data given in the *Annual Survey of Industries*, 1960.

Note: The factories covered by the A.S.I. are those registered under the Indian Factories Act, 1948 which employ 50 or more workers with the aid of power or 100 or more workers without the aid of power, including those which did not work during the year. The term "salaries and wages" includes all payments made in cash as compensation for work done during the year, e.g., basic wages, dearness allowance, over-time payments, shift allowance, leave wages, wages for paid holidays, all bonuses such as profit-sharing bonus, production bonus good attendance bonus, etc., and other cash payments made from time to time, regular and *ad hoc*, contractual or *ex gratia*. Materials and fuels consumed exclude any fuel or material manufactured within the factory and consumed in it, e.g., electrical energy generated and consumed within the factory. The coal used in generating the energy is however, included since it is brought into the factory from outside. Materials consumed for repair and maintenance are included. The value of material, etc., consumed is the cost at the factory. It includes the purchase price, transport charges and other incidental cost. Depreciation has been calculated at the rate allowed by the Income-Tax authorities for assessing taxable income. Output is the aggregate value of products and by products manufactured for sale and of work done for the customers and has been adjusted for the difference in stocks of semi-finished goods at the beginning and at the end of the survey year.

maintenance and manufacturing work done by other concerns have not been accounted for in our computations. Even when these are accounted for, there will remain a gap to be imputed to the interest charges, rent and margin of profits, etc. As such the cost components worked out by us fall short of the gross value of output in the case of as many as 40 industries treated of in this table—in some the gap is very wide, in some it is very narrow, in the rest it is just average. On the other hand, in the case of four industries, viz., edible oil (other than hydrogenated oils), jute textile, railway rolling stock, and inorganic fertilizer the total of the main cost components exceeds the gross value of output. How are we to account for this? Evidently, the constituent factories, for several reasons, incurred loss, or alternatively, were indebted to other or owned inventories already paid for.

It would be fruitful to interpret the cost data in relation to the existing difficulties of the different industries enumerated earlier in this chapter. We can divide the industries in three broad categories in accordance with the figures being on the high side in respect of wages and salaries, fuel and power, materials consumed, and depreciation. In industries with serial numbers 1 to 6, 9-10, 12, 16-17, 28, 33 and 35-37 material cost constitutes two-thirds or more of the total cost. In industries with serial numbers 8-9, 14 (relatively to material cost), 20-22 (relatively to material cost), 24, 26, 27 (relatively to material cost), 30-32, 34-35, 38 and 41 (relatively to material cost) wage cost constitutes one-fifth or more of the total cost. In industries with serial numbers 25 and 43 power cost constitutes approximately one-sixth or more of the total cost. Power cost is proportionally low in most of the metallic and chemical industries, which in Bihar are not sufficiently modernised and mechanised, and hence do not use proportionally more power and fuel. Less mechanised and almost obsolete techniques persist in them. Depreciation cost constitutes one-tenth or more of the total cost in industries with serial numbers 3 (in relation to material cost), 9 (in relation to wage cost), 15, 19, 25 and 42.

The policy implication of the above analysis is that the prices of materials and the rates of fuel and power consumed and the salaries and wages of the people finding employment in the industries need to be regulated and prevented from rising (or rising unduly or excessively), if the prices of their products and those of industries linked to them have to be kept steady. The light shed by this analysis will prove to be helpful in rationalising our economic policy towards these industries.

STATE GOVERNMENT MEASURES FOR DEVELOPMENT OF LARGE AND MEDIUM INDUSTRIES

1. In the interest of industrial development and with a view to reducing the existing imbalance in the levels of development in different regions of the State, the State Government has lately announced a *'package of incentives'* for facilitating the establishment of new large and medium industries in Bihar. These are:

(i) *Licence*—The Government would give suitable assistance to parties in the matter of supply of basic information regarding the availability of industrial raw materials and other facilities in Bihar, and would also assist them as far as possible in securing the necessary licence under the Industries (Development and Regulation) Act, 1951 as well as the release of the foreign exchange required to set-up the industry.

(ii) *Land*—In the six industrial complexes, to start with, viz., (i) Patna, (ii) Adityapur, (iii) Patratu, (iv) Ranchi, (v) Barauni, and (vi) Bokaro, and in other developing areas to be founded later, land will be acquired and developed with water, power and communication facilities as State cost. Factory plots in each such developed area will be settled with entrepreneurs of long-term lease and only token rent will be realised from them annually. Full cost of acquisition and development of land will be recovered from the parties in convenient instalments spread over a period not exceeding three years from the date of allotment of the land.

(iii) *Revolving Fund for Building Materials*—In order to help new industries in procuring building materials in time and thereby to help them in expeditious completion of their construction programme, the Government will create a revolving fund of building materials like cement, iron and steel, etc. These building materials will be made available to industry on no-profit-no-loss basis against cash payment, and the stock will be replenished out of the separate revolving funds sanctioned of the purpose.

(iv) *Store Purchase*—In all States purchases or purchase by bodies subordinate to or controlled by the State Government, preference will be given to the products of all large and medium industries located in Bihar.

(v) *Finance Assistance*—In order to enable new industries to raise requisite finance, the Government may consider favourably the question of under-writing of shares, equity financing and grant of loan and guarantee of loans to be raised by industries.

(vi) *Project Report*—The Government shall give 50 per cent contribution towards the cost of preparation of the Project Report provided it is made through an agency approved by the Government. After the project is accepted for implementation, the Government's contribution towards the preparation of the Project Report will be converted into Government's contribution towards share capital of the project.

(vii) *Sales Tax*—In order to help a new industry to compete with an established industry during the initial period of its production: (a) The Government shall grant exemption on all purchases of raw materials needed in the process of manufacture for a period of 5 to 10 years as may be decided by the Government in each case from the date, the unit goes into production, and (b) exemption from multi-point sales tax at the first stage of sale by the manufacturer.

(viii) *Housing*—Under the subsidised industrial housing scheme, 50 per cent of the amount is given as loan, 25 per cent is allowed as subsidy while 25 per cent of the total cost of construction has to be met by the industry concerned. New industries have to provide housing facilities to some of their skilled workers and they may not be in position to go ahead with the housing programme in the initial stages. In order to help them in this respect the Government will subsidise industries to the extent of 10 per cent out of the 25 per cent of the industry's share which they are now required to contribute.

(ix) *Water Royalty*—Wherever industries lift water from sources maintained by the Government, water will be supplied to such industries on no-profit-no-loss basis.

(x) *Electricity Tariff—In* the case of electro-chemical and electro-metallurgical industries where electric power is used as raw material, power will be supplied on no-profit-no-loss basis. At present subsidy on power consumed by small-scale industries is available only to the units located in North Bihar, subject to the maximum of 9 paise per unit provided the maximum connected load does not exceed 20 H.P. This concession will now be extended throughout the State. In suitable cases the Government may also exempt new industries from payment of electricity duty under the Bihar Electricity Duty Act.

2. Since the aim is to encourage and foster such industries as are specially needed to benefit the economy of the State as a whole, the above concessions will normally be available only to the scheduled industries, except small-scale industries qualifying for power subsidy throughout the State. The Government may, however, add more industries to the schedule from time to time.

3. In the case of large and medium industries all the incentives mentioned above may initially be made available for a period of 10 years from the commencement of production, or for a period of 12 years from the date of the grant of licence/letter of intent, as the case may be.

4. While concessions to medium industries will generally be confined to the six industrial complexes (Patna, Patratu, Adityapur, Ranchi, Barauni and Bokaro areas) to utilize capital investment by the Government in acquiring and developing factory sites in the above areas, special cases of medium industries for grant of similar concessions, if located outside these areas, may be considered on merit. In the case of large industries, however, these incentives will be available to the units throughout the State.

5. The Government will have the right of withdrawing any area from being eligible to these incentives depending on the industrial development achieved in that area.

In order to facilitate quick and easy distribution of loans under the State Aid to Industries Act, the power to sanction loans has been decentralised. For example, loans up to Rs. 5,000 for any single industry can be had from the Project Executive Officer in a community development block, from the Community Project Officer (Industries) in areas covered by a pilot project, and from the Sub-divisional Officer in other cases, in whose jurisdiction the industry has to be set-up. The Collectors and Additional Collectors can sanction loans up to Rs. 10,000 and the Director of Industries and the Additional Director of Industries up to Rs. 20,000 in any single case. Loans exceeding these amounts are sanctioned by the Government. The Community Project Officers in charge of the rural industries projects at Buxar and Dumka can also sanction loan up to Rs. 10,000 in each case. The State Government has set-up a Board of Industries under this act. All applications for loans exceeding Rs. 20,000 are put up before this Board for advice. The Board also advises the Government as regards the policy to be followed in financing different kinds of industries. Loans up to Rs. 50,000 are granted at concessional rates of interest of 2.5 per cent for the co-operative societies and of 3 per cent in other cases.

For procuring controlled raw materials such as steel (including sheets and plates), copper and other non-ferrous metals, the small-scale units have to approach the Director of Industries of the State for necessary allocation of quotas. Since there is a shortage of these raw materials, the demand of the existing units may not be fully met. Therefore, before setting up units requiring such raw materials, small industrialists are advised to contact the Director of Industries of the State with a view to finding out if they can secure the required raw materials after they make a start. The position regarding some of the important raw materials is as follows:

(a) *Iron and Steel*—There is an over-all shortage of iron and steel *vis-a-vis* the total demand. In the case of small-scale industries, allocation is made under two quotas, viz., (i) Steel Processing Industries quota, and (ii) Small-scale Industries quota. Under the first, allotment is made of prime steel materials to the organised industries engaged in the processing of steel which are operated by skilled technicians. The second is received and is distributed by the Director of Industries to small-scale industrial units or fabricators. Allotments under these two quotas are made annually.

(b) *Tinplate*—Tinplates of various categories are allotted to the Director of Industries by the Development Commissioner (Small-Scale Industries), Government of India on a six-monthly basis. It is distributed to the small-scale industrial units manufacturing tin containers, school boxes, etc.

(c) *Non-ferrous Metals*—(i) With a view to conserving the scarce raw materials and putting them to most judicious use according to the present needs, the Government of India has promulgated the Scarce Industrial Material (Control) Order, 1965 from the 14th September, 1965 onward. The order covers scarce metals, namely, copper, zinc, lead and tin and scrap of these metals. Zinc, mozak and other zinc die casting alloys have also been controlled. The control order, however, does not apply to fabricated or wrought items like plates, sheets, bars, rods, wires, powders, cast or forged components, (ii) The order lays down that any acquisition, purchase, sale, transfer or even use for any purpose of any of these scarce metals/scrap is fully controlled and can be given effect to only after obtaining an appropriate permit from the controller, (iii) Quotas of copper, zinc, tin, lead and electrolytic grade aluminium are allotted by the Development Commissioner (Small-Scale Industries), Government of India to the State Director of Industries for meeting the requirements of small-scale industries. The Director of Industries issues the permits for copper, zinc, tin and lead to the small-scale industrial units of the State. Recommendations are sent to the Development Commissioner (Small-Scale Industries), Government of India, for the issues of permits and authorisation for electrolytic grade of aluminium. The requirements of the small-scale units engaged in the execution of orders of the Defence Ministry, the Post and Telegraphs Ministry and the Railway Ministry of copper, zinc, lead and tin are met directly by the Controller of Scarce Industrial Materials, Office of the Director-General of Technical Development, Government of India on the recommendations of the sponsoring authorities. The Director of Industries is the sponsoring authority for the small-scale units.

(d) *Coal and Coke*—The small-scale units receive their quota of coal and coke from the State Coal Controller on the recommendation of the State Director of Industries. Allotments are made to industrial units under different classes of industries such as engineering, glass, chemical, pottery, soap and leather.

(e) *Chemicals and Pharmaceuticals*—Chemicals and Pharmaceuticals, both indigenous and imported, are allotted by the State Trading Corporation of India. Some of the important items under this category which are available to small-scale industrial units are as follows: (a) Camphor for tableting and medical purposes, (b) Soda ash for manufacture of sodium silicate and allied industries, (c) Caustic soda for use in soap industries and aluminium industry, (d) Aluminium of carbonate for biscuit industry, (e) Menthol for chemical units, (f) Sodium nitrate for preparation of acids, (g) Carbon black for chemicals and paints, and (h) Ultramarine blue for repacking.

3. In order to store in bulk and sell the above raw materials to small-scale industries, the State Government has set-up a number of raw material depots. These depots are located at Patna, Ranchi, Monghyr and Darbhanga. For new depots are being established at Gaya, Jamshedpur, Muzaffarpur and Katihar.

Actual user applications from small-scale industries for import of iron and steel materials including alloy-tool and special steel and ferro-alloys are submitted to the Director of Industries, who is the sponsoring authority for the purpose, in the prescribed form, with an advance copy to the Iron and Steel Controller, Calcutta who is the licensing authority in the above cases. For import of items such as B.S.P. Sheets, G.P. Sheets and wire rods, an advance copy has also to be sent to the M.M.T.C., as the import of these items is also effected by it. The Director of Industries forwards these applications with his recommendations in accordance with foreign exchange ceiling placed at his disposal to the above licensing authority. These allotments are made for a period of one year in terms of import policy in force. According to the new procedure, applications for import of raw materials (other than iron and steel), components, spare parts and machinery of value less than Rs. 5,000 (rupees five thousand) are required to be submitted to the Joint Chief Controller of Imports and Exports, Calcutta, through the respective sponsoring authorities. In the case of small-scale industries except those relating to textile engineering, Pharmaceuticals, handloom, fishery and fruit and vegetable preservation, the Director of Industries functions as the sponsoring authority. In respect of the expected items mentioned above, the sponsoring authorities are the Textile Commissioner, Bombay; the State Drug Controller; the State Director of Handloom; the State Director of Fisheries and the Director of Marketing and Inspection, Ministry of Food and Agriculture, Government of India, Nagpur respectively. No separate application is required to be submitted for grant of the essentiality certificate as heretofore. The prescribed form of application is itself an application-*cum*-recommendation form. These applications are forwarded by the sponsoring authorities mentioned above to the Joint Chief Controller of Imports and Exports, Calcutta, with their recommendation, keeping in view the foreign exchange ceiling.

Cottage Industry

The objectives of developing the small (cottage and small-scale) industries, according to the Indian planners, are the following:

(1) To provide whole-time employment by the creation of new employment opportunities and to provide part-time subsidiary employment in the rural areas, thus, reducing unemployment and augmenting agricultural income;

(2) To revive and strengthen the existing crafts by encouraging the gradual progress in the techniques of production in the unorganised sector of industries without causing any large-scale technological unemployment;

(3) To promote the production of a large variety of goods, specially consumer goods, through the labour-intensive methods, by correlating them with the production programmes of the large-scale industries, wherever necessary; and

(4) To ensure greater dispersal and ruralisation of industries so as to ensure: (a) a more equitable distribution of the national income, (b) an effective mobilisation of the

capital and the skill which may otherwise remain unutilized, and (c) to avoid the ills stemming from unplanned urbanisation.

The following cottage industries come under the purview of the Khadi and Village Industries Commission, Bombay and the Bihar State Khadi and Village Industries Board, Patna:

(1) Khadi:
   (i) Traditional and Ambar Khadi (Cotton).
   (ii) Woollen Khadi.
   (iii) Silk Khadi.
(2) Village Oil Industry.
(3) Village Leather Industry.
(4) Village Pottery Industry.
(5) Processing of Cereals and Pulses Industry.
(6) Gur and Khandsari Industry.
(7) Palmgur Industry.
(8) Hand-made Paper Industry.
(9) Cottage Match Industry.
(10) Bee-keeping Industry.
(11) Village Fibre Industry.
(12) Non-Edible Oils and Soap Industry.
(13) Lime-stone Industry.
(14) Carpentry and Blacksmithy.
(15) Methane Gas Industry.

The cottage match and carpentry industries could not succeed in Bihar and their performance may accordingly be treated as negligible. The lime-stone and methane gas industries are new industries and the Board has not taken up these so far.

Only what might be called pilot schemes were attempted during the First Plan in Bihar, consisting chiefly of schemes of assistance to the handloom weaving industry. The funds for the development of the khadi and village industries come from the Central Plan through the Commission. The Third Plan of Bihar had provided for Rs. 32.50 lakhs for meeting the expenses envisaged by the Bihar State Khadi and Village Industries Board and not provided for in the Central Plan. Rs. 200 lakhs were to be spent on the development of the handloom industry; Rs. 60

lakhs on that of sericulture; and Rs. 35 lakhs on that of handicrafts during the Third Plan (State and Central).

THE HANDLOOM WEAVING INDUSTRY

In 1958 there were more than 2 lakh handlooms in Bihar and some 10 lakh people earned their livelihood from the handloom weaving industry. The first Weavers' Co-operative Society was set-up in Bihar in 1930 at Biharsharif. The State Government sanctioned the necessary technical and supervisory staff for the proper guidance, organisation and supervision of the Weavers' Co-operative Societies. The growth of the co-operative movement was slow, though steady, till 1953, when the Cess Fund Scheme was introduced. By 1958, 786 primary weavers' co-operative societies had been organised in the State with a membership of 1,06,420. These societies supplied yarn to the weavers, took back the finished products and arranged for their sale. It was for coordinating the activities of these societies and to pool their resources that the Bihar State Handloom Weavers' Co-operative Union Ltd.—the apex society—was formed in 1948. This apex organisation purchases raw materials for the primary societies, supervises production, ensures the manufacture of goods consistent with standard specifications, arranges the marketing of finished goods, gives financial aid to the societies and carries on scientific publicity for boosting the sales of the products. The following Table 4.1 shows the progress of these societies:

TABLE 4.1

Years	*Number of Societies*	*Membership*
1952-53	136	15,000
1953-54	329	34,475
1954-55	429	79,211
1955-56	488	88,123
1956-57	786	1,06,420

With a view to enabling the weavers to come under the cooperative fold various schemes of financial assistance were sanctioned by the Government. A loan of Rs. 15 per cotton handloom weaver was advanced to enable him to purchase one share of his society valued at Rs. 20 and Rs. 100 respectively. Upto 1956-57 a sum of Rs. 15,18,715 was granted as share capital loan to the weavers. Keeping in view the meagre resources of the societies, a sum of Rs. 26,23,000 was given as working capital loan to the primary societies and Rs. 7,00,000 to the apex society out of the Cess Fund grants.

Besides this, the State Government also gave a sum of Rs. 3 lakhs as working capital loan to the apex society. It was decided by the Government of India that with effect from April 1, 1957 credit facilities would be available only from the Reserve Bank of India and the Government would advance only towards the share capital loan. During 1957-58 a sum of Rs. 10 lakhs was proposed to be advanced to the apex society and Rs. 40 lakhs to the primary societies towards their working capital through the Reserve Bank of India. The Government also sanctioned a grant of Rs. 2,18,000 during 1957-58 to be given to the societies in the form of improved appliances.

Bihar is placed in the most disadvantageous position in respect of yarn supply to its handloom industry, dependent as it is on distant mills in Bombay and South India. The price at which yarn is supplied to the weavers is very high on account of the rapacious activities of the middle-men. Besides, there are vagaries in the supply to yarn. This difficulty has been removed to a certain extent since the apex Union started the yarn business. The Union is able to make direct contact with the whole-sale agents and on account of its better bargaining power, it is able to purchase yarn at the competitive rates and to supply the same to the primary societies. In 1957 it was running 23 yarn depots, situated at places with concentrations of the handloom weavers.

The State Government also launched to schemes during the Second Plan to ease the yarn supply position under the long-term scheme and proposed to set-up a co-operative spinning mills of 12,000 spindles at Mokameh as a joint venture of the weavers' co-operative societies. For meeting the immediate need a cash credit of Rs. 3.5 lakhs was sanctioned by the Bihar State Cooperative Bank to the Gaya Cotton Mills to help it in augmenting the output of low count yarn for the handloom weavers.

For Bihar the target under the Second Plan was fixed at 75 million yards for 1957-58 and 85 million yards for 1958-59. Out of these, the co-operative sector had to produce 55 million yards and 70 million yards in 1957-58 and 1958-59 respectively.

Like all other industries, the handloom weaving industry too can thrive only when what is produced is sold and consumed; otherwise, there will be a pilling up of stocks, resulting in the impoverishment of the weavers. Hence, any plan of increased production is meaningless without creating a corresponding increase in the demand for the handloom products.

To find an outlet for the increased production of the primary societies 100 emporia had been opened in all parts of the State by 1956-57 and were being managed by the apex society. Government assistance on a sliding scale was available on the maintenance of staff, etc. Because of their dealing only in standard quality products at fixed and competitive rates, these emporia soon came to earn the goodwill of the people, thus, boosting the demand for handloom cloth, as would be evident from the following figures:

TABLE 4.2

Years	*Number of Emporia*	*Sale Proceeds (In '000 Rs.)*	*Sale through the Co-operative Societies (In lakh yards)*
1952-53	1	37.6	7.0
1953-54	18	107.2	40.0
1954-55	55	1,424.4	170.5
1955-56	70	1,749.8	181.0
1956-57	100	2,125.4	222.7

The total number of cotton handlooms registered in India during 1960-61 was 27,61,494. A detailed statement of handlooms registered is given in Table 4.3.

The following Table 4.4 gives the distribution of handlooms in the co-operative fold among the various States as on March 31, 1963. It shows that the number of registered cotton handlooms in Bihar had gone up from 1,36,227 in 1960-61 to 1,38,492 in March 1963.

The Reserve Bank scheme of handloom finance which extends the concessions regarding subsidy towards interest and guarantee of losses to working capital loans to the weavers' co-operative societies came into operation from the 1st April 1957.

TABLE 4.3

States/Union Territories	*Number of Handlooms*
Andhra Pradesh	4,01,712 (3)
Assam	5,06,138 (1)
Bihar	1,36,227 (7)
Gujarat	46,766(13)
Maharashtra	1,46,991 (6)
Madhya Pradesh	42,877 (14)
Madras	4,66,366 (2)
Orissa	1,11,366 (9)
Punjab	47,468 (12)
West Bengal	1,28,494 (8)
Uttar Pradesh	2,61,791 (4)
Mysore	1,02,355 (11)
Rajasthan	41,069 (15)
Kerala	1,03,750 (10)
Delhi	846 (18)
Manipur	2,00,258 (5)
Tripura	14,949 (16)
Pondicherry	3,256 (17)
Total	27,62,679

Note: Figures in Brackets Indicate Ranks.

Under this scheme, Madras and Andhra Pradesh have received the bulk of the accommodation. Uttar Pradesh, West Bengal, Assam, Punjab, Rajasthan, Bihar and Gujarat have either availed themselves of the facility to a very small extent or not availed themselves of it at all.

The State-wise physical progress achieved in the implementation of the conversion of handlooms into powerlooms scheme at the end of the 31st March 1961 was as follows:

The cloth business of the Bihar State Handloom Weaver's Co-operative Union is done through its 88 Sales Emporia and 8 Regional Depots. With these sales emporia and regional depots the Union effected the following sales of the handloom cloth during the last few years:

TABLE 4.4

States	*No. of Hand-looms (Cotton) Registered*	*Number of looms in the co-operative fold*			
		Cotton	*Silk*	*Art Silk*	*Woollen*
1	2	3	4	5	6
Andhra Pradesh	4,01,712 (3)	2,58,015 (1)	2,121(4)	—	20,482(1)
Assam	6,06,138 (1)	34,430(10)	—	—	—
Bihar	1,38,492 (8)	1,14,779 (4)	5,700(2)	9,790(1)	641(4)
Gujarat	46,385(14)	25,247(13)	547(6)	180(6)	
Maharashtra	1,55,502 (6)	80,564 (6)	517(7)	15(4)	2,828(3)
Madhya Pradesh	48,462(13)	33,389(11)	—	—	—
Madras	5,16,086 (2)	2,24,704 (2)	3,132(3)	1,269(2)	—
Orissa	1,11,385 (9)	53,460 (8)	752(5)	—	—
Punjab	63,102(12)	12,782(14)	—	—	—
West Bengal	1,39,140 (7)	77,000 (7)	—	60(3)	300(5)
Uttar Pradesh	2,61,791 (4)	2,00,619 (3)	—	—	—
Mysore	1,02,355(11)	82,833 (5)	5,875(1)	—	15,097(2)
Rajasthan	41,069(15)	27,687(12)	—	—	—
Kerala	1,09,185(10)	49,216 (9)	—	—	—
Delhi	846(18)	794(18)	—	—	—
Himachal Pradesh	—	21(20)	—	—	15(8)
Manipur	2,00,272 (5)	6,270(15)	—	—	—
Tripura	14,494(16)	3.252(16)	—	—	—
Pondicherry	3,338(17)	2,916(17)	—	—	—
Jammu & Kashmir	—	120(19)	130(8)	—	65(7)
Total	20,59,754	12,88,098	20,774	11,134	39,608

Note: Figures in brackets indicate ranks.

TABLE 4.5

States/Union Territories	*Number of looms sanctioned*	*Number of looms ordered*	*Number of looms received*	*Number of looms installed*
Assam	230 (11)	150 (10)	150 (9)	30 (9)
Bihar	1,300 (5)	900 (3)	800 (3)	341 (4)
Maharashtra & Gujarat	3,100 (1)	1,152 (2)	1,024 (1)	1,007 (1)
Kerala	1,500 (4)	500 (6)	—	—
Madhya Pradesh	467 (9)	258 (8)	258 (6)	258 (6)
Madras	15 (14)	15 (14)	15 (11)	15 (11)
Orissa	1,200 (6)	512 (5)	489 (5)	300 (5)
Mysore	2,000 (2)	1,280 (1)	900 (2)	488 (3)
Punjab	500 (8)	188 (9)	188 (8)	180 (7)
Rajasthan	400 (10)	130 (11)	100 (10)	75 (8)
Uttar Pradesh	1,000 (7)	268 (7)	268 (7)	27 (10)
West Bengal	1,605 (3)	745 (4)	735 (4)	735 (2)
Union Territories:				
Delhi	26 (13)	16 (13)	—	—
Manipur	1 (15)	—	—	—
Pondicherry	125 (12)	30 (12)	—	—
Total	13,469	6,144	4,927	3,456

Note: Figures in brackets indicate ranks.

TABLE 4.6

Years	*Number of Emporia*	*Sale of cloth (Rs.)*	*Sale of yarn (Rs.)*
1960-61	122	27,48,190	21,42,860
1961-62	117	25,53,540	25,67,183
1962-63	105	21,46,112	17,45,212
1963-64	88	19,00,000	12,46,197

All the varieties of the handloom fabrics, marketed by the Union, are sold throughout the State. Some of them even command foreign markets. The Union is alive and alert to the changing colours and designs, patterns, fashions, tastes and demand of the public. Its most popular varieties are the furnishing fabrics of Biharsharif, the *dhotis* and *thans* of high counts of Madhubani and the silk of Bhagalpur.

To popularise more and yet more the varieties marketed by it, the Union participated in many exhibitions held outside the State. It won prizes and appreciations for its products. Among the exhibitions the Union participated, mention may be made of the World Agricultural Fair, New Delhi; Indian Exhibition, 1958, New Delhi; and Exhibition at Durgapur, 1964. All these helped the Union in stabilising its worth and raising its prestige in the eyes of the consumers.

It may be mentioned here that the entire cost of maintenance of the 88 emporia used to be borne by the Government upto 1956. After this year, the Government decided to transfer the emporia to the charge of the Union and laid down the maxim that the Government would meet the cost of maintenance of these emporia on a sliding scale thenceforth. The Union raised objections and expressed its inability to take up this heavy responsibility. But due to the decisions of the Government the Union had no option but to take up the responsibility of running these emporia. After a lapse of four years, the subsidy on the majority of the emporia began vanishing and the Union had to close down many of them and retrench its staff from time to time to balance its expenditure. Due to the paucity of funds the Union had been facing great difficulty and it drew the attention of the Government from time to time but since its inception a total sum of Rs. 10 lakhs only was given to it as working capital loan. This meagre amount was insufficient for running the above emporia and depots as well as to manage the sale of products of all the weavers under the cooperative fold. The immediate attention of the Government was drawn so that it came to the rescure of the Union and save the one lakh and forty thousand weavers' families. The Union was not able to get the Reserve Bank loan due to the non-completion of audit. The date for the repayment of the State Government loan required to be extended upto at least such time as the Reserve Bank of India loan assistance became available to the Union demanded that the date of repayment of the instalments of the Cess Fund loans should also be extended upto at least such time as the Reserve Bank of India loan assistance to which the Union was legitimately entitled became available to it. An additional working capital loan of at least Rs. 40 lakhs required to be made available to the Union. 25 lakh for the supply of raw materials and 15 lakhs for marketing the handloom goods.

The Union requires to be given a subsidy of Rs. one lakh and fifty thousand per year to meet the deficit. The handloom industry has not reached that stage when it could be self-sufficient. It still needs the help and guidance of the Government. Silk, particularly *tasar* silk, is a very important handloom industry of this State. *Tasar* goods are very popular in the United States of America and other countries. It is an important means of earning foreign exchange, particularly the dollar. The handloom sector is not able to push up the sale of the silk goods as no rebate is admissible on the sale of silk in the handloom sector.

The rebate scheme of the Government has helped a great deal in bringing about the development of the handloom industry inasmuch as it has helped the sale of the handloom products at par with the mill products of other States which are much cheaper than those of Bihar. The rebate on the handloom cloth is allowed in other States without any restriction. The Union demanded that the restriction imposed by the Bihar Government be immediately withdrawn to save lakhs of weavers from starvation.

In August, 1965 fifteen powerlooms were reported to be lying idle at Noorsarai for the last three years. Fifty powerlooms were brought there from Madhubani in 1962 and were to be given on loan for installation in the individual houses of the weavers there on a co-operative basis. A working capital of Rs. 1,000 was also to be given to them. But, in the mean-while, a controversy arose between the Co-operative and the Industries Departments of the Bihar Government over distribution to a single or to two cooperative societies. It took a long time to settle the issue and consequently, the looms remained idle. At last one more co-operative society had to be formed because at that time there was only one society at Noorsarai. Twenty-five looms were given to each society. Thirty-five of them were recently commissioned. The rest were lying idle.

About 125 powerlooms in all were diverted to Noorsarai from Madhubani, after lying idle for about two and a half years there. The loams were meant for distribution among the weavers there but the weavers could not be enthused to take the looms on loan. Meanwhile, the Government of India was reported to have withdrawn the distribution of the powerlooms along with the working capital of Rs. 1,000 on loan basis. As a result, the weavers had to purchase the looms at the rate of Rs. 1,000 each.

THE KHADI INDUSTRY

The first two Five-Year Plan's attached great importance to the organisation and development of khadi in Bihar. The First Plan witnessed the origin of the All-India Khadi and Village, Industries Board in 1953. Apart from being an agency for raising national income and employment, the Board made a bold attempt to weld together the stray co-operative societies and institutions engaged in the production of khadi. During the Second Plan it went ahead further. At the end of the Plan the number of institutions and co-operative societies had risen significantly. The sphere of the khadi industry had expanded. By 1960-61, 55 certified khadi institutions had already gone into production on the State. Even though the level of activity attained by the end of the Second Plan could not correspond to the expectations of the planners, it had no doubt become evident that the khadi industry had come to stay in Bihar.

A new era of development started during the Third Plan. The number of certified institutions and co-operative societies in Bihar multiplied from year to year. Consequent upon the rise in their number, the production and sales of the different varieties of khadi increased steadily in the State.

.The following tables contain data on the organisational set-up of the khadi industry and production and sales of khadi in Bihar in recent years, coming under the purview of the Khadi Commission:

TABLE 4.7

Organisational Set-up

Years	*State Board*	*Registered Institutions (including Government centres)*	*Co-operative Societies*	*Total*
1958-59	1	18	17	36
1959-60	1	18	30	49
1960-61	1	19	35	55
1961-62	1	18	35	54
1962-63	1	26	76	103

During 1963-64 Bihar occupied the second position among

the States in both production of khadi and its retail sales coming under the jurisdiction of the Khadi Commission. Table 4.10 is illustrative of this.

TABLE 4.8

Production of Khadi

(Lakh Sq. Yds)

Years	*Traditional (Cotton)*		*Ambar*			
	For Sale	*Self-sufficiency*	*(Cotton)*	*Woollen*	*Silk*	*Total*
1957-58	59.85	0.80	7.69	0.07	4.08	72.47
1958-59	56.09	7.61	21.94	1.18	4.77	91.59
1959-60	96.61	0.69	23.67	2.53	5.91	129.41
1960-61	72.29	0.26	24.97	6.12	3.89	107.53
1961-62	76.61	0.18	35.28	4.81	4.28	121.16
1962-63	92.42	0.18	52.73	3.98	3.79	153.10
(Lakh sq. mts.)						

TABLE 4.9

Value of Sales of Khadi (Traditional and Ambar)

(Rs. lakhs)

Years	*Retail*	*Wholesale (outside the State)*
1956-57	67.62	N.A.
1957-58	71.28	26.07
1958-59	59.97	22.80
1969-60	87.18	17.42
1960-61	178.98	45.17
1961-62	289.94	N.A.

The reasons for a general slump of activities during 1963-64 was the presence of certain bottlenecks operating against the development of the khadi industry, the removal of which was quite necessary for the level of production to again catch up the momentum. The accumulation of stocks of khadi in the godowns of the institutions largely exercised a drag on funds available for further investment, rendering it difficult for the institutions to increase their production.

TABLE 4.10

Khadi Industry—Ranking of States During 1963-64

States	*Khadi Production*	*Retail Sales of Khadi*
Andhra Pradesh	5	6
Assam	16	16
Bihar	2	2
Gujarat	9	7
Jammu & Kashmir	11	15
Kerala	12	13
Madhya Pradesh	14	12
Madras	4	3
Maharashtra	15	10
Mysore	8	9
Orissa	13	14
Punjab	3	5
Rajasthàn	6	8
Uttar Pradesh	1	1
West Bengal	10	11
Delhi	7	4

As regards the volume of the export of khadi of certain specific varieties of relatively higher counts from this State, there is dearth of statistical information and it cannot be precisely assessed how far the same increased as compared with the previous years. The exports during 1962-63 and 1963-64, however, amounted to Rs. 81,39,563 and Rs. 76,49,963 respectively.

Likewise, owing to the dearth of precise statistical information, it is difficult to indicate the magnitude of employment, given to the different categories of workers in the khadi industry during different years. However, a rough picture of the total employment given and its composition during 1962-63 and 1963-64 is contained in Table 4.11. Leaving aside the spinners, who can be safely classified as partially employed, khadi offered full-time employment opportunities to the weavers, various categories of artisans and supervisory and managerial personnel, numbering 16,509 in 1962-63 and 13,649 in 1963-64 in Bihar. During the same

TABLE 4.11

Years	*Spinners*		*Weavers*		*Others*		*Total*	
	Number Employed	*Wages (Rs.)*	*Number Employed*	*Wages (Rs.)*	*Number Employed*	*Wages (Rs.)*	*Number Employed*	*Wages (Rs.)*
1962-63	3,62,618	84,76,662	11,583	49,39,761	4,926	33,24.794	3,79,127	1,67,41,217
1963-64	1,69,076	71,32,065	9,832	45,59,332	3,817	31,04,344	1,82,725	1,47,95,741

period wages paid to those classified as fully employed amounted to Rs. 82,64,555 and Rs. 76,63,676 respectively an average income of such persons as were fully employed worked out at Rs. 41.75 and Rs. 46.79 respectively in 1962-63 and 1963-64. Part-time employment was offered to 3,62,618 spinners and Rs. 84,76,662 were paid as wages to them in 1962-63 whereas 1,69,076 spinners received part-time employment in 1963-64 and Rs. 71,32,065 were paid to them as wages.

It appears from the foregoing analysis that the magnitude of employment in the khadi industry is substantial in Bihar and hence the feasibility of raising its volume is still greater.

In the early years of the Third Plan the work of khadi production and sales in the districts of Purnea, Monghyr, Santhal Parganas and Gaya was decentralised and the management was entrusted respectively to Ranipatra Ashram, Purnea; Khadi Gramodyog Sangh, Monghyr; Gramodyog Samiti, Dumka; and Gram Nirman Mandal, Gaya.

A number of khadi institutions have done a great deal to step up production during the last few years. Mention may be made of the Khadi Kendrit Rachnatmak Samities of Narsingpur, Patepur, Baghakhal, Tilak Maidan and Waijitpur in Muzaffarpur district and the Congress Rachnatmak Samiti, Monghyr and several other small institutions. Due to the efforts of all these institutions khadi worth about Rs. 3 crores was sold throughout the State during 1961-62 through 632 sales emporia.

Attempts were made during the Third Plan to open at least one sales centre in every community development block to be run either by the institutions or by the Bihar State Khadi and Village Industries Board. Plans were drawn up to open large-scale sales emporia in the urban areas.

In view of the national emergency steps were taken up to establish small emporia all along the northern border. The idea to make not only cloth but also other articles of daily need available to the community through these emporia.

By 1963 altogether 73,806 Ambar charkhas and 2,79,800 traditional charkhas has been distributed among the spinners in the State. The khadi industry provided part-time and whole-time employment to nearly 5 lakh families of spinners, weavers and other artisans, salesmen and other workers.

The Bihar Khadi and Village Industries Board like the All-

India Khadi and Village Industries Commission, decided in October 1963 that it too would not involve itself in the production of khadi but would just help in the production activities of the institutions and the co-operative societies by means of financial and technical assistance. Accordingly, the Board transferred its production activity to the regional institutions and societies such as the Sarvodaya Ashram at Ranipatra in Purnea, the Gram Swarajya Sangh in Monghyr, the Gramodogya Samity in Santhal Parganas, the Gram Nirman Mandal in Gaya, and so on. The following table shows the contribution made by the different leading institutions to the progress of khadhi in Bihar during 1963-64.

During 1962-63 total expenditure through the Board was Rs. 24,37,187 out of which Rs. 2,33,398 were on the Ambar charkha; and Rs. 20,27,902 on the traditional charkha, Rs. 1,75,886 were incurred on exhibitions. In 1962-63, 108 co-operative societies and institutions were given financial help. During 1963-64 yarn production went down by 25.4 per cent as compared to that during 1962-63 whereas cotton cloth production went down by 4.7 per cent. Severe floods were the most important reason for this. In 1963-64 there were 78 sales centres in Bihar—9 in Patna, 19 in Tirhut, 21 in Bhagalpur and 29 in Chotanagpur divisions.

In February 1963 Acharya Vinoba at a meeting suggested that the rebate on the sale of khadi be replaced and twelve yards of cloth be woven free of cost on yarn being supplied by the spinners so as to ensure self-sufficiency in cloth, specially in the rural areas, and to impart inducement in the defence strategy of khadi production and to revive and to foster the khadi spirit everywhere. Vinoba's suggestions are under the consideration of the Bihar Government. It is, however, apprehended that the withdrawal of rebate may reduce the sale of khadi, khadi being dearer than mill cloth. So that this is averted, a gradual removal of the rebate is advocated instead in the hope that the purchasing habit of the people might change in the long-run and increasing demand in the urban areas might offset whatever fall there is in the demand in the rural areas. But all this is crystal-gazing and the apprehension might not be baseless, as for the successful implementation of the khadi scheme it is essential to extend weaving facilities to the villages through the aegis of the

TABLE 4.12

	Names of Institutions	*Production (In lakh Rs.)*	*Sale (In lakh Rs.)*	*Employment*			
				Spinners	*Weavers*	*Workers*	*Wages (In lakh Rs.)*
1.	Bihar Khadi Gramodyog Sangh	232.33	189.93	2,49,642	12,541	2,440	137.70
2.	Bihar State Khadi & Village Industries Board (and other institutions and societies)	16.90	50.55	18,226	664	294	9.79
3.	Sarvodaya Ashram and Kshetra Samiti, Ranipatra	2.16	8.39	1,178	210	86	1.70
4.	Gram Swarajya Sangh, Monghyr	5.64	17.62	24,884	235	542	11.75
5.	Narsingh Khadi Kendrit Rachnatmak Sahyog Samiti	4.44	2.28	3,627	301	181	3.47
6.	Santhal Parganas Gramodyog Samiti	1.24	3.90	507	82	55	1.03
7.	Gram Nirman Mandal	8.52	9.34	5,616	340	219	6.50
	Total	271.23	278.95	3,03,780	14,373	3,817	171.80

panchayats. At the moment such facilities are provided by about 1,000 centres, leaving the vast majority of villages untouched.

The khadi industry has not made any real difference to the economic and social conditions of the spinners, the weavers, the artisans and the rural economy as a whole. Its impending problems are: (a) fall in the level of real wages as compared with the prewar level, (b) development of khadi production without any reference to the incidence of unemployment and local demand and market, (c) complete non-participation of the producers in the plans for the development of khadi and their execution, (d) growing resistance of the customer to the prices of khadi, (e) lack of any improvement in the technique of spinning in what is called traditional khadi and non-utilization and under-utilization of the Ambar charkha and the resulting huge wastage of capital resources, (f) failure of khadi to make any material impact on the rural unemployment, (g) hardly any evidence of social earnestness among the bulk of the field workers and even among the newly appointed supervisory staff, (h) inability of the khadi workers to identify themselves with the village communities or to assume any role in their development, and (i) exclusion of the poor peasants and landless labourers from the range of khadi production.

During the Third Plan steps were taken to implement two different kinds of schemes for the all-round development of the villages. These were the Gram Ekai Scheme of the Khadi Commission and the Rural Industrialisation Scheme of the State Government to be implemented through the State Board and the khadi institutions. The Khadi Gramodyog Sangh was to implement these schemes in the Pusa area and the Gram Nirman Mandal of Shekhodeora, Gaya was to implement it in the Warsaliganj and Kaokol areas. The Gram Ekai Scheme aimed at the intensive development of the village industries and the linking up of this activity with the development of agriculture and animal husbandry.

Under this scheme units of areas known as Gram Ekais with an average population of 5,000 were selected for such an integrated development. The whole of Madhubani sub-division and portions of Sitamarhi and Samastipur sub-divisions, including the Pusa area, were taken up for development under this scheme. Besides, 168 Gram Ekais in other areas were selected. The work of survey in all these areas was in progress and the development work was to be undertaken shortly.

The Bihar State Khadi and Village Industries Board has been playing an important role in the development of the village industries. The Board discharges its main functions through the industrial co-operative societies. The total number of the registered village industries co-operative societies in Bihar was 2,304 in 1963-64, out of which 1,557 were given all possible economic and financial help. These societies produced Rs. 5,08,28,000 worth of consumer goods, gave employment, part-time or full-time, to 95 thousand people and spent Rs. 119 lakhs on wages. A detailed account of the different village industries of Bihar is given below.

PROCESSING OF CEREALS AND PULSES INDUSTRY

Bihar is the classic home of traditional deviced for the processing of cereals and pulses. Hand-pounded rice still constitutes the bulk of the rice consumed in Bihar particularly in its rural areas, though a continuous decline has been noticeable notwithstanding the nutritive value which hand-pounded rice, hand-processed flour and pulses claim to have. It was to curb this tendency and to provide gainful employment to the people that the Khadi and Village Industries Commission undertook the protection of this industry. Financial assistance to institutions and co-operative societies has been extended by the Commission ever since its inception to rehabilitate these traditional industries. Such assistance was directed mainly towards paddy stocking, construction of godowns and marketing depots. A sizable portion of the rural population has already been brought under the cooperative fold. The keen reaction of the people has been reflected in commendable progress in the organisational set-up of the industry. The following tables bring out this clearly.

The progress achieved under the different Five-Year Plans in terms of production, sales and employment, as presented in these tables clearly indicates an upward rising trend. This trend, however, got reversed in 1963-64 which witnessed a general slump of activities owing to the presence of various bottlenecks. It cannot be precisely said whether the continuous lead given by Bihar to other States ever since 1955-56 was maintained during 1963-64 or not.

TABLE 4.13

Institutional Progress

Years	Co-operatives	Registered Institutions	Total
Upto 1955-56	22	5	27
1956-57	58	14	72
1957-58	57	18	75
1958-59	61	18	79
1959-60	135	20	155
1960-61	194	19	213
1961-62	270	23	293
1962-63	281 (working)	13 (working)	294 (working)
	217 (reporting)	11 (reporting)	228 (reporting)
1963-64	376 (working)	13 (working)	389 (working)
	207 (reporting)	—	207 (reporting)

TABLE 4.14

Extent of Financial Assistance
(Disbursements made by the Commission)

(In Lakhs of Rupees)

	Upto the end of First Plan	During Second Plan	First Year of Third Plan
Grant	Nil	6.87	1.13
Loan	1.20	34.69	11.43
Total	1.20	41.56	12.56

As regards production, the progress attained during the Third Plan period lagged behind that at the close of the Second Plan. It is encouraging to note, however, that some sort of *Status quo* has been maintained and the volume of activities promises a better future.

Sale of hand-pounded rice in Bihar has not posed much of a problem whatsoever and the godowns created out of the funds available from the Commission have proved to be ideal storage centres in their respective localities. The table below gives the sales effected in the State by the co-operative societies alone:

TABLE 4.15

Paddy Dehusked

Years	*Quantity (In Lakhs of Mds.)*
1955-56	0.55
1956-57	2.15
1957-58	2.47
1958-59	1.82
1959-60	3.59
1960-61	7.56
1961-62	6.59
1962-63	6.99 (2.65 quintals)
1963-64	1.29 (quintals)

TABLE 4.16

Years	*Sales (In Lakhs of Mds.)*
1959-60	1.88
1960-61	4.14
1961-62	4.04
1962-63	3.42 (or 1.28 quintals)
1963-64	0.77 (quintals)

Likewise, the Table 4.17 gives a rough idea of the volume of employment offered by the co-operative societies:

TABLE 4.17

	1956-57	*1957-58*	*1958-59*	*1959-60*	*1960-61*	*1961-62*	*1962-63*	*1963-64*
Full-time	1,009	—	1,112	3,808	6,886	5,008	3,123	N.A.
Part-time	3,254	—	1,087	2,828	5,208	2,539	2,350	7,990
Total wages paid (Rs.)	—	—	—	4,30,940	8,35,890	7,21,694	7,38,697	N.A.

The extent of the distribution of the improved implements for the growth of this industry in Bihar during the different Plan periods is given by Table 4.18.

TABLE 4.18

Implement	*Upto 1955-56*	*During the Second Plan*	*First three years of the Third Plan*
Paddy Chakkis	43	1,365	2,457
Winnowing Fans	1	58	2
Dhekis	—	125	6
Atta Chakkis	26	468	612
Paddy Chakkis	—	—	2,457

The objectives of developing the hand-pounding of rice industry are: (a) to provide part-time employment for at least 150 days in a year specially to women, (b) to pound maximum rice from paddy, (c) to protect the nutritive properties of rice, and (d) to prevent rice from breaking. The chief troubles of this industry originate from the mill and the huller competition. With these ends in view the Khadi Board distributes through the cooperatives improved tools and implements such as the ball-bearing chakki, the Assam dhenki, the flying wheel, and so on. A large number of mistries have been appointed at Muzaffarpur, Balia-kothi, Darbhanga and Bhagalpur by the Khadi Board for giving technical advice and assistance to the hand-pounders. Fair price shops have been started for dealing in hand-pounded rice. Centres for the manufacture of the improved tools and implements have been set-up at Dumka, Muzaffarpur, Ranchi and other places. In 1962-63 the total number of the co-operative societies of hand-pounders in Bihar was 475. They processed 4,54,780 maunds of rice, out of which 3,41,536 maunds were sold for Rs. 73,48,217. 3,123 persons found full-time employment among whom Rs. 5,41,424 were distributed as wages. 2,350 persons were employed part-time among whom Rs. 1,97,272 were distributed as wages. During 1963-64 Bihar topped the list among the States in both production and sale of dehusked paddy, as revealed by the following Table 4.19.

The main objectives of encouraging the atta chakki industry (i.e., the hand-grinding of flour industry) are the same as in the case of the hand-pounding of rice industry and the measures adopted for the purpose are also more or less of similar nature. The Khadi Board gives financial help for the purchase of improved tools and implements to the extent of 50 per cent of their total cost,

TABLE 4.19

Processing of Cereals and Pulses Industry Ranking of States during 1963-64

States	*Paddy Dehusked*	*Sales*	*Employment*	
			Full-time	*Part-time*
Andhra Pradesh	3	3	—	6
Assam	9	10	—	2
Bihar	1	1	—	3
Gujarat	7	11	9	8
Kerala	6	4	.2	10
Madhya Pradesh	5	12	4	7
Madras	4	2	1	—
Maharashtra	8	13	10	4
Mysore	11	8	6	11
Orissa	2	6	—	5
Punjab	8	7	3	9
Rajasthan	12	14	7	—
Uttar Pradesh	10	9	5	—
West Bengal	10	5	8	1

the remaining 50 per cent of the total outlay on organisation, replacement and contingencies is borne by the Board. Likewise, for the construction of godown a sum of Rs. 5,000 is advanced by the Board, half of it as loan and half as aid. Loans are advanced also for meeting the expenses on account of research and training at the sales centres.

VILLAGE OIL OR GHANI INDUSTRY

The village oil industry is one of the oldest cottage industries of our State. The preference of many people for ghani oil has been a potent factor contributing to its survival inspite of the high price. Its rehabilitation has been the chief concern of the Commission and the Board in this State. Financial and technical assistance has been extended to the co-operative societies and the institutions for the purpose. The Table 4.20 contains data on financial assistance. The responsibility for further assistance to the oilmen's co-operatives or other institutions rests with the Bihar State Khadi and Village Industries Board. The funds released to other institutions on the direct list of the Commission for the purpose are utilized by such institutions.

While it cannot be claimed that the financial and technical assistance extended by the Commission has already succeeded in realising the desired object or corresponded to the amount necessary for the rehabilitation of this industry, yet the fact that by now the industry has been able to revive itself and to march on the road to success cannot be denied. The gradual transformation in the institutional set-up, the rising volume of production and sales of oil through the efforts of the Commission and various other agencies including the State Board, and the sizable increase in the number of persons employed in this industry bear testimony to the above contention.

The institutional set-up existing before 1958-59 was characterised by the predominance of the primary co-operative societies of oilmen, developed as a suitable agency for the consolidation of their activities. The year 1958-59 was remarkable in that during it 601 primary co-operatives of oilmen, 31 multi-purpose co-operative societies, 85 registered institutions and 9 ghani manufacturing workshops were in operation. Table 4.21 depicts the changing institutional set-up of this industry in the succeeding years.

Whereas at the close of the First Plan there were only 965 registered ghanis, the number at the close of the Second Plan had increased to 7,033 (2,501 being improved ghanis) and to 8,558 in 1963-64 (4,963 being improved ghanis).

TABLE 4.20

(In Lakhs of Rupees)

	1956-57	*1957-58*	*1958-59*	*1959-60*	*1960-61*	*1961-62*	*1962-63*	*1963-64*
Grant	2.26	2.85	4.32	6.10	7.67	13.64	7.44	4.43
Loan	5.41	13.35	7.49	13.28	23.81	21.80	12.74	3.08
Total	7.67	16.20	11.81	19.38	31.48	35.44	20.18	7.51

Bihar happens to be the largest single producer and seller of the different varieties of edible oils in India. In 1961-62 it had a

TABLE 4.21

Years	*Primary co-operative societies*	*Multipurpose co-operative societies*	*Registered institutions*	*Ghani manufacturing sheds*	*Model centres*
1959-60	754	43	56	9	12
1960-61	877	57	46	10	11
1961-62	947	46	57	8	12
1962-63	989	17	58	9	10
1963-64	1,005	17	58	12	12

lion's share both in respect of the total production and the total sale effected in the country. Production of oil in Bihar constituted nearly 25.8 per cent of the total production of edible oils in the country in 1961-62 and nearly 27 per cent of that in 1962-63. Except during 1963-64 both production and sales increased at an extraordinary pace. The upward rising trend in production was, however, abruptly reversed in 1963-64, so much so that the level of production and sales during 1963-64 corresponded to level attained as early as 1959-60. In order that this retrogade tendency was arrested extra efforts were needed to plug the points where leakages had occurred.

The development programme for the village oil industry consists of the following measures: Extension and publicity of the improved gharri and the hand filter, arrangement for their manufacture, provision for loans to the co-operative societies, registration of the sales centres for stimulating production, establishment of the co-operative societies of the oil-men, arrangement for their training, construction of godowns and formation of their unions at the district and the State levels.

As would appear from the Table 4.24, during 1963-64 Bihar occupied the topmost position among the States both in the production and sale of village oil.

VILLAGE LEATHER INDUSTRY

The prime difficulty of the village leather industry stems from the unscientific exploitation of the animal carcasses. One solution

TABLE 4.22

Production of Oils and Oilcakes

(Quantity in Lakhs of Mds.) (Value in Lakhs of Rupees)

Variety	*1957-58*		*1958-59*		*1959-60*		*1960-61*		*1961-62*		*1962-63*		*1963-64*	
	Qty.	*Value*	*Qty.*	*Value*	*Qty.*	*Value*	*Qty.*	*Value*	*Qty.*	*Value*	*Qty.*	*Value*	*Qty.*	*Value*
Oils	0.59	58.73	2.18	192.86	3.23	—	4.14	410.17	5.01	449.60	5.82	615.05	2.83	391.05
Oil-cakes	—	—	4.22	50.56	6.61	—	8.26	82.58	9.94	99.64	11.90	121.55	6.90	78.26

TABLE 4.23

Sales of Oil in Bihar

(Qty. in Lakhs of Mds.) (Value in Lakhs of Rupees)

	1957-58	*1958-59*	*1959-60*	*1960-61*	*1961-62*	*1962-63*	*1963-64*
Quantity	0.58	1.77	2.57	3.66	4.45	—	3.22
Value	61.97	156.14	240.76	366.94	438.05	520.32	363.73

of this will lie in the Government's declaring them as State property and entrusting the task of collecting them to the village panchayats.

The Khadi Board has taken the following steps for the development of the industry. It has established centres for procuring carcasses and for their flaying, one each for eight to Jen

TABLE 4.24

Employment in the Village Oil Industry

	1957-58	*1958-59*	*1959-60*	*1960-61*	*1961-62*	*1952-63*	*1963-64*
Full-time	3,093	4,769	9,283	10,352	10,675	11,258	7,857
Part-time	962	2,005	3,372	2,710	2,739	6,758	2,877
Casual	—	—	—	—	3,708	—	24

TABLE 4.25

Village Oil Industry Ranking of States

States	*Production of Oil*	*Production of Oil-cake*	*Sales*
Andhra Pradesh	5	6	5
Assam	13	13	14
Bihar	1	1	1
Gujarat	6	7	8
Kerala	8	11	9
Madhya Pradesh	9	9	10
Madras	3	3	3
Maharashtra	2	2	2
Mysore	7	8	7
Orissa	11	10	12
Punjab	10	9	11
Rajasthan	4	5	4
Uttar Pradesh	5	4	6
West Bengal	12	12	13

villages, falling within an area of five to seven miles. It has also established model tanning centres and co-operative village tanning centres. Schemes for chrome-cleaning and re-cleaning with chemicals and finishing have been implemented. Similarly, there is provision for establishing co-operative sales centres and fertilizer (made from bones) producing, saresh-producing and shoe-making units. The Board gives grants and loans for promoting the industry for digging new pits and repairing the old ones, for settling up sales, flaying, model village and co-operative tanning and chrome-treating centres and for saresh-producing, bone utilizing and chrome-cleaning units.

The tables, given below, contain significant data on the construction of pits, production and sales of tanned hides and skins and leather goods and employment in the village leather industry.

TABLE 4.26

Construction of Pits

Years	*New*	*Total*	*Old*	*Total*
1957-58	170	170	110.	110
1958-59	50	220	100	210
1959-60	50	270	25	235
1960-61	70	340	50	285
1961-62	135	475	—	285
1962-63	65	540	50	335

Bihar occupied during 1963-64 one of the lowest positions among the States in respect of production and sales of leather goods.

There are some 3,00,000 heads of cattle in Bihar. This should prove to be an asset for the progress of this industry. Unfortunately, however, it is difficult to organise this industry on modern lines because of the poverty, illiteracy, traditions, taboos and superstition-mindedness of the people engaged in it. In 1963-64 there were 55 co-operative societies of the tanners and they produced between them leather goods valued at Rs. 3,24,000, 980 people got employment, full-time or part-time. Rs. 52.000 was distributed among them as wages. The fertilizer unit turned out in 1962-63 fertilizer weighing 56,913 lbs.

On the basis of the live-stock population of Bihar and the figures of export of hides and skins from Bihar to the world marked it can be enjoined on the Bihar State Financial Corporation that it should finance a chain of up-to-date tanneries in every part of this State. The success of this scheme would, however, turn on the extent to which fallen cattle carcass processing could be organisad on proper lines by the Khadi and Village Industries Commission and Board and other agencies. The Bihar Unemployment Committee (1954) had examined this scheme in detail and had calculated that on the basis of the live-stock census of 1956 and its mortality figures there would be some 28 carcasses daily within a radius of ten miles, apart from the hides and skins from the slaughter houses available for processing and curing. Each carcass has three hundred uses and its processing should create employment for certain categories of the population which are mostly without land. An organised and vigorously executed

TABLE 4.27

Production

(Value in Rs.)

Years	*Flaying centres*	*Bone crushing units*	*Model Tanneries*	*Training-cum-production centres*	*Total*
1957-58	3,403	55	18,984	14,855	37,297
1958-59	4,086	309	38,492	46,542	89,429
1959-60	17,028	707	28,600	1,17,932	1,64,267
1960-61 (Rs. lakh)	0.22	0.01	0.35	1.56	2.14 (+0.12 I.A.S.)*
1961-62 (do)	—	—	—	—	2.29
1962-63 (do)	—	—	—	—	4.32

* Income from Auxiliary Sources.

TABLE 4.28

Employment

Years	*Full-time*	*Part-time*
1957-58	34	149
1958-59	37	32
1959-60	73	37
1960-61	79	31
1961-62	91	169

TABLE 4.29

Sales

(Rs. Lakhs)

Years	*Value*
1959-60	1.02
1960-61	1.75
1961-62	4.30
1962-63	3.65

TABLE 4.30

Village Leather Industry
Ranking of States during 1963-64

States	*Production and Sales*
Andhra Pradesh	6
Assam	15
Bihar	12
Gujarat	5
Kerala	13
Madhya Pradesh	4
Madras	8
Maharashtra	3
Mysore	9
Orissa	11
Punjab	7
Rajasthan	2
Uttar Pradesh	1
West Bengal	10
Delhi	14

scheme of carcass utilization would, thus, create additional industrial employment, which would, in its turn, ease the pressure for further land fragmentation and land distribution, besides providing cured hides and skins for setting up tanneries. These tanneries should provide leather for the small-scale and the cottage units for the manufacture of footwear and other leather goods for home consumption and for export.

Besides, if scientific methods of tanning could be introduced, some new markets for tanned leather might possibly be found in Africa and Asia even though the more advanced countries prefer raw hides and skins. Again, India is likely to have a stable market for the export of footwear to the countries in which the pig rather than the bovine population is the more important source of meat. But a stable export trade in footwear can be fostered only if the quality of craftmanship and finish is of high order and is standardised by the use of good tanning technique and high-class mechanical appliances even in the cottage industries.

GUR AND KHANDSARI INDUSTRY

The sugar mills apart, the gur-khandsari industry is an important industry of Bihar. The greatest shortcomings of the industry are an uneconomic use of fuel and the dependence on out-moded karahs (pans) and kolhus (expellers). Improved karahs and kolhus are distributed among the producers by the Khadi Board through their co-operative societies.

The Table 4.31 gives the production of gur and khandsari in Bihar in recent years.

TABLE 4.31

(Quantity: Lakh Mds.) (Value: Rs. Lakhs)

Year	*Gur*		*Khandsari*		*Rab Value*	*Molasses Value*
	Qty.	*Value*	*Qty.*	*Value*		
1957-58	0.50	6.08	—	—	—	—
1958-59	0.13	2.29	0.03	0.81	0.38	0.6
1959-60	0.30	—	0.05	—	—	—
1960-61	0.52	—	0.04	—	0.51	0.09
1961-62	0.92	—	0.08	—	0.93	0.02
1962-63	0.68	0.01	—	—	—	—
(Lakh quintals)						

A gur-khandsari scheme was started in 1955 and was later merged with other schemes sponsored by the Bihar Khadi and Village Industries Board. There were in 1963-64 nearly 16 exhibition centres at the following places: Pirpati, Kahalgaon, Banka, Tarapur, Barbigha, Jamui, Islampur, Bikram, Hariharganj, Jainagar, Saharsa, Rajkhand, Khizarsarai, Sherghati, Dumraon, and Bihta. For about 72 villages there is one such centre, one centre being composed of six sub-centres. These impart training to the peasants in the operation of the kolhus, run by oxen or motor engines.

In 1963-64 the total number of the co-operative societies was 1,19,208 oxen-driven kolhus and 748 pans were distributed. Gur and khandsari worth Rs. 48,51,000 were produced. 21 persons were given technical traing. In the previous year 823 kolhus and 829 pans had been distributed.

PALMGUR INDUSTRY

The tables below show the progress of the palmgur industry in Bihar in recent years in terms of productions and employment and the institutional progress and the position of Bihar among the States in regard to the palmgur industry during 1963-64.

TABLE 4.32

Institutional Progress

Years	*Number of Co-operatives*	*Membership*	*States Federation*
1956-57	25	N.A.	—
1957-58	32	580	—
1958-59	60	1,170	1
1959-60	62	1,200	1
1960-61	86	3,360	1
1961-62	190	2,809	1
1962-63	192	3,000	1
1963-64	192	3,000	1

TABLE 4.33

Production and Employment

Years	*Quantity (Lakh Mds.)*	*Employment (Number)*
1956-57	0.05	212
1957-58	0.05	—
1958-59	0.04	360
1959-60	0.08	406
1960-61	0.16	2,207
1961-62	0.09 (or 0.03 lakh quintals)	—
1962-63	0.09 (do)	1,383
1963-64	0.04 (do)	2,968

TABLE 4.34

Palmgur Industry
Ranking of States during 1963-64

States	*Production*	*Employment*
Andhra Pradesh	5	2
Assam	—	13
Bihar	6	7
Gujarat	8	4
Kerala	3	3
Madhya Pradesh	—	12
Madras	1	1
Maharashtra	—	11
Mysore	4	4
Orissa	6	9
Rajasthan	7	10
Uttar Pradesh	7	8
West Bengal	2	5

SOAP-MAKING FROM NON-EDIBLE OIL INDUSTRY

Soap-making from non-edible oils has a bright future in Bihar. In Champaran district and Chotanagpur division non-edible seeds grow abundantly. The Khadi Board is executing a scheme under which oils are being extricated from non-edible seeds. Others schemes for the development of this industry are more or less the same as in the case of other village industries.

The Tables 4.35 to 4.38 given below trace out the progress of the non-edible oils and soap industry in recent years in Bihar from the standpoints of production of oil and soap and employment provided. During 1963-64 Bihar occupied an extremely low position among the States so far as the production and sales of soap made from non-edible oils were concerned.

HAND-MADE PAPER INDUSTRY

There are in Bihar four units producing hand-made paper. Three of them are medium-sized. These are located at Patna (at Sadaquat Ashram), Biharsharif and Ranchi. The fourth one, a small-sized unit, is located at Muzaffarpur.

TABLE 4.35

Production of Soap

Years	*Quantity (Lakh Lbs)*	*Value (Rs. Lakhs)*
1956-57	0.48	0.36
1957-58	0.98	0.67
1958-59	1.71	1.26
1959-60	3.14	2.31
1960-61	2.61	1.93
1961-62	2.45	1.80
1962-63	1.54 (Lakh (Kgms)	2.40 (Lakh Rs.)
1963-64	1.99 (do)	2.70 (do)

The following Table 4.39 shows the organisational progress of this industry.

The financial assistance extended to the Bihar State Khadi and Village Industries Board and the Bihar Khadi Gramodyog Sangh, Muzaffarpur taken together under the first two Plans and during the first three years of the Third Plan is presented in the Table 4.40.

Production of high-grade, high quality paper is the prime

TABLE 4.36

Production of Non-edible Oils

Years	*Seed Collection*		*Oil Production*	
	Quantity (*Lbs.*)	*Value* (*Rs.*)	*Quantity* (*Lbs.*)	*Value* (Rs.)
1958-59	40,030	5,174	13,070	9,639
1959-60	—	—	22,728	17,533
1960-61	2.05 (Lakh lbs)	—	0.27 (Lakh lbs)	0.21 (Rs. Lakhs)
1961-62	0.33 (Lakh kgms)	0.18 (Rs. Lakhs)	0.22 (do)	0.21 (do)
1962-63	0.39 (do)	0.24 (do)	0.05 (Lakh kgms)	0.09 (do)

concern of the hand-made paper industry. In Bihar production has tended to consist of high-grade writing paper and printing paper, blottings, covers and boards, etc. The Table 4.41 gives figures of production.

TABLE 4.37

Employment

Years	*Full-time*	*Part-time*
1956-57	26	3,895
1957-58	14	1,591
1958-59	35	497
1960-61	71	1,710
1961-62	40	—
1962-63	42	1,001

TABLE 4.38

Non-edible Oils Soap Industry
Ranking of States During 1963-64

States	*Production*	*Sales*
Andhra Pradesh	1	1
Bihar	10	9
Gujarat	3	2
Kerala	5	5
Madhya Pradesh	9	10
Madras	4	4
Maharashtra	7	7
Mysore	8	8
Rajasthan	6	6
Uttar Pradesh	2	3
West Bengal	11	11

TABLE 4.39

Type of unit	*At the end of the First Plan*	*At the end of the Second Plan*	*Under the Third Plan*
Medium	1	2	3
Small	1	1	1

TABLE 4.40

(in lakhs of Rs.)

	First Plan	*Second Plan*	*First 3 years of the Third Plan*
Grant	0.14	1.35	1.55
Loan	0.15	1.90	1.70

It is evident from the Table 4.41 that in the first three years of the Third Plan production had more than doubled compared to that during the Second Plan.

TABLE 4.41

	First Plan	*Second Plan*	*Three years of Third Plan*
Quantity (Kgms)	—	24,399	57,091
Value (Rs.)	—	72,022	1,86,472

The hand-made paper industry enjoys more or less a monopolistic position with respect to quality paper needed by the universities for certificates and degrees. The durability of such paper is between three hundred and five hundred years. There has been an upward rising trend in its sales under the different Five-Year Plans, as shown by the following Table 4.42.

Although the volume of employment offered by the industry does not look substantial, yet seen against the limited scope of the activities undertaken it cannot be dismissed as unsatisfactory. Table 4.43 gives the number of persons employed in the industry during different years.

TABLE 4.42

	First Plan	*Second Plan*	*Three years of Third Plan*
Quantity (Kgms)	—	16,739	32,753
Value	—	48,493	1,19,872

The employment potential of this industry is limited because it has to remain confined within the bounds of certain institutions only and does not admit of the possibility of organisation along the co-operative lines.

BEE-KEEPING INDUSTRY

The prospect for the bee-keeping industry in Bihar is bright. According to an estimate, nearly 30 thousand acres in Bihar are such that some 15,000 maunds of honey can be produced every year. Regional effects have been opened for promoting this industry. Their main functions are to establish sub-stations or sub-centres, to assemble appliances and to supply them to these sub-centres, to help the producers in the sale of honey and wax and to impart training to the staff of the regional workers. Tables 4.44 and 4.45 contain figures of production and employment in recent years in Bihar.

TABLE 4.43

	1957-58	*1958-59*	*1959-60*	*1960-61*	*1961-62*	*1962-63*	*1963-64*
Full-time	—	—	30	42	31	119	70
Part-time	—	—	8	15	20	6	—
Causal	—	—	3	5	—	14	—

TABLE 4.44

Production of Honey

Years	*Quantity (Lbs.)*
1956-57	2,946
1957-58	6,276
1958-59	10,493
1959-60	15,369
1960-61	21,517
1961-62	43,130
1962-63	36,662 (Kgms)

TABLE 4.45

Employment

Years	*Part-time Bee-Keepers*
1956-57	401
1957-58	428
1958-59	644
1959-60	827
1960-61	1,128
1961-62	1,491
1962-63	2,681

In 1962-63 there were 75 such centres in Bihar. The Head Office for the sale and purchase of honey is located in Bombay in the office of the Khadi Commission, having one marketing officer. In the regional offices the marketing supervisors conduct the whole affair, assisted by a number of workers who gather honey for sale and do the packing. Besides technical and financial help, the bee-keepers are given 50 per cent of the cost of the necessary instrument as subsidy and 50 per cent of the cost of storage of honey as loan. The aparists are imparted training at the Central Bee-keeping Research Institute at Poona, as established and maintained by the Khadi and Village Industries Commission.

The industry has a bright future in North Bihar, particularly in Muzaffarpur, Champaran and Darbhanga, and in Chotanagpur, particularly in Ranchi, where the raw material is abundant. In Muzaffarpur and Champaran districts several families depend on this industry for their livelihood, each family earning Rs. 3,000 to Rs. 4,000 per year. Honey could be a good foreign exchange earner. In Bihar in 1963-64 the total production of honey was nearly one lakh pounds valued at Rs. 2,63,000. Bihar's rank among the States from the point of view of this industry was fairly high as shown in following Table 4.46.

VILLAGE POTTERY INDUSTRY

The village pottery industry is a declining industry in Bihar due to the growing use of substitutes made of metal and china-

TABLE 4.46

Bee-Keeping Industry Ranking of States

States	*Production*	*Employment*
Andhra Pradesh	6	7
Assam	7	6
Bihar	4	5
Gujarat	14	14
Jammu & Kashmir	11	11
Kerala	3	3
Maharashtra	12	12
Madhya Pradesh	15	—
Madras	2	2
Mysore	1	1
Orissa	5	4
Punjab	10	10
Rajasthan	13	13
Uttar Pradesh	9	9
West Bengal	8	8

clay, lack of organisation and technical advice and finance, and so on. The Bihar Unemployment Committee (1954) recommended that the facilities given to the potters of taking earth from the land or to the people for taking dry wood, leaves and other minor forest produce from the State forests given previously be restored. Effects are being made to rehabilitate this industry by removing all these difficulties. Production and marketing, research and training are being organised. In 1963-64 there were in this industry 56 co-operative societies. The value of total production was Rs. 62,000 and about 10,589 persons were engaged partially or fully in it. Wages claimed Rs. 2,78,000. The following tables give the figures of production, sales and employment in the previous years. During 1963-64 Bihar occupied a fairly good position among the States so far as this industry was concerned.

FIBRE INDUSTRY

The fibre industry has an important place among the village industries of Bihar. It is spread almost in all parts of Bihar, though in different forms. It is being developed through the introduction

TABLE 4.47

Production and Sales

Years	Production (Value Rs.)	Sales (Value Rs.)
1957-58	17,697	13,329
1958-59	29,160	27,437
1959-60	42,899	27,784
1960-61	90,853	42,226
1961-62	2.19 (Lakh Rs.)	1.78 (Lakh Rs.)
1962-63	4.19 (do)	3.20 (do)

TABLE 4.48

Employment
(Number)

Years	Full-time	Part-time	Casual
1957-58	278	245	—
1958-59	44	67	136
1959-60	90	43	—
1960-61	163	1,035	—
1961-62	242	87	—
1962-63	560	217	—

of the new techniques of production. The co-operative societies engaged in it are provided the necessary funds for the purchase of these techniques—50 per cent by way of loan and 50 per cent by way of grant. Model training centres have been set-up. There is one Organiser, one Director and one Assistant Registrar in each centre for its management. There is provision for starting a centre for training in silk work and for distributing rope-making machines and training workers in it and for constructing godowns.

In 1963-64 there were two production-*cum*-training centres and ten persons had been selected for training. There were about 19 co-operative societies. 37 rope-making machines had been distributed among them. The total production of the industry including ropes and other articles was valued at Rs. 23,000. About

TABLE 4.49

Ranking of States

States	Production	Sales	Employment	
			Full-time	Part-time
Andhra Pradesh	6	5	5	5
Assam	16	16	13	11
Bihar	5	6	4	7
Gujarat	2	2	1	2
Jammu & Kashmir	13	15	15	14
Kerala	1	1	3	3
Madhya Pradesh	14	13	10	13
Madras	4	3	2	—
Maharashtra	9	4	9	9
Mysore	7	7	7	15
Orissa	15	14	11	12
Punjab	11	10	14	8
Rajasthan	8	8	6	1
Uttar Pradesh	3	4	6	1
West Bengal	10	12	12	4
Delhi	12	11	16	10^

500 people were engaged, part-time or full-time, in this industry. Three production units—one each at Sultanganj, Bairgania and Saharsa—were run by the Khadi Board. Goods valued at Rs. 18,383 were sold. Rs. 5,275 were distributed as wages.

The following tables show the progress of this industry in Bihar in respect of production, sales and employment in recent years. Bihar's position among the States remains low so far as this industry is concerned.

TABLE 4.50

Production and Sales

(Value Rs.)

Years	Production	Sales
1958-59	29,160	27,437
1959-60	42,899	27,784
1960-61	0.02 (Rs. Lakhs)	0.02 (Rs. Lakhs)
1961-62	—	—
1962-63	0.24 (do)	0.19 (do)

TABLE 4.51

Employment

Years	Part-time
1960-61	20
1961-62	39
1962-63	120. (full-time and seasonal)

TABLE 4.52

Fibre Industry
Ranking of States

States	Production	Sales
Andhra Pradesh	10	7
Bihar	9	8
Gujarat	13	9
Jammu & Kashmir	11	—
Kerala	4	3
Madhya Pradesh	6	2
Madras	12	10
Maharashtra	14	—
Mysore	7	5
Orissa	8	—
Punjab	1	1
Uttar Pradesh	5	4
West Bengal	2	6

CARPENTRY AND BLACKSMITHY

These are complementary and supplementary to each other and have an important place in the village economy in providing employment but they are handicapped by the use of out-moded appliances. The Khadi Board is endeavouring to open a large workshop in every block and a small one in every village with a view to manufacturing the tools and implements used by the different village industries. The workshops will be supplied the necessary raw materials as well as given the necessary financial aid and loan by the Khadi Board. 'Class A' workshops will, thus, receive Rs. 16,500 each, two-thirds by way of loan and one-third by way of grant. This is in addition to the provision for the supply of working capital. 'Class B' workshops will receive Rs. 7,500 each by way of grant for the buildings and appliances and another Rs. 7,500 by way of loan and Rs. 3,000 for meeting the expenses on organisation by way of aid. 'Class C' workshops will receive Rs. 3,500 as aid and Rs. 2,500 as loan. Lastly, 'Class D' workshops will receive Rs. 8,250 as aid and Rs. 4,250 as loan. The money is proposed to be disbursed through the co-operative societies. Artisans are entitled to loans for paying their share capital to their societies.

From what has been said above it does not necessarily follow that all is well with the khadi and village industries. It is pointed out that the purpose of encouraging the khadi and village industries is being spoiled by their being continuously sustained through special subsidies. Gandhiji thought of khadi as a means of stopping the imports of textiles from abroad and wanted the development of the village industries as a means to supplementing the limited income of the rural population whereas today both the khadi and village industries have become a vested interest with the result that there are big jobs for the big and easy jobs for a host of others and nobody is really concerned about marketing the goods produced by these industries or even about producing what is required because of the provision of subsidies. It is further pointed out that the actual work done so far for the protection and promotion of the village industries has been meagre, being largely exploratory in nature. Many of the units of such industries are not located at proper places. The coverage of the artisans is small even in the areas in which the work has been organised. The quality of work done generally has been poor. The impact of the developmental programmes on the problem of underemployment of those already engaged in these industries has been at best trivial. The organisational machinery at the headquarters and in the field lacks unity of purpose, clarity of approach and rationalisation of functions. The earnings of the artisans are known to be exceedingly low and have, as a general rule, not increased owing to the developmental efforts in the past one decade.

The integrated development of the village industries would involve pooling of all resources in the villages, planned allocation of the available manpower consistent with a budget of needs and resources, regionalisation of the plans of development, and federalisation and co-operativisation of the agencies responsible for their development. There should be a clear demarcation between the spheres of activity of the village industries, small-scale industries and large-scale industries. The competition between them calls for some kind of systematic regulation. At present whatever is done to develop the village industries is being neutralised in some degree by letting the processing industries like rice-hulling, oil expellers, spinning and sugar mills grow indiscriminately and without plan notwithstanding the regulative legislation in cases like oil and rice.

The fact remains that rural industrialisation on a decentralised basis cannot be a sound and developing process unless it is carried out with the use of modern science and techniques in order to raise productivity, increase earnings and create a surplus for the capital formation without creating any technological unemployment.* The development of agricultural processing industries and *mandis* as nuclei of the new agro-industrial centres could also profoundly influence the rural-urban migration trends that are denuding the rural areas of some of their best talents.

Co-operation and panchayati raj have been forged by local leadership into a potent force that is shaping a new agro-industrial society in Sangli and Kolhapur districts of Maharashtra. Everywhere in Maharashtra the break-through in co-operative sugar processing has created a nucleus of growth backed up by a well-knit organisation, financial resources, technical know-how, managerial skill and above all, an exhilarating sense of self-confidence. That is significant. In it, is the conviction that if co-operation is to fulfil its essential purpose, it must go all the way and permeate and pervade all aspects of the lives of the people.

SILK INDUSTRY

The most important producers of non-mulberry silk are

* Gyan Chand, *Socialist Transformation of Indian Economy,* New Delhi, 1965. We have examined the whole issue of choice of technique in our previously published book (being our Cambridge Ph.D. thesis), *Technological Choice Under Developmental Planning,* Popular Prakashan, Bombay, 1963.

Assam, Madhya Pradesh, Orissa and Bihar. While Assam produces the entire quantity of *muga* silk and major portions of *eri* silk, *tasar* silk is produced mainly in Bihar, Madhya Pradesh and Orissa.

Whereas in 1953 Bihar claimed to be the second biggest silk-producing State in India, the figures placed before the Tariff Commission in 1958 revealed that Mysore, Kashmir, Assam and West Bengal had forged ahead of it. During 1959, 100 hectares of land were brought under mulberry cultivation in Bihar. In that year the requirement of mulberry silk-worm seed in the State was placed at 23.8 kgms. The production of mulberry raw silk was 1,125 kgms. The production of *tasar* silk in the State was 70,200 kgms during the year. Besides, 15,862 kgms of *eri* silk yarn were also reported to have been produced.

Bihar contributes about 40 per cent of India's total *tasar* silk production. It is also the biggest *eri* silk-cultivating State next to Assam. It carried on also small *mulberry* silk production. *Tasar* cultivation is carried on in the districts of Hazaribagh, Santhal Parganas, Singhbhum, Dhanbad, Palamau and Ranchi, chiefly by the Adivasis, Santhals, Pahadias and other tribes and castes. Bihar produces over 80,000 kgms of *tasar* raw silk annually and for its development the Government has set-up 9 *tasar* seed supply stations, 20 sub-stations, 7 training centres, 2 marketing centres and 15 co-operatives. There is a Silk Institute at Bhagalpur. *Eri* silk-worm rearing is essentially practised as a subsidiary occupation. *Eri* silk production is about 9,000 kgms per annum. It is spun by taklis, spinning wheels and improved pedal spinning machines. There are at present 4 *eri* seed supply stations, 25 demonstration units and one research centre at Ranchi. The two tables that follow contain important data on the silk industry in Bihar *vis-a-vis* other States.

HANDICRAFTS

By handicrafts are meant those cottage industries which produce goods of artistic value by the use of traditional skills. Among the important handicrafts of Bihar are brass and bell-metal works, fibre products like sikki and jute mats, jari lace, lac-painted wooden goods, toys and stonewares. At the end of the First Plan as many as twenty-one schemes consisting of training centres,

TABLE 4.53
Silk Industry

States	*1956 (in lbs.)*		*1960 (in Kgms)*		*1963 (in Kgms)*	
	Mulberry raw-silk products	*Non-Mulberry raw-silk products*	*Mulberry raw-silk products*	*Non-Mulberry raw-silk products*	*Mulberry raw-silk products*	*Non-Mulberry raw-silk products*
1	2	3	4	5	6	7
Andhra Pradesh	253 (11)	—	225 (11)	338 (8)	292 (12)	495 (7)
Assam	27,619 (11)	666,762 (1)	11,250 (4)	1,55,153 (1)	13,800 (6)	2,33,750 (1)
Bihar	2,550 (8)	1,19,000 (3)	1,125 (7)	83,262 (2)	1,136 (8)	88,978 (3)
Jammu & Kashmir	1,72,982 (2)	—	84,437 (3)	—	19,000 (5)	—
					71,966 (3)	
Madhya Pradesh	N.A.	1,40,000 (2)	270 (9)	83,250 (3)	586 (10)	1,10,000 (2)
Madras	1,22,416 (4)	—	1,242 (6)	—	998 (9)	—
Maharashtra	2,550[a] (9)	—	—	958 (6)	—	1,112 (6)
Mysore	15,72,592 (1)	—	8,30,958 (1)	14,878 (4)	10,20,000 (1)	—
Orissa	—	1,00,000 (4)	—	—	2,478 (7)	18,571 (4)
Punjab	13,239 (6)	—	4,539 (5)	—	404 (11)	—
Uttar Pradesh	3,000 (7)	—	873 (8)	134 (9)	2,11,578 (2)	73 (9)
West Bengal	1,62,151 (3)	5,877 (5)	2,18,833 (2)	6,452 (5)	68,000 (4)	11,894 (5)
Himachal Pradesh	444 (10)	—	96 (12)	—	130 (14)	—
Manipur	—	—	234 (10)	913 (7)	253 (13)	369 (8)
Tripura	—	—	—	—	7 (15)	—

a Including Gujarat.

Notes: (1) Mulberry raw-silk includes filature, dupion, etc., whereas non-mulberry silk includes *tasar, eri, muga*, etc.
(2) Figures in brackets indicate ranks.

TABLE 4.54

Silk Industry

States	*1956 (in lbs)*		*1960* (in *Kgms)*		*1962 (in Kgms)*	
	Mulberry silk waste products	*Non-Mulberry silk waste products*	*Mulberry silk waste products*	*Non-Mulberry silk waste products*	*Mulberry silk waste products*	*Non-Mulberry silk waste products*
Andhra Pradesh	—	—	113 (10)	170 (7)	150 (10)	1,050 (6)
Assam	13,312 (15)	5,55,955 (1)	5,265 (4)	88,154 (1)	6,000 (4)	94,000 (1)
Bihar	2,550 (7)	60,000 (3)	1,125 (6)	50,580 (2)	1,136 (6)	61,364 (2)
Jammu & Kashmir	1,44,000 (3)	—	71,068 (3)	—	62,503 (3)	—
Madhya Pradesh	—	1,30,000 (2)	135 (9)	33,750 (3)	200 (9)	40,000 (3)
Maharashtra	—	—	582 (8)	611 (6)	—	744 (7)
Madras	74,619 (4)	—	—	—	927 (7)	—
Mysore	6,62,005 (1)	—	3,54,500 (1)	—	4,68,150 (1)	—
Orissa	—	55,000 (4)	—	5,443 (4)	—	4,814 (4)
Punjab	5,266 (6)	—	1,465 (5)	—	1,740 (5)	—
Uttar Pradesh	—	—	873 (7)	32(8)	379 (8)	33 (8)
West Bengal	2,38,243 (2)	470 (5)	1,45,925 (2)	1,950 (2)	1,75,086 (2)	2,575 (5)
Himachal Pradesh		—	23 (12)	—	90 (11)	—
Manipur	—	—	68 (11)	—	87 (12)	29 (9)

Note: Figures in brackets indicate ranks.

production centres and common facility service centres were in operation for the revival of the decadent traditional crafts and the training of the artisans. For all these schemes a sum of Rs. 26 lakhs was provided in the Second Plan against which total expenditure up to March, 1961 amounted to Rs. 14.88 lakhs. The shortfall was chiefly due to the full amount having been not utilized under most of the schemes.

The most notable among the handicraft schemes implemented in the State during the Second Plan was the establishment of the Institution of Industrial Designs at Patna. Set-up more or less on the model of the Institute of Industrial Arts, Tokyo (Japan), this institute is of immense help to the cottage and the small-scale units of the State which cannot, afford to employ their own designers, by giving them new and modern designs and also by advising them on improved techniques of production. The designs as well as the new processes developed at the institute are made available to craftsmen. The institute also imparts training to the traditional artitsans and the supervisory staff. During the Second Plan 3,020 paper designs and 5,624 sample designs were evolved by the institute. 7,100 paper designs and 2,749 sample designs were sent out to various training institutions, industrial co-operatives of artisans and State-owned production centres, etc. In addition, 253 persons were also trained in various crafts, mainly with a view to upgrading their skill. A Designs Selection Committee meets every month to scrutinise the new designs involved in the previous month. The new designs and samples approved by the committee are sent out to the artisans and institutions for execution. On demand some designs are also sent to other States. Once in every two months an exhibition of the designs produced at the institution is organised. Local craftsmen and also craftsmen from different areas in the State are invited to witness, scrutinise and appreciate the samples.

For the development of the tribal crafts it was decided in the concluding year of the Second Plan to locate an institution of tribal designs in Ranchi from the savings of welfare funds provided by the Home Ministry of the Government of India.

On the eve of the Third Plan we had at different places in Bihar toy development centres and palmyraleaf, sikki goods, papier-mache goods, calico printing, lacquerware and lac-painted goods, bamboo works, flower-bowl, tikuli, traditional furniture, mat-making, bamboo works, kasida work and applica work production centres besides decorative pottery, wooden carving and inlay work, doll-making training centres and procurement-*cum*-sale depots.

The measures proposed in the Third Plan for the development of the handicrafts for sale in domestic markets and for export included the following: (i) Provision of advanced training to practising craftsmen, comprising training and demonstration of improved processes and techniques; (ii) Establishment of production centres for selected handicrafts for commercial production of quality goods; (iii) Schemes of research and design development, mainly through the expansion of the existing Institute of Industrial Designs, located at Patna; and (iv) Raw material depots for bulk purchase of raw materials for sale to craftsmen at a reasonable price, etc.

Handicrafts, being hard selling items, emporia, sales depots and shops and stalls at important railway stations, airports and places of tourist's interest were proposed to be set-up to assist in their marketing. To the same end provision was also made for expenditure on publicity, exhibition and schemes of quality marking. In order to enable the private banking institutions to meet the credit requirements of the artisans, provision was made as well for the establishment of a Credit Insurance Fund for guaranteeing repayment of the loan advanced on the recommendation of the Working Group constituted by the Government of India for handicrafts. As handicraft workers were mostly illiterate and disorganised, in order to encourage formation of their co-operatives, managerial and technical assistance on a sliding scale, for a maximum period of four years was proposed to be given. Important schemes worth mention were the folk art museum at Patna and a commercial museum in each division. The establishment of the rural arts and crafts museum at Patna would greatly assist the traditional artisans not only by making their existing skill widely known but also by making it possible for the Designs Institute to introduce modifications in the existing patterns so as to make these more attractive and acceptable to modern taste. The idea behind the commercial museum at the divisional level was to keep a representative collection of handicraft goods produced in the area ever ready for inspection by foreign or outside buyers as a prelude to purchase orders. A provision of Rs. 35 lakhs for the handicrafts schemes was made in the Third Plan.

RECENT DEVELOPMENTS IN HANDLOOM WEAVING AND SERICULTURE

The schemes for assistance to the handloom weaving industry during the Third Plan would be in accord with the general principles laid down by the All-India Handloom Board. Rs. 200 lakhs —the total outlay under this head—represented expenditure on schemes of marketing, including provision of Rs. 70 lakhs for payment of rebate on sales through State-owned emporia and other agencies. The proposed outlay also included schemes in the nature of technical assistance and those of training and research. Some of the important schemes for cotton weaving were:

> (i) Provision of share capital loans to the weavers; (ii) State participation in the share capital of the Bihar State Handloom Weavers' Co-operative Union; (iii) Expansion of two finishing plants; (iv) Establishment of a fancy yarn-making plant; (v) Expansion of the Co-operative Spinning Mill at Mokameh and establishment of a new spinning mill in the co-operative sector; and (vi) Building up of a housing colony for the weavers.

Those for silk weaving included a designs centre and reorganisation of silk weaving and opening of a dyeing section in the Nathnagar Silk Institute. For wool weaving, it was proposed to set-up a woollen carding and spinning plant—a scheme included in the Second Plan but not taken up in the absence of clearance from the All-India Handloom Board. It was further proposed to advance share capital loans of Rs. 1.00 lakh and working capital loan of Rs. 5.00 lakhs to the woollen weavers during the Third Five-Year Plan. Provision was also made for the grant of loans of the order of Rs. 1.50 lakhs to the woollen weavers during this period. For the whole plan period, the estimated cost for the scheme under this section was Rs. 200.00 lakhs.

Schemes proposed in the Third Plan for further development of sericulture in Bihar comprised the following:—

(i) Establishment of new tasar seed supply stations and substations; (ii) Assistance to the tasar rearers' co-operative societies; (iii) Marketing organisation for the purchase of tasar cocoons to prevent exploitation of the tasar growers by middlemen; and (iv) Establishment of training-*cum*-production centres for tasar-rearing and spinning. For assistance to the eri-silk rearers, following measures were proposed in the Third Plan: (i) Establishment of two new eri-seed supply stations, (ii) Establishment of 20 eri demonstration centres, and (iii) Setting up of a marketing organisation for purchase of eri cocoons. Already a mulberry farm has been established and Roshna in the district of Purnea for supply of disease-free layings to the rearers free of cost. Improved varieties of mulberry saplings and cuttings were also distributed from this farm, and training given to rearers. In view, however, of the suitability of the climate and soil of the Gangetic plain in Bihar for mulberry cultivation, production subsidy was suggested in the Third Plan for increasing the production of mulberry silk. For these new schemes a provision of Rs. 58.50 lakhs was made in the Third Plan. A small provision of Rs. 1.50 lakhs also existed for the spill-over schemes.

Small-Scale Industry

GOVERNMENT POLICY

Assistance generally to the cottage and the small-scale industries is provided by the Government either directly or more often through the Industries Department. A part of the assistance is under the Bihar State Aid to Industries Act, 1956 and takes the form of: (a) a loan; (b) guarantee of case credit, overdraft or fixed advance with a bank; (c) taking of shares or debentures: (d) guarantee of minimum returns on the whole or part of the capital of a joint stock company; (e) grant of favourable terms of land, raw materials or other property vested in the State; (f) payment of subsidy for: (i) establishment or expansion of small-scale industry, and (ii) the conduct of research; (g) supply of machines on hire-purchase system; and (h) supply of electrical energy at concessional rates. However, State aid in the forms specified above is not to exceed in amount or value Rs. 50,000 to any one firm. Generally, loans are granted to the cottage and the small-scale industries. Subsidies are granted upto 50 per cent of the cost of establishment, running, expansion or development in the case of the small-scale industries and upto 50 per cent of the cost of research or purchase of machinery in the case of any other industry. Better conditions are available to the co-operative societies and persons trained in particular trades at the Government cost.

The Bihar State Financial Corporation was incorporated in 1954 to meet the requirements for long-term finance to the small-scale industries. It is authorised to grant credit to any party upto Rs. 10 lakhs at $6^1/_2$ per cent interest per annum. A rebate of $^1/_2$ per cent is allowed, if the interest and instalment of principal are paid on the due six-monthly date. Financial accommodation is granted to new industrial concerns, which have a reasonable amount of capital but require additional funds to fully implement their scheme or to old concerns for expansion and modernisation purposes.

There were in 1960-61, 15 State Financial Corporations in the country, one in each of the States of Madias, Punjab, Bombay, Gujarat, Kerala, West Bengal, Assam, Uttar Pradesh, Bihar Rajasthan, Madhya Pradesh, Andhra Pradesh, Orissa, Mysore and Jammu and Kashmir. The capital of these corporations was fixed by the States concerned subject to a minimum of Rs. 50 lakhs and maximum of Rs. 5 crores. The share capital of the State Financial Corporations could be subscribed by the public to the extent of 25 per cent and the rest was subscribed by the State Government, Reserve Bank, Scheduled Banks, Co-operative Banks, Life Insurance Corporation and other financial institutions. They could also issue bonds and debentures to augment their financial resources.

The State Financial Corporations provided financial assistance of the following types:

(i) Granting loans or advances or subscribing to debentures of industrial concerns repayable within 20 years; (ii) Guaranteeing loans raised by industrial concerns repayable within 20 years; and (iii) Underwriting shares and debentures, etc., to be disposed of in the market within 7 years.

Unlike the Industrial Finance Corporation of India (IFC) they could grant loans even to private limited companies, partnerships and firms, and even individual enterprises. The maximum amount of loans that could be granted to a single concern was 10 lakhs or

TABLE 5.1

Operation of State Financial Corporations

(Lakhs of Rupees)

Corporation	*Capital as at the end of March 1961*	*Outstandings of Bonds issued as at the end of March 1961*	*Loans sanctioned during 1960-61(a)*	*Loans disbursed during 1960-61*
1	2	3	4	5
Andhra Pradesh (b)	150 (2)	—	56 (6)	27 (7)
Assam	100 (4)	55 (5)	68 (5)	56 (4)
Bihar	100 (4)	100 (4)	51 (7)	36 (5)
Bombay	200 (1)	114 (2)	176 (1)	83 (1)
Gujarat	50 (5)	—	38 (10)	19 (10)
Kerala	100 (4)	55 (5)	42 (9)	23 (8)
Madhya Pradesh	100 (4)	—	37 (11)	7 (12)
Madras	132 (3)	136 (1)	112 (3)	71 (2)
Mysore	100 (4)	—	44 (8)	21 (9)
Orissa	50 (5)	—	25 (14)	7 (13)
Punjab	100 (4)	102 (3)	128 (2)	57 (3)
Rajasthan	100 (4)	—	27 (13)	10 (11)
Uttar Pradesh	100 (4)	55 (5)	78 (4)	35 (6)
West Bengal	100 (4)	100 (4)	30 (12)	21 (9)
Jammu & Kashmir	41 (6)	—	4 (15)	2 (14)
Total	1,523	717	916	475

TABLE 5.1 *(Contd.)*

Corporation	*Loans Outstanding as at the end of March 1961*	*Loans sanctioned as on March 31, 1964*	*Loans disbursed as on March 31, 1964*	*Loans outstanding as on March 31, 1964*
1	*6*	*7*	*8*	*9*
Andhra Pradesh (b)	82 (9)	657 (5)	291 (7)	219 (7)
Assam	154 (5)	552 (7)	384 (5)	303 (5)
Bihar	149 (6)	414 (9)	319 (6)	242 (6)
Bombay	196 (2)	1,357 (2)	837 (2)	582 (2)
Gujarat	19 (13)	234 (12)	144 (13)	140 (13)
Kerala	138 (7)	340 (11)	276 (8)	172 (9)
Madhya Pradesh	44 (11)	629 (6)	248 (9)	191 (8)
Madras	389 (1)	1,438 (1)	1,094 (1)	737 (1)
Mysore	34 (12)	223 (13)	180 (12)	157 (12)
Orissa	18 (14)	194 (14)	119 (14)	106 (14)
Punjab	171 (3)	976 (3)	574 (3)	428 (3)
Rajasthan	54 (10)	341 (10)	210 (11)	165 (10)
Uttar Pradesh	103 (8)	505 (10)	235 (10)	158 (11)
West Bengal	157 (4)	784 (4)	493 (4)	396 (4)
Jammu & Kashmir	2 (15)	32 (15)	18 (15)	16 (15)
Total	1,710			

Notes: Figures in brackets indicate ranks.

(a) Includes in respect of some corporation loans subsequently declined by industrial concerns or cancelled or reduced by the corporations.

(b) Figures upto 1955-56 relate to the Hyderabad State Financial Corporation.

These figures were taken from the annual reports of the different State Financial Corporations which also contain the industry-wise distribution of the loans and advances and other relevant information relating to their recovery and default, etc.

10 per cent of the paid up capital whichever was less. Generally speaking, the State Financial Corporations assisted the medium-scale and the small-scale industries, which did not fall within the scope of the IFC. Till the end of 1960-61 their total outstanding loans and advances stood at a figure of Rs. 17.10 crores. The foregoing Table 5.1 shows the operation of the State Financial Corporations.

Further financial assistance is provided under the pilot schemes launched by the State Bank of India to give short-term credit to the small-scale industries for working capital.

Under the Stores Purchase (Preference) Rules, the Bihar Government has decided to give preference to the products of the cottage and the small-scale industries to meet the requirements of all departments. This will include concessions in price, standard of the products, period allowed for the supply of stores, security deposit required and the time of payment for stores supplied.

The opinion survey conducted among the industrialists by the NCAER brought to light the following weaknesses of the above assistance programme:

> (1) The supply of scarce materials was not prompt and efficient. (2) The supply of power was short and was at high rates. (3) The financial assistance given was not adequate to meet the credit requirements. (4) The procedure involved in getting a loan was too cumbersome and acted as a deterrent to the potential investors. (5) The technical aid provided was insufficient and was not well-publicised. (6) The specific assistance given in marketing and techniques of production was inadequate. (7) The supply of machines on hire-purchase basis was not efficient. (8) There were difficulties in the acquisition of land.

The authors of the Techno-Economic Survey Report suggested the following measures for promoting the small industries of Bihar:

> (1) The establishment of Investment Trusts with Government guarantee entrusted with the function of guidance and actual investment, (2) the formulation of a common production programme for the development of the small-scale industries

by sub-contracting components of the large-scale ones, (3) the setting up of a cell in the Government to make available information regarding investment opportunities in the State, (4) the establishment of a marketing Corporation at the State level with chain stores, (5) a detailed survey of the position of the cottage and the small-scale industries, (6) the strengthening of the Geological Department of the Government, and (7) the examination and periodic review of the utilization of the mining leases granted and prevention of the abuse of these facilities through delaying mining operations for speculative purposes and a definite stipulation as to the period within which the leases should become operative with the right on the part of the Government to cancel the licences after that period.

Industrial estates were set-up during the Second Plan period at Patna, Ranchi, Darbhanga and Biharsharif for the expansion of the small-scale industries and for creating a technological bias which was expected to grow rapidly because of the advantage of the location of the large-scale industries in Bihar. Pilot projects were started in these areas for giving encouragement to their industrial potential. Production-*cum*-training centres in the blocks were set-up for a large variety of the cottage industries like lock-making, carpentry, tailoring, etc. A sum of Rs. 1.19 crores was advanced till 1959-60 to the small industrialists. Industrial surveys were conducted in different districts with a view to ascertaining their particular demands and potentials.

A scheme for the establishment of rural industrial estates was taken up and necessary exploratory surveys were conducted. Towards the end of the Second Plan period the scheme for the setting-up of Industrial Areas was taken up, under which necessary overheads of industrial development were to be provided over specified areas and enterpreneurs were invited accordingly. Organisation of co-operatives for the marketing of goods produced through the production-*cum*-training centres and tuition classes numbering 467 was taken up.

The Third Plan proposed to set-up a lac seed supply station to expand the research station at Chaibasa, and to establish suitable production-*cum*-training centres, to expand and reorganise the Industrial Designs Institute and to purchase in bulk raw materials for sale at reasonable rates with a view to developing handicrafts in brass, bell-metal work and fibre products, and to train 8,948 additional craftsmen.

The Third Plan proposed to provide two more large industrial estates for towns with a population of 50,000 and above, for small industrial estates for towns with a population of 20,000 to 50,000, ten smaller industrial estates for townships with a population of 5,000 to 20,000 and fifty workshop sheds for rural towns of less than 5,000 population. It proposed to augment the Industrial Extension Service by the Small Industries Service Institute of the Government of India which would open more branch institutes for the small-scale industries and additional extension centres. The State Government was to set-up an Institute of Engineering Designs as a service organisation to help the designing of industrial products, especially in the light engineering industries. A directory of goods produces by the small-scale industries was to be prepared and the sale of the goods organised through emporia.

To cover areas, where power is not available but where willing entrepreneurs can be located, a provision of Rs. 15 lakhs was made in the Third Plan for the installation of diesel-operated electricity generating sets in accordance with the recommendation of the working group set-up by the Government of India.

The Third Plan provided for industrial extension services, services-*cum*-common facility workshops, pilot production centres, industrial pilot projects, training, financial assistance, marketing, dispersal of industrial growth, subsidy rent, guarantee fund, managerial assistance, and so on.

The Bihar State Small Industries Corporation was formed in 1961 for promoting the important small-scale and medium-scale industries in Bihar by taking up the management of industrial estates and other commercial schemes including marketing.

Among the small-scale industrial units we have the grey iron castings in Jamshedpur and automobile leaf springs manufacturing units in Dhanbad and Jamshedpur, glass and glass-ware units in Hazaribagh, Dhanbad and Singhbhum, cement-making units in Palamau, Dhanbad, Singhbhum and Dhanbad, stone-dressing and crushing units in Singhbhum and Dhanbad; bricks and tiles works in Dhanbad, and concrete hume pipe works in Palamau, Ranchi and Singhbhum.

DIFFICULTIES AND PROBLEMS OF THE SMALL-SCALE INDUSTRIALISTS

The private industrialists have to face difficulties relating to the acquisition of land for prospective industrial sites at reasonable prices, the supply of cheap electric power at rates comparable to those in the neighbouring States, sales tax on raw materials, duties on finished products as compared to those in the neighbouring States, disposal of applications for loans from the State Financial Corporation, road and railway transport facilities, and so on.

Industrialists running the medium-scale and the small-scale units in Bihar complain that they suffer mostly from an inadequate allotment of raw materials and the unsatisfactory overall supply position of non-ferrous metals. They adduce cases where these units have been left to starve from the short supplies of ferrous and non-ferrous raw materials with the result that their given capacities remain largely unutilized. Even when the essentiality certificates have been secured based on actual assessment of the working capacity of the units, the office of the Joint Chief Controller of Imports and Exports has not hesitated to slash their requirements, causing formidable difficulties to them as they can thrive on the imported raw materials alone. They contend that there was no sense in the Government's giving permission to set-up such units and taking the responsibility to supply them the basic raw materials, if this were to happen.

The small-scale industrialists complain that at present non-ferrous raw materials are not being distributed among them by the Industries Department on the basis of their installed capacity with the result that in one and the same industry factories having much lower capacity obtain much larger quantities of these raw materials than those having much higher capacities. They suggest that the raw materials should be distributed strictly on the basis of the installed capacities of these units. They claim that the small-scale industries have received a discriminatory treatment in the allotment of these raw materials. It is further pointed out that B.P. sheets and G.C. sheets have not been allotted to them for some years. Acute shortage of machinery and components was another difficulty holding up their expansion and growth. The allocation of copper to the small-scale units in Bihar is believed to be the lowest as compared to that in other major States. In the supply of zinc Bihar's place was seventh; in that of lead ninth; in that of tin eighth; and in that of aluminium fifth. The allotment of foreign exchange to the small-scale units in Bihar was only 1.3 per cent of the total allotment as against 28.6 per cent to Maharashtra, 14.2 per cent to Madras, 13 per cent to West Bengal and 11.9 per cent to Gujarat.

Certain categories of sheet and plate have lately been brought under the Government control. This control is posing a problem to both the traders and the manufacturers. A retention period may, therefore, be fixed for an early liquidation of their stocks.

The Estimates Committee of the Vidhan Sabha of Bihar regretted in its report of August 1965 that the raw materials obtained for the small industries were mostly disposed of in the black market by the permit holders. The Committee gave concrete instances of how certain persons obtaining licences had sold the entire quota of copper and zinc in the black market. An industrial concern at Bhagalpur had also misused its quota. The Committee recommended that the licence holders should swear affidavits before the order was made. This would make the prosecution of those charged with the misuse of their permits and quotas easier. It also laid down a procedure for the grant of loans to the entrepreneurs. It pointed out that loads had been misused in almost all the districts of the State and a huge amount of the Government money was blocked in the loans. It expressed deep concern over the future of the small industries in the State due to these bunglings in the State due to these bunglings in permits, licences and loans.

The small-scale industrialists have stressed the need for establishing a Raw Material Bank, which should function like any other bank dealing in raw materials. They make out a case for an organisation like the Raw Material Depot, which will cater to their needs and responsible for their minimum requirements. They suggest that the industrial requirements should be adjudged and planned buying should be undertaken. To avoid any accumulation of stocks, the entrepreneurs should be asked to pay the Depot commitment charges so that it might act as a deterrent to such entrepreneurs as requisition large quantities of raw materials but not use them all. Suitably qualified officers should be employed to see that the right sorts of raw materials and spares for the plant and equipment are bought, stored and made available to the small-scale industrialists. The procedures for the licensing of industrial units should be simplified; and adequate and better allotment of raw materials should be ensured; land acquisition procedures should be expedited and better co-ordination between the different departments of the Government should be effected.

The Bihar Government has recently appointed two whole-time liaison officers, one in Calcutta and the other in Delhi, to ensure the supply of iron and steel and other non-ferrous metals.

Not many industrialists come forward to take advantage of the loan facilities extended by the State Government under the Bihar State Aid to Industries Act. The Government alleges that the response on the part of the medium-scale industrialists has not been as encouraging as in other States. This is attributed to the dearth of local business leaders at various levels and to the fact that it is so much easier to make money through commercial transactions quickly and with lesser risks of serious leakages of raw materials any misutilization of funds. Moreover, the handicaps facing the new industrialists are numerous, arising usually from the administrative set-up in a centrally planned economy necessitating a system of pre-promotion and post-promotion servicing, on the one hand and of policing to prevent malpractices, on the other. There are reports that in several cases discrimination was practised in giving loans by the Government (under the State Aid to Industries Act) and the Bihar State Financial Corporation and those, who had no approaches in higher circles, could never hope to get loans for their industrial enterprises. The small-scale industrialists have expressed a note of despondency on the working of the Bihar State Financial Corporation for its failure to keep pace with the required development programmes concerning them. The various rules and overhead charges such as inspection fees of the Corporation are stated to be extremely taxing. A comparative study of the workings of some of the State Financial Corporations shows that while buoyancy and enthusiasm is noticeable in Punjab and Assam, there is a note of dispondency in Bihar. Information obtained from the annual reports for 1963-64 of the respective State Financial Corporations shows that in Punjab the Corporation received 114 applications for an aggregate amount of Rs. 3.56 crores, out of which 61 loan applications worth Rs. 1.84 crores were sanctioned and only 14 applications worth 21.36 lakhs were declined. 39 applications were withdrawn and rest were under consideration. In Assam out of 116 applications for consideration, 47 applications worth Rs. 1.18 crores were sanctioned and only one application worth Rs. 2 lakhs was rejected, 37 applications were withdrawn and 31 applications were under consideration. By contrast, in Bihar of the 48 applications received, 17 applications worth Rs. 35 lakhs were sanctioned and 6 applications were rejected. The rest of the applications were supposed to have lapsed.

It is further alleged that the existing scheme of price preference for the products of the small-scale industries entitling them to a price preference of the order of 12£ per cent in matters of stores purchased by the Government Departments is followed more in breach than in fulfilment and is not very enthusiastically taken into account by the purchase departments in general and by the autonomous bodies like the Bihar State Electricity Board, in particular. The State Government at present purchases nearly a hundred goods, the suppliers of which have their manufacturing units located generally outside Bihar. On the other hand, Uttar Pradesh, Maharashtra, Punjab, Orissa and Madras have got their centralised purchase units. The purchase sections of the public sector projects in Bihar are located either at Calcutta or at Delhi. This does not help in the development of the local ancillary units.

The products of the Indian Wire Products and the Cable Company are sold at the same price in the industrial markets of Maharashtra and West Bengal as in Bihar. This policy is proving to be a limiting factor in the industrial growth of Bihar, conductive as it is to the interest of the country as a whole. Thus, a divergence has arisen between the State and the national interests. Likewise, as a result of the pool price, iron and steel are available of the same price throughout India. The advantage to Bihar of the location of iron ore mines has to a great extent, been neutralised by this. Meterological coal found in Bihar is reserved for the public sector enterprises. Lime-Stone deposits are reserved for the Hindustan Steel Limited.

The small-scale industries face considerable difficulty in the marketing of their finished goods. The Government of India has established the National Small Industries Corporation Limited (NSIC) which purchases the goods manufactured by these industries. A recent review made by the Corporation indicated that the number of units registered with it from Bihar was very low. It was only 336 from Bihar as compared to 2,049 from West Bengal, 1,683 from Maharashtra and 1,346 from Madras with the result that the Bihar units got orders worth about Rs. 33.7 lakhs, the Punjab units worth Rs. 10.41 crores, the Uttar Pradesh units worth Rs. 6.36 crores, and the Delhi State units worth about Rs. 4.07 crores in 1963-64. Tables 5.2 and 5.3 illustrate this.

The Government takes too much time in sanctioning the acquisition of land for the small-scale units. Delay in the allotment of land in the Industrial Areas dampens the enthusiasm of the entrepreneurs. Even after the sanction is given, the physical handing overtakes too much time. After the handing-over is done, the villagers create difficulties and do not allow the industries to function on their lands.

The small-scale industrialists of Bihar allegd that in the matter of granting licences the Central Government treats them unfairly and licences are often not granted.

The supply of power is short and is at high rates. The Bihar Electricity Duty (Second Amendment) Act, 1963 has imposed a very heavy burden on the mining and manufacturing concerns situated in the State, which has adversely affected the existing industrial units.

The continued levy of a sales tax on iron and steel is a serious impediment to the growth of industries in Bihar. One solution of this will be replacement of the sales tax by an excise duty. Hosiery goods and handloom durries industries have to suffer from the levy of a general sales tax of $^1/_2$ per cent and a special sales tax of 4 per cent on them. For example, the number of units in the hosiery industry at Muzaffarpur declined from nine to one on account of these taxes. Units elsewhere are contemplating of shifting to other States. By remaining in this State they cannot hope to complete with their rivals in West Bengal which are exempt from such taxes. The sales tax on potato and potato seeds is reported to be affecting their trade adversely in Bihar as they are not subject to such taxation in other States. Disparity in the rates of sales tax on certain commodities like kerosene oil between the neighbouring States such as Bihar, Assam, West Bengal, Orissa and Uttar Pradesh leads to undesirable consequences. In the eastern zone Bihar used to have a monopoly in linseed and oil used to be extracted from it in the State itself. But when the State

TABLE 5.2

Number of Units Enlisted with NSIC Year-wise and State-wise

States	*Till April 1959*	*1959-60*	*1960-61*	*1961-62*	*1962-63*	*1963-64*	*Total*
Andhra Pradesh	180	68	52	52	113	168	633(7)
Assam	22	13	12	22	24	—	93(14)
Bihar	78	67	62	46	83	—	336(12)
Delhi	352	178	185	113	228	218	1,274 (6)
Gujarat	—	—	97	309	67	113	586 (8)
Goa	—	—	—	—	—	21	21(17)
Jammu & Kashmir	20	2	10	5	6	15	58(15)
Kerala	95	99	141	18	28	83	464(10)
Madhya Pradesh	93	45	31	123	52	39	383(11)
Madras	358	200	242	199	166	181	1,346 (5)
Maharashtra	782	281	206	—	139	275	1,683 (2)
Mysore	190	21	96	85	76	60	528 (9)
Orissa	6	6	15	8	6	—	42(16)
Punjab	774	152	106	112	220	86	1,450 (4)
Rajasthan	26	13	41	38	30	26	174(13)
Uttar Pradesh	471	157	131	169	244	391	1,553 (3)
West Bengal	628	330	219	264	178	430	2,049(1)
Total	4,075	1,632	1,647	1,563	1,660	2,106	12,683

Note: Figures in Brackets Indicate the Ranks of the States.

TABLE 5.3

Ranking the States with Respect to the Value of Contracts Secured by Units Enlisted with NSIC

States	*1957-58*	*1958-59*	*1959-60*	*1960-61*	*1961-62*	*1962-63*	*1963-64*
Andhra Pradesh	7	8	9	11	11	12	12
Assam	—	—	—	—	—	—	14
Bihar	9	10	12	8	7	9	8
Delhi	2	3	3	3	5	5	5
Gujarat	—	—	—	7	9	10	10
Kerala	8	9	7	9	8	8	9
Madhya Pradesh	—	11	11	12	13	11	11
Madras	3	6	6	6	7	7	7
Maharashtra	6	5	2	2	1	1	4
Mysore	—	—	8	13	12	13	12
Orissa	—	—	—	—	—	14	15
Punjab	5	4	4	5	3	4	1
Rajasthan	—	7	10	10	10	6	6
Uttar Pradesh	1	1	5	4	2	3	3
West Bengal	4	2	1	1	4	2	2

Government levied a sales tax on linseed, linseed began to move to West Bengal as there was no such sales tax on it there, and oil was extracted from it there with the result that for linseed oil we have now to look to West Bengal. The paint industry has not developed in Bihar for want of linseed oil. The sales tax on sewing thread balls and tubes is a peculiarity of Bihar and its existence has depressed their sale.

The Department of the Director-General, Supply and Disposal and the Railways have not given the small-scale industries of Bihar their due share, presumably due to lack of vigorous follow-up activity in this regard by the State Government. States like Punjab and Maharashtra have got a lion's share of their requirements.

The introduction of the telescopic rates by the Railway Ministry favours industries situated at distant places and discriminates against those within this State. This has to some extent neutralised the advantage to Bihar of the location of coalfields.

There is great scope for the development of industries manufacturing paints, varnish, plastic goods, organic pigment, ink, etc., but the dearth of technical personnel and advice is arresting their development. The establishment of the Bihar Technical Consultant Bureau is, therefore, a step in the right direction.

Difficulties are experienced by the flour mills of this State in respect of the supply of wheat which is restricted. Wheat products are neither properly distributed nor are lifted timely. Consequently, there is frequent accumulation of stocks. Restriction on extraction of fine flour maida and suzi to the maximum of 10 per cent results in the economic hardship of the flour mills. Biscuit manufacturers and bakeries are particularly adversely affected due to the short supply of maida and suzi. The production of wheat barn is quite substantial. But there is no proper arrangement for its distribution.

There is no restriction on the inter-State movement of pulses in other parts of the country. In the neighbouring States of Uttar Pradesh, Madras and West Bengal there are no restrictions whatsoever. There is, however, a ban on the movement of pulses from this State to other States and, more often than not, pulses from this State are smuggled to the neighbouring States causing loss to the cultivators and the State by reducing its revenue.

The State Government decided to supply two months' food-grains at the time direct to the industries, but no arrangement for this has so far been made by the Department of Supply and Commerce.

Difficulties are encountered by the wholesale distributors of sugar in the matter of supply of raw sugar as it is not lifted by the allotees in time. The quality of raw sugar is not popular in the market either. Besides, heavy shortages in transit and storage occur. Steps should, therefore, be taken for the immediate disposal of such stocks of raw sugar, and future supplies of sugar of this quality should be stopped. As regards crystal sugar, it may be noted that local authorities take a long time to dispose of the same, causing heavy accumulation and blockade of capital and space. The traders thereby stand to lose and artificial scarcity of sugar is the result.

According to Section 3(ii) of the Bihar Edible Oil Wholesale Dealers' Licensing Order, 1964, any person who stocks edible oil in any quantity exceeding eight quintals at any one time, unless the contrary is proved, is deemed to be carrying on business as a wholesale dealer of edible oil. This clause has, however, created difficulties to the retailers. It is not clear from it whether a dealer desiring to purchase 16 kilograms or more but less than 8 quintals and purchase edible oil without licence or shall have to obtain a licence for this. Again, it is not clear from it whether a dealer without a licence can keep 8 quintals of each kind of edible oil or 8 quaintals of all edible oil taken together. Moreover, it is clear whether a dealer is bound to obtain a licence if he keeps a stock of less than 8 quintals of edible oil but sells 16 kilograms or more at a time to an individual customer.

According to a recent circular of the Supply and Commerce Department of the Bihar Government (Circular No. 5869/SC, dated the 2nd April 1965), the levy on the rice millers having more than one huller would be compoundable at the rate of 185 quintals, that is, 500 maunds of rice per huller per month, or at the rate of 148 quintals, that is, 400 maunds per huller, as the case may be; whereas the rice millers, having only one huller, are to compound levy at the rate of 25 quintals of rice per month. Thus there is great disparity between the two types of millers, one having one huller, and the other having more than one huller. This has caused an anomalous situation inasmuch as the millers having more than one huller will not in view of the aforesaid circumstances, be able to procure paddy at a reasonable price, their competitive ability having been adversely affected thus, as compared to the millers with one huller. As a result, the procurement of rice from these mills may not be so encouraging as the scheme of compounding levy on the rice mills envisages. The payment of the price of rice supplied by the millers under the aforesaid scheme is not very prompt. This is also causing under harassment to the millers.

There is undue delay in the disposal of cement and the Government should, therefore, allow the disposal of cement as per its notification, that is, after 3 weeks' retention period and subsequently after one week's notice. By serving notice the dealer should be free to dispose of the cement and thus, unnecessary stocking of cement should be avoided in the interest of the dealers as well as the consumers alike.

The supply of all other qualities of salt in Champaran district has been banned except iodised salt from the Sambhar Lake. It has often been reported that no arrangement to ensure a regular supply even of this variety of salt to Champaran district has been made as a result of which shortages are experienced.

There is also need for quality control of goods which can be exercised through the marketing committees formed in different *mandis*. Uniform trading practices have to be evolved and quality standards fixed for different cereals and pulses in all the recognised *mandis*.

North Bihar is a particularly backward area of this State, and the entrepreneurs and industrialists have to face great difficulties in either setting up or in running their industries there due to the excessively high power rate. In this connection the transport bottle-neck in North Bihar needs special mention. The Rajendra Bridge at Mokameh has eased the situation only to a limited extent.

The discontinuance of the practice of issuing quota certificates of iron and steel to the registered steel fabricator has entailed great disappointment among the owners of the small-scale industries.

In 1965 an officer of the Commissioner's ranks was appointed by the Bihar Government to look after the liaison function for it at Delhi. The private industrialists cannot approach the officer concerned for assistance. It is reported that a similar officer of the Punjab Government stationed at Delhi, looks into the problems of the private industrialists as well and does liaison work in obtaining orders from the Department of the Director-General, Supply and Disposal and the Railways. A similar arrangement in this State, too, for the convenience of the private industrialists would be a welcome feature.

It is suggested that the State Purchase Committee on the lines of the Department of the Director-General, Supply and Disposal should be formed so that the small-scale units may not have to experience difficulties in supplying goods to the Government Departments.

It is alleged that various provisions of the Factories Act, Bonus Ordinance and other forms of labour legislation are such as to cause great difficulties to the small-scale units in complying with their requirements. It will, therefore, be quite appropriate if steps are taken to simplify and modify these so as to enable the small-scale units to conveniently comply with their requirements.

The mining industries of this State are believed to be experiencing a great deal of difficulty due to the non-co-operative attitude of the Indian Bureau of Mines, Nagpur, so much so that cement and G.I. sheets are hardly made available to the intending miners. The miners assert that considerable amount of foreign exchange could have been earned, had the aforesaid materials been supplied to them in time. For the construction of additional working space and the erection of godowns the mine owners often require corrugated sheets which are allotted to them by the Industries Department after due recommendation by the Mines Commissioner, the District Industries Officer and other officials concerned. Due to the non-allotment of corrugated sheets for these purposes the mining industries have to face various difficulties.

The revised scheme by the State Bank of India on advances against orders from the Director-General of Supply and Disposal beginning from procurement of raw materials to discounting of supply bills should be given effect to immediately. Credit facilities to the small-scale industries should be further liberalised within the framework of the rules already prescribed.

For the convenience of the labour colonies ought to be constructed around industrial estates.

EXAMPLE OF PUNJAB

The inhabitants of Bihar can taken a lesson from those of Punjab in their effort to develop their small-scale industries. The position of the small-scale industries in Punjab is reported to be very strong. The ingenuity of the Punjabi worker is unique. He can produce anything if he has just a model. He is eager to learn new techniques. This is why Punjab had a head-start in the production of durable consumer goods on small-scale basis. Its economy is efficiently served by both rail and road transport. Power resources are ample. The absence of coal is compensated by the large hydro-power potential, which is estimated to be around 3 million KW. The level of literacy in urban centres is as high as 57 per cent as against 45 per cent in all-India. The diet of the people is nutritive; climate healthy; and the standard of general health of the people high. The administrative machinery is satisfactory. The enterprising nature and the industry-mindedness of the people have contributed to a rapid growth of industries in Punjab in recent years. Non-factory industries predominate in the industrial structure. To every factory worker there are six non-factory workers. Of the total industrial employment, agriculture, live-stock and forest-based industries together engage over 72 per cent. Of this 40 per cent are engaged in textiles. 16 per cent in industries processing farm products and 16 per cent in forest industries. Engineering industries employ 12 per cent of the working force in industry. Mineral, chemical and miscellaneous industries employ the remaining 16 per cent. The pattern of agro-industries are traditional. In the production of assembly goods (small machine tools, bicycles, sewing machines, electrical instruments) Punjab has the advantage of an early start and these goods have bright expansion prospects. The engineering industries are generally small in unit size, light in character and varied in the nature of their products. Punjab is perhaps foremost in India in the development of engineering industries in the small-scale sector. Cement is the only industry in Punjab which lies in the mineral-based sector. With the exception of the new large-scale units engaged in the manufacture of cotton textiles, woollen textiles, sugar, cement, paper, bicycles and a few other items, all the registered units come under the category of the small-scale industries. With the predominance of the small units, industrial employment is fairly evenly distributed throughout the State. By far the largest growth has been in the consumer goods industries. This growth has strengthened the inter-dependence of agriculture and industry inasmuch as agriculture provides raw materials for the production of consumer goods as also rising purchasing power for their purchase.

ANCILLARY INDUSTRIES

It is an avowed policy of the Government, both at the Centre and in the State, to encourage the small-scale industries to become as far possible ancillary units to the large-scale ones. It is, therefore, suggested that a survey be conducted to find out which of the small-scale industries might serve as ancillary units to the large-scale industries either in the private or in the public sector situated in this State. The Government has not been able so far to foster the proliferation of the small-scale industries as ancillaries to the large-scale mineral and metallurgical industries in Bihar.

Whatever ancillary units Bihar has got suffer from both financial and non-financial impediments, which necessarily hamper their development. The problems of raw material and power shortages have assumed added significance in recent years. One problem of finance always existed and still exists because most of these units are small proprietorship and partnership concerns. But lately due to import restrictions and the system of priority and controls the ancillary establishments are hard pressed for strategic raw materials and because of the difficulties of procuring the necessary raw materials they find it unusually hard to fulfil their production plans within the prescribed time schedule. As a result of this they run the risk of dishonouring their commitments made to the parent firms. The following table shows the percentage shares of Bihar, Bombay, Madras and West Bengal in the ancillary units in the manufacturing industries.

The Table 5.4 shows that the share of Bihar was quite negligible in 1957 (as it is even at present). The Table 5.5 shows that in 1957 in Bihar 0.34 per cent of all factories were ancillary. The corresponding figures for Madras and West Bengal were 1.65 and 4.47 respectively. In the same year the ancillary units in Bihar gave 0.19 per cent of the total employment given by all the factories. The corresponding figures for Madras and West Bengal were 1.39 and 1.35 respectively.

TABLE 5.4

Number of Units

States	*1955*	*1956*	*1957*
Bihar	4.65	4.56	4.53
Bombay	16.09	20.35	19.80
Madras	11.25	10.49	10.66
West Bengal	22.27	19.62	20.03
Total	54.26	55.02	52.02

TABLE 5.5

(Year: 1957)

States	*Number of Working Factories*	*Average Daily Employment (in '000)*	*Number of Working Ancillary Units*	*Average Daily Employment (in '000)*	*Total Investment (in lakh Rs.)*
Bihar	5,507	189	19(0.34)	0.37(0.19)	14.09
Madras	5,682	325	94(1.65)	4.52(1.39)	400.05
West Bengal	4,116	723	195(4.47)	9.83(1.35)	146.02

The first four positions were taken up by the following categories of the ancillary industries: industrial machinery, agricultural machinery, machine tools and industrial instruments. Bihar recorded a maximum concentration in the Rs. 10,000 to Rs. 1,00,000 range. Roughly speaking, all the units had less working assets than fixed. The average working capital for all the units in Bihar was 43 per cent of total production capital. The proportion of debt to investment was 23.8 per cent. The units appeared to rely more on private sources such as friends and relatives. Raw materials accounted for 42 per cent of total working capital.

The emergence and existence of the ancillary industries hinge mainly on a fundamental law of comparative cost advantage. The decision-making of a manufacturer depends on the answer to the question: Whether one should manufacture the product in its entirely or purchase certain parts and components from outside, and if so, how much ? If the manufacturer decides to produce the entire product, an ancillary unit cannot take up a separate entity. It is only when the decision favours the alternative course that the ancillary units comes to the fore. It means that the growth of the ancillary units is not dependent on the growth of industries as such, but on the growth of that group of units which prefer to buy inputs from outside. This is further conditioned by several other factors, such as cost deferential, if any for the same product if brought from outside and manufactured within, regularity in supply, and so on.

The basic malady of the situation lies in the acute difficulty, faced by the ancillary units, in obtaining an adequate and regular supply of raw materials. Most of the ancillary units have a peculiar type of cost-structure in which capital cost is high and almost constant; raw material cost is also high and varies within a wide range; and labour cost is comparatively low and more or less constant. In most of the units three exists a good deal of excess capacity. This partly accounts for the high capital cost. The basic policy should be to utilize fully such excess capacities. This is vital now since we are facing a national emergency and since increased production is the precondition of success—both from the point of view of our defence requirements and from that of our development needs. Utilization of excess capacity in the ancillary units will increase both capital productivity and labour productivity and will make the cost-structure more favourable for the ancillary units, provided high and fluctuating raw material cost does not meanwhile upset the picture.

This means that ultimately the problem boils down to the availability of and the smooth and regular flow of raw materials to the ancillary units. But these units are not in a position themselves either to procure or to hold a buffer stock of raw materials so as to meet the work orders which they receive from their parent units. This is because neither do they possess enough finance for purchasing at a time all the materials they require for meeting the work orders nor do they have sufficient storage capacity for inventory accumulation purposes.

Looking at Japan, where ancillary-parent relationship is both direct and strong, we find that there the parent units themselves directly assess the raw material requirements of the ancillary units and make suitable arrangements for the supply of raw materials to them. There the development of ancillary-parent relationship has mainly hinged on the direct contracts which the ancillary units have had with the parent firms and all this was strengthened through a system of bilateral exchange of intelligence, ideas and methods of organisation. Unfortunately, in the case of our country we do not find such a direct relationship between the activities of the ancillary units and the work done by the parent firms. In the way of achieving this relationship, the first difficulty is that the parent firms in our country are much too busy putting their own house in order, following the impact of new and additional taxes. The second difficulty is that in a situation of emergency it will be a somewhat wishful proposition to expect that the raw material problem of the ancillary units will have a quick solution even when the parent units volunteer, as they do in Japan, and are determined to provide direct help to the ancillary units.

INDUSTRIAL ESTATES

Bihar so far has only four approved industrial estates, the lowest number among the major States, as would appear from the Table 5.6 on next page. The establishment of industrial estates has already come to be recognised as a positive means of achieving decentralisation and dispersal of industry, particularly in areas which are industrially less developed. The four industrial estates set-up at Patna, Biharsharif, Darbhanga and Ranchi during the Second Plan have been helpful in building up in Bihar, an industrial outlook and in stimulating investment in consumer goods industries. During the Third Plan two industrial estates one each in Muzaffarpur and Bhagalpur and two semi-industrial estates one each in Purnea and Daltonganj and ten other estates were opened. The Heavy Engineering Corporation has, at the request of the State Government, agreed to set-up an industrial estate at Ranchi for letting out sheds to the ancillary units on hire-purchase basis.

A rural industries project at Pusa and two pilot projects one each at Siwan and Kishanganj have been started to develop suitable industrial programmes and to intensify them in compact areas.

TABLE 5.6

Approved Industrial Estates

States	*Number*
Andhra Pradesh	19 (5)
Assam	5 (12)
Bihar	4 (13)
Gujarat	14 (6)
Jammu & Kashmir	24 (3)
Kerala	7 (10)
Madhya Pradesh	13 (7)
Madras	10 (9)
Maharashtra	21 (4)
Mysore	11 (8)
Orissa	7 (10)
Punjab	29 (2)
Rajasthan	13 (7)
Uttar Pradesh	63 (1)
West Bengal	6 (11)
Delhi	2 (14)
Himachal Pradesh	1 (15)
Manipur	1 (15)
Pondicherry	1 (15)
Tripura	4 (13)
Total	255

Note: Figures in brackets indicate ranks.

A fair correlation can be found between the size of the industrial estates and their location. In the functioning category the average number of sheds is 41 for the urban estates (near cities with population over 50,000), 22 for the semi-urban estates (near population centres in the 5,000-50,000 range) and 18 for the rural estates (less than 5,000 persons). Within each category, however, there is a surprising range between the smallest or the largest number of sheds. Thus the range for urban estate is from 223 sheds to 1; for semi-urban estates from 52 to 5; and for rural estates from 42 to 6. The non-functioning estates are consistently smaller, the average being 13 sheds for the urban estates, 8 for the semi-urban and 9 for the rural. The evidence seems to indicate that most of these non-functioning estates may not have come to function at all. At any rate, whereas for the functioning estates there are only small disparities between the shed targets and the number of completed sheds, there is a tremendous difference between the targets and the completed sheds in the non-functioning category; indeed expect for Punjab and Rajasthan (where there is an identity between targets and completed sheds), only 55 per cent of the target number of sheds were built in these 50 completed but not functioning estates.

For these estates, as on June 30, 1964, the utilization is shown in Table 5.7. All in all, it is rather poor performance, since only two-thirds of the completed sheds are being utilized. A few States, however, show a fairly satisfactory utilization ratio: Delhi with 91.7 per cent (for its single estate); Madras with an average utilization of 88.2 per cent for 9 estates; Andhra Pradesh with 83.9 per cent; Gujarat with 79.3 per cent. But off-setting these creditable figures, there is Rajasthan with 44.1 per cent utilization, Assam with 45.3 per cent and West Bengal with 48.5 per cent.

The rural utilization average (62.6 per cent) is considerably worse than that of the urban located estates (70.3 per cent) but by no means as bad as the utilization ratio of the semi-urban estates (52.4 per cent). There are extremely wide variations in utilization and in cost-benefit ratios within each of the three groupings. There are, unfortunately, no discoverable performance norms; a survey of 12 estates, using output per rupee of capital cost as a test of estate performance, revealed variations of eleven-fold. What is abundantly clear is that the general location is only one of many factors that can influence the success or failure of an industrial estate. Almost without exception, they have been small, fairly capital-intensive, manufacturing enterprises that use electric power and modern machinery. A study based on data supplied by 206 of these estate-based factories revealed that almost half of them employed less than 10 workers, about a third hired from 10 to 40 workers and only a sixth employed more than 40 persons. They are, then, predominantly small-scale firms engaged in small operations in India.

TABLE 5.7

Utilization of Industrial Estate Sheds
(As on 30th June 1964)

No.	*States*	*Completed*	*Occupied*	*Working*	*Utilization (per cent)*	*Enterprises*
1	*2*	*3*	*4*	*5*	*6*	*7*
11	Andhra Pradesh	243	223	204	83.9	162
2	Assam	75	65	34	45.3	29
4	Bihar	140	136	101	72.1	71
1	Delhi	36	36	33	91.7	34
7	Gujarat	493	427	391	79.3	334
1	Himachal Pradesh	10	9	6	60.0	5
8	Kerala	238	211	151	63.4	86
10	Maharashtra	318	307	245	77.0	242
7	Madhya Pradesh	242	199	164	67.8	156
9	Madras	237	235	209	88.2	143
9	Mysore	182	155	120	65.6	76
5	Orissa	148	128	86	58.1	63
1	Pondicherry	6	6	4	66.6	4
6	Punjab	349	317	270	77.3	243
9	Rajasthan	304	217	134	44.1	93
2	Tripura	28	27	16	57.1	15
8	Uttar Pradesh	331	301	229	69.2	230
3	West Bengal	66	46	32	48.5	25
4	Jammu & Kashmir	114	75	59	51.7	39
107	Total and Average	3,540	3,020	2,378	67.1	19 per state

Notes: (a) The utilization rate in column 6 is a very crude one. This merely relates the working with the completed sheds. It does not measure how effectively factory space is utilized. The calculations are based on data provided by the Office of the Development Commissioner (Small-Scale Industries), Ministry of Industry, Government of India.

(b) The disparity between the occupied and the working sheds is there either because the Government agencies are using sheds for storage or other purposes, or because certain opportunities have rented facilities not for actual use but in order to give entrepreneurs a claim on raw material allocations which they use elsewhere.

The existing industrial estates in Bihar are reported to be sickly; they exist merely because they have to exist. They are criticised for their unsatisfactory administration. The working of the raw material depots situated in the industrial estates is not at all satisfactory and complaints are received from the small-scale industrial establishments that they are not getting their requirements adequately and in time. Generally, no action is taken even when complaints are made. It is suggested that the raw material depots should be made to function like the raw material banks and to supply the needed raw materials to the small-scale units as and when required on producing a prescribed requisition form.

The allotees of the industrial estates are experiencing great difficulty as the terms and conditions on which the sheds had originally been allotted to them have not been finalised as yet. In the beginning the entrepreneurs had been given to understand that they would ultimately become the owners of the sheds. Now they are given to understand that whatever amount had been paid by them would be taken into account towards rent and perhaps they would never be made the owners of the sheds. In view of this non-ownership character of the sheds they cannot develop their business as the banks would not be in a position to advance loans against such sheds.

Some time ago it was alleged in a section of the local press that for years the Industries Department of the Bihar Government had been the centre of inaction and corruption. Its main preoccupation had been, by and large, to grant loans to undeserving persons, to issue or to recommend permits for scarce raw materials to industries which existed mostly on paper only and to purchase junks in the name of machinery. Only a thorough anti-corruption drive can expose the racket and improve the situation. In selecting the site for the industrial estate at Biharsharif no account was taken of the availability of raw materials, transport facilities, supply of technical personnel, sale of goods to reliable parties, accommodation for the technical staff that will run the imported machines, quality of the recruited staff and various other factors that constitute the industrial process. In this industrial estate the cycle parts unit failed on account of high cost of production and difficulties in marketing the products. This was not expected. Biharsharif itself is not in the heart of the industrial area where goods of various types are bought and sold and sent out into the interior. The products have to be bought by wholesalers from whom retailers make their purchases for sale to customers. The industrial estate itself cannot undertake retail selling. If it does, the products will become costlier. It is reasonable to believe that wholesalers, who care for their reputation as well as profit, will not venture to come to Biharsharif, one of the filthiest towns in Bihar, unless they are assured of a good bargain, which they cannot ordinarily expect from a Government establishment.

The cycle parts unit in question was later shifted to Patna but that did not by itself ensure its profitability or utility, unless its cost of production was brought down and the products competed in the market without subsidy from the Government. It might be as much a failure at Patna as it was at Biharsharif. The point to emphasise here is that the country has not yet made up its mind about the type of implements its different regions require. Again, the implements made must be within the reach of the small farmer for whom they are meant.

If it is a fact that the Marketing Union gave only two months' time to the Biharsharif industrial estate to manufacture 6,000 ploughs, than it means that the Union placed orders under pressure from some people and had no intention to make the purchase. Even if the ploughs had been brought, they could not have been sold to the individual farmers and would have been stocked in some so-called co-operative store. If the unit was set-up without ascertaining the nature of the demand and suitability of Biharsharif for the purpose, then there was no alternative but to face these anomalies. The loss of a few lakhs of rupees is not a small thing for a poor State like ours.

Policy regarding the industrial estates needs re-examination. The idea is basically sound. But in some cases there is either mislocation or a wrong choice of industries. The development of the small industries must be dispersed but with discrimination. A small unit will always remain a hot-house growth unless it is linked to the larger unit as an ancillary producer or caters to particular local demand in a local market, naturally protected by transport costs or enjoys the advantage of local raw materials or engages in the production of a conspicuous product based on a particular type of raw material or traditional skill not available elsewhere.

The Directorate of Industries, Bihar suggests the following guidelines for the future development of industrial estates in the State:

1. Past experience suggests that in cities and large towns the Government may confine itself to the provision of developed site with basic facilities like water, power, etc., leaving the construction, management and day-to-day administration of the estates to the co-operatives or a suitable association of the local entrepreneurs as the case may be. Such industrial estates will have, therefore, to be developed in the private sector and can be called 'assisted industrial estates'. In cities and large towns where local entrepreneurs do not come forward to organise an association or a co-operative for construction of the industrial estates and the dimension of growth potentiality is large our aim should be to set-up an industrial area instead of an industrial estate.
2. So far as the location of industrial estates in backward regions, including rural areas, is concerned, the initiative and responsibility for sponsoring, construction, management and day-to-day administration will have to be borne by the Government at least for a few years to come.
3. As regards the selection of the area sites, careful pre-planning is most essential which implies assessment of the feasibility and of the pre-requisites like labour, power, water, raw materials, marketing, etc., and other supporting facilities and industrial growth prospects of the different alternative areas with a view to selecting locations and eventually the sites of the estates.
4. A State-wide survey to select places having comparatively sound infra-structures, etc., based on the feasibility of the estate is necessary. Even the places so selected should be listed in order of priority according to the potentiality of the areas. While deciding for the apportionment of land, adequate provision should be made for extra land, if possible, for future expansion and the same consideration will have to be borne in mind while preparing the lay-outs of the industrial estates.

5. The degree of success of an industrial estate depends on the availability of entrepreneurs. The backward regions or rural areas suffer from several handicaps, viz., high initial cost, lack of supporting facilities and services, long delay in reaching the efficiency level and difficulties in obtaining the requisite volume of skilled labour. In a situation like this local entrepreneurship will have to be stimulated with inducements and incentives such as exemption of raw materials and machinery from octroi duty, subsidised rent on sheds for a longer period than five years, concession in railway freight, etc. These concessions, while they are very necessary, should be provided for a temporary period only, otherwise such concessions would tend to perpetuate high-cost firms in the industrial estates which will involve a permanent burden on the State exchequer.
6. Functional industrial estates can be located even at places remote from marketing centres and away from the large-scale industries; but they must be located in the areas which have good potentiality. A functional industrial estate not only provides small-scale units of the estate economies and efficiency but also assists in the solution of then marketing problems. Such estates may be suitable for the co-operative venture.
7. In order to create an industrial complex in backward areas a deliberate policy needs to be pursued for locating medium and large-scale industries in those areas. Advantage can be taken of the recent development of road connections in North Bihar, namely, construction of lateral roads connecting the high-ways with the rich agricultural lands of North Bihar where difficulty of power has been removed by now and water is available anywhere in the area in abundant measure. Only about 15 years ago there were just 10 towns and villages in Bihar where one could see the flicker of electric bulbs. But today power supply has covered, besides towns of various sizes, almost 4,000 villages in our State. It is expected that by the end of the Fourth Plan almost 14,000 villages would have been covered by the electrification scheme. The chief purpose of rural

electrification is to provide facilities on attractive terms to the owners of small industrial units to install power-using techniques of production and to the cultivators for irrigating their lands. A uniform power tariff was introduced throughout the State with effect from the 1st of January 1966. Prior to this date the tariff was much higher in North Bihar since power requirement in that region was being met by generation from small diesel sets.

8. The actual execution of the schemes of industrial estates and industrial areas very much needs to be speeded up.
9. Financial assistance to the units should be made available with much greater speed.
10. It is very necessary to cultivate great vigilance and promptness in the supply of raw materials to the industrial units. The raw material depots set-up by the State Government may be re-organised, if necessary. Associations and co-operatives may also be organised to undertake the supply of raw materials.
11. In matters of marketing the Government will have to introduce a comprehensive quality marketing scheme, undertake publicity and take measures to push up the sale of the products of small-scale industries in the public sector as well as in the general market. In this task the enlightened co-operation of small manufacturers will be indispensable.
12. Small-scale industries in Bihar have not so far benefited appreciably from export opportunities and defence production. The quality marking scheme and the common facility service of the Small Industries Service Institute and the State Government will have to be geared to win a good share of export market and defence production.
13. The units in the industrial estates, besides working independently of each other for their respective fields of demand, should constitute small consortiums to undertake manufacture of complete industrial machinery, machine tools or sophisticated types of agricultural implements for internal consumption and for export. In other words, they should assume the role

of ancillaries to their own consortiums.

14. The units should undertake a regular programme of training within the factories and productivity probe which will enable them to adapt themselves to the fast changing techniques of production and emerging needs of the economy.
15. A design centre should be organised on the Japanese model of design centres for popularising good designs and for promoting research and improvement in the existing products and for undertaking manufacture of new products in small-scale units.
16. Industrial estates and industrial areas should organise themselves into associations not only to mobilise prompt assistance of the Government and the Government-sponsored institutions but also to deal directly with the varied problems such as marketing, finance, supply of raw materials and techniques of production.
17. The aforesaid associations should bring their constituents into very close touch with medium and large-scale industries and develop very cordial relations with them to go hand in hand with their production programmes.
18. Besides giving preference in placing orders with the small-scale units, rules should be adopted against delayed payments to small-scale units and to ancillaries by the Government departments and large-scale industries. Delayed payment reduces the turn-over of a factory to a large extent.
19. The present policy of the Government of India needs re-orientation to subserve the objective of decentralisation of industry and growth of ancillary industries. Certain components which could be manufactured by small-scale units should exclusively be reserved for ancillary industries.

The high prices of agricultural products, the inflated prices of land, both rural and urban, and the profits from even small trades and commerce are bringing funds into the hands of certain classes of people which should be productively invested. The Bihar State Financial Corporation can extend financial assistance to cooperative enterprises which may be set-up by persons of moderate means, as suggested by Professor Gorakhnath Sinha. If we succeeded in drawing these funds into productive channels, we would be strengthening contra-inflationary mensures along two lines: first, by diverting funds away from the consumer market and socially sterile investment in the rural and urban land transactions, and second, by raising the volume of production. The inflation of the land values is distinctly a social evil and one of the objectives of the Unit Trust of India is to prevent the money coming in the hands of small and moderate savers from spilling over into sterile channels.

RECENT DEVELOPMENT

Although the importance of the small-seals industries in providing new employment opportunities had been admitted at all times, yet it was only during the Second Plan period that extensive programmes for the growth and development of these industries were undertaken and implemented. The First Plan of Bihar had spent Rs. 34.70 lakhs on these industries whereas its Second Plan provided for an aggregate outlay of Rs. 366 lakhs. The industrial estates came to be recognised as a means to achieving decentralisation and dispersal of industry, particularly in the undeveloped and underdeveloped areas of the State. Accordingly, Rs. 60 lakhs were provided for them for the first time and a total expenditure of Rs. 48.29 lakhs was incurred over their establishment at Patna, Ranchi, Biharsharif and Darbhanga—Rs. 42.9 lakhs on the construction of sheds and Rs. 5.37 lakhs over the acquisition of land. The ten Government-sponsored industrial units located in the industrial estate at Patna were the bicycle assembly workshop, the common facility service workshop, the model foundry for non-ferrous castings, the raw materials depot, the electric motor unit, the auto-battery unit, the sports goods unit, the electrical accessories units, the mechanical toys unit and the radio components unit, all except the first four being manufacturing units with the provision of training as well. The Government-owned common facility service workshop manufactures tools and dies required by other Government units and private enterprises also. Facilities of machines and supplies of dies and tools are provided on no-profit and no-loss basis. The bicycle assembly workshop has a production programme of 15,000 to 30,000 bicycles per year. The production rate achieved is 30 bicycles per day and nearly 60 persons are employed in this unit. Six private units located in the estate have taken steps to supply ancillary parts to this workshop. The raw materials depot stocks raw materials commonly used in the engineering industries, particularly the controlled commodities like iron, steel and non-ferrous materials, for sale to the Government-owned schemes and the State-sponsored private units. In the industrial estate at Ranchi the Government-owned units are the small tools producing unit, the sports goods producing unit, the electroplating unit and the wooden toy development centre, all these being commercial units with the necessary provision for training also. The Government-owned units in the Biharsharif industrial estate are carpentry, the agricultural tools producing unit, the mechanical trades unit, the bicycle parts manufacturing unit and the common facility centre for footwear. These too are commercial units with the provision for training as well. Finally, the Darbhanga industrial estate has the following Government-owned commercial units with the provision for training also— model black-smithy, model carpentry, the footwear manufacturing unit and the sports goods unit. These industrial estates have subserved the purpose of building up an industrial outlook in the areas where they are located.

Other schemes concerning the small-scale industrial units can be broadly classified into three categories, namely, model workshops, industrial groups and pilot projects. The object of the model workshops is to train the artisans of the urban and the semi-urban areas in the use of modern tools, modern equipments and small tools of improved designs. In these workshops they are also taught modern manufacturing processes and better designs. The training imparted throughout is oriented towards the production of consumer goods of diverse types like agricultural implements of improved variety and other articles of common utility. There were in 1960-61, 24 such schemes located in different parts of the State. These included model blacksmithy, carpentry and tannery, improved blacksmithy-*cum*-worskshop, mobile blacksmithy and carpentry, vans, saw mill-*cum*-mechanised carpentry, manufacture of agricultural implements, cutlery and carpentry goods. Out of these, the model blacksmithy centre at Bhagalpur and the model carpentry centre at Gaya were started from the welfare funds and are exclusively meant for the benefit of the training of people belonging to scheduled castes and other backward classes. At both the centres there is provision for the training of 50 persons at a time. A model carpentry centre at Chakradharpur and another at Daltonganj were also sanctioned during the closing years of the Second Plan as centrally sponsored schemes out of the welfare funds. The industrial group schemes are for developing related industries, including the provision of common facility services. There were during the Second Plan 19 schemes in this group. These included wood working-*cum*-training centres, sales-*cum*-stores depots, raw material depots, sports goods centres, radio components, electrical accessories, bicycle assembly workshops, model foundry, common facility service workshops, electric motors, common service facility organisation for the mother-of pearl button industry, pottery, development centres, central finishing workshops and linseed fibre research centres. Lastly, the pilot projects have been established with the object of demonstrating the technical and economic feasibility of the small-scale enterprises, specially the small manufacturing industries so that entrepreneurs may set-up similar industries in other parts of the State. Twenty-one units under the above group of schemes were sanctioned in the Second Plan. These include at present leather goods manufacture, a model tannery, a footwear unit, a common facility centre for footwear industry, a fancy leather goods centre, a mechanical toys manufacturing unit, a mechanical trades unit, a bicycle parts manufacturing centre, a small tools manufacturing centre, an electroplating and black enamelling centre, aluminium wares manufacturing centres, a tiles factory, an auto-battery manufacturing unit, a lock factory, a timber seasoning plant, a saw mill-*cum*-wood seasoning plant, a saltpetre refinery, a fruit-preservation centre and a dehydration of lichis plant.

A village industries experimental workshop was proposed to be established during the Second Plan period at Samastipur for taking up various kinds of researches and experiments for the benefits of the village industries. The work was to be divided in three broad sections, namely, leather, engineering and chemical.

The quality marking scheme aims at encouraging production of quality goods in the small-scale sector. In order to increase the competitive strength of the products of the small-scale industries in the market, the supply of cheap power to the small units is an essential first step. Hence, a scheme for the subsidisation of cost on power in favour of certain selected industries was drawn up during the Second Plan and a sum of Rs. 50,000 was transferred to the Bihar State Electricity Board for that purpose. A substantially large provision was made in the Third Plan.

Three pilot industrial projects at Biharsharif, Pusa and Ranchi were started in the Second Plan to serve mainly as testing grounds for determining the types of schemes of the cottage and the small-scale industries suitable for development in different parts of the State. Work in the Biharsharif project started in July 1956, while the other two projects at Pusa and Ranchi came into operation in March 1957. On the basis of the experience gained by the implementation of the schemes in these projects, a schematic progamme of rural arts, crafts and industries was outlined for implementation in the community development areas. Till March 1961, 472 industrial co-operatives had been organised in these projects with a total membership of 13,222 and a paid-up share capital amounting to Rs. 2.51 lakhs. Introduction of improved tools and equipments formed an important adjunct of the industries programmes in these projects. The total value of goods produced and marketed till March 1961 amounted to Rs. 289 lakhs and Rs. 252 lakhs respectively. The total value of orders secured for the cottage and the small-scale units located within the project areas under the Stores Purchase (Preference) Rules till March 1961 amounted to Rs. 12.31 lakhs out of which orders worth Rs. 10.25 lakhs were executed. Schemes of raw material depots were also established in these projects for sale of scarce and controlled raw materials to the artisans and their co-operatives. Raw materials worth more than Rs. 4 lakhs were supplied to the artisans through the three raw material depots located in the projects. Women industrial co-operative societies were organised and through them orders of the Bihar police for woollen garments were executed. Wollen hosiery, using small knitting machines, is a new industry in Bihar, developed mainly from the work done in the project areas. For the training of the rural artisans, training-*cum*-production centres and tuitional classes were started.

The Government of India appointed a high-powered committee (known as the Rajnath Committee) to study the working of the training-*cum*-production centres all over the country which recommended steps for making the rural artisans' training programmes more effective and useful. The Government of Bihar accepted its recommendations, according to which the existing training-*cum*-production centres were to be replaced by the institutional training centres of the cluster type, where training in four to five crafts at one place would be imparted with better staff and equipment. With each such training centre would be attached eight to ten mobile demonstration parties, for upgrading the skill of the rural artisans in such traditional crafts as could not be clustered at one place. These centres would be of the peripatetic type and undertake training of the rural artisans in their existing concentrations or very close to them. During 1961-62, 20 cluster type training institutions were to be set-up, the ultimate aim being the location of one such centre in every sub-division of the State by the end of the Third Plan.

For the follow-up of the training given, Industrial co-operatives of ex-trainees have been organised as far as possible. Besides the provision of technical and financial assistance to individual ex-trainees and their co-operatives, there is provision for the supply of improved tools and equipment to them at subsidised rates. But even with the best of efforts with a very large number of persons the chief incentive for undergoing the training has been the wages or the stipend paid for it. It is, however, hoped that in the cluster centres, both the training and the extension aspects of the programme will be more closely supervised than what had been possible in the loose and widely dispersed training-*cum*-production centres.

For the training of women, precedent to the Second Plan, two women's industrial schools in the State were located at Ranchi and Monghyr. Both the schools were of an itinerant nature. During the Second Plan these two schools were sanctioned on a permanent basis. In addition, four more schools were established at Muzaffarpur, Gaya, Purnea and Daltonganj. All these schools have an admission capacity of 60 trainees each. The duration of the course is one year. Training is imparted in the following six trades: tailoring and cutting, embroidery, knitting, fancy leather work, cane and bamboo work, and toy and doll-making. During the Second Plan period about 600 trainees passed out from these institutions and a good many of these ex-trainees found employment as instructors and skilled artisans in the training-*cum*-production centres started throughout the State in knitting and embroidery and tailoring crafts for the village women. From the savings under the scheme three more schools were established from the 1st January 1961 at Bhagalpur, Arrah and Darbhanga. During the Third Plan it was proposed to cover every district by one such school.

Nearly half of the provision meant for the small-scale industries during the Third Plan was to be spent in the rural areas, i.e., in villages having a population of 5,000 and below. Establishment of rural industrial estates and workshop sheds under the industrial estates group, establishment of rural workshops and women's industrial schools so as to cover each district, establishment of a Small Industries Corporation for operating all commercial schemes including schemes of marketing, quality marking, State participation in capital formation of the private enterprises, establishment of raw materials depots in all districts and grant or organisational assistance to the industrial co-operatives under the small-scale industries group were some of the important schemes sanctioned in the Third Plan.

As stated at the outset the schemes under the category of the small-scale industries for the Third Plan comprised of: (i) Technical Assistance, (ii) Training, (iii) Financial Assistance, (iv) Marketing, (v) Industrial Co-operatives, (vi) Other services, (vii) Dispersal of industrial growth with State participation in capital formation, and (viii) Establishment of an autonomous corporation for the small-scale industries. Below is being given a detailed study of these.

(I) *Technical Assistance (Rs. 73.50 lakhs):*

1. *Industrial Extension Services*: These comprised schemes for the establishment of: (i) two Branch Institutes, one each in the North Bihar and the Chotanagpur regions, subordinate to the existing Small Industries Services Institute at Patna, (ii) two workshops attached to the aforesaid Branch Institutes for the purpose of providing necessary technological assistance to the industrial units in a practical and effective manner, (iii) additional extension centres to serve the needs of local units in selected districts, (iv) common facility service centres in order to provide technical assistance and common

facility services to specific industries, close to their existing concentrations and thereby to improve the technical efficiency of the artisans and to encourage them to adopt improved devices in production, management and marketing, and (v) the establishment of an Institute of Engineering Designs for the designing and the redesigning of the industrial products, including components and parts to make them more effective, durable and competitive in price. As the scheme mentioned against [i], [ii] and [iii] were to be the direct responsibility of the Small Industries Organisation at the Centre, no provision of funds for these schemes was made in the Third Plan.

2. *Rural Workshops (Maintenance and repair facilities—Establishment of 60 Service-cum-Common Facility Workshops)*: The community development programme had brought within its wake the technological advancement of the rural areas through the introduction of improved agricultural implement and varieties of equipments, e.g., tractors, diesal engines, electric motors, pumping sets, sprayers, cane-crushers, sewing machines, bicycles, radios, fans, etc. For the maintenance and repair of all these equipments and implements suitable facilities were to be developed in the rural areas. It was, therefore, proposed to set-up sixty rural workshops at suitable places in the State.
3. *Pilot Production Centres:* The object of these pilot production centres is to encourage by actual working of the units private entrepreneurship in the fields so far unexplored by the small-scale industries. It was considered expedient to set-up such pilot units (a) for the production of articles which are considered basic and essential such as hoe lasts, surgical instruments and laboratory appliances for which private entrepreneurs might not be forth-coming, and (b) to develop entrepreneurial talent in interior areas where people are not eager to come forward to set-up new industries, although such places might hold sufficient potentialities.
4. *Establishment of Industrial Pilot Projects:* As in the Second Plan, so in the Third Plan it was proposed to establish

pilot projects for industries in three new areas of the State, for integrated development of the small-scale and the cottage industries.

(II) *Training (Rs. 175.76 lakhs):* In a developing economy the need for organised training programmes to promote the skills, technical knowledge and related information, which were essential for the successful working of the small units at a particular level cannot be over-emphasised. One of these programmes was training of workmen which would be of two types—(i) For those who wished to become qualified for employment in a trade; and (ii) For those who were pursuing the trade and needed supplementary training in technical and other related subjects for being better suited for their jobs.

Training programmes were, therefore, to be organised by the State Directorate in trades like blacksmithy, carpentry, leather work, tanning, shoe-making, tailoring, etc., which were not covered by the Craftsmen's Training Programmes of The Ministry of Labour, Government of India. These training programmes were to be executed mostly through: (i) twenty-four permanent tuitional classes, which were to be reorganised, both in their existing set-up and working details, in the light of the recommendations of Rajnath Committee set-up by the Government of India, (ii) twenty production centres, which would serve as focal points for the dissemination of improved techniques and commercial intelligence among practising craftsmen as well as for demonstration and supply of improved tools and equipments to the artisans, selected ones from amongst whom were to be employed in these production units, (iii) fifteen model workshops in trades like carpentry, blacksmithy, leather goods-making, etc., in the urban or the semi-urban areas having electricity as well as concentration of artisans requiring advanced training in these trades, (iv) rural artisans' cluster-type training centres in each sub-division of the State in the light of the recommendations of the Rajnath Committee, (v) twelve new women's industrial schools (in addition to the existing six such schools so as to cover every district in the State) for imparting training to women in useful crafts like tailoring and cutting, cane and bamboo work, knitting and embroidery, fancy leather work, etc., (vi) expansion of the existing women's industrial schools, and (vii) sanction of grants-in-aid to private institutions engaged in women's crafts training.

Provision in the Third Plan was made for thirty-four cluster-type training institutions only at an estimated cost of Rs. 80 lakhs. More of such institutions were to be set-up gradually from the savings under other schemes as the Plan progressed from year to year so as to cover each sub-division in the State.

(III) *Financial Assistance (Rs. 115.00 lakhs):* One of the major factors that had hindered the growth and development of the small-scale industries in the State till the end of the Second Plan was the lack of credit facilities. The co-operative banks or private banks had not yet started granting loans to the small-scale industries on an appreciable scale. The credit facilities available to them through the State Bank of India were also relatively meagre. Their credit requirements were, therefore, proposed to be met largely out of the provision for grant of loans under the State Aid to Industries Act. Accordingly, a provision of Rs. 100.00 lakhs for such loans was made in the Third Plan. In addition, a provision of Rs. 15 lakhs was also made for grant as subsidy under the aforesaid Act for the developmental purposes.

(IV) *Marketing (Rs. 36.50 lakhs):* It had long been recognised generally that any form of assistance that the Government might extend to the small-scale industries in marketing their products should inevitable be indirect and the Government should not generally undertake direct marketing responsibility. But publicity measures to popularise the products manufactured by the small-scale units constituted important marketing aid which the state had to extend. The schemes in the Third Plan under this head, therefore, covered: (a) compilation of a directory of all small-scale manufacturing units, (b) a concise survey of immediate industrial potentialities in each district, as had been done by States like Punjab and West Bengal, (c) participation in exhibitions and fairs, (d) introduction of schemes of quality marking, and (e) establishment of sales emporia.

Assistance for the establishment of the Bihar State Small Industries Corporation: The State set-up the Bihar State Small Industries Corporation during the Second Plan period. This corporation functions more or less on the lines of the National Small Industries Corporation. The main functions of the corporation are: (i) Assistance for participating in the State Government's Stores Purchase Programme, (ii) Development of the small units as ancillaries to the large ones, (iii) Promotion of sales of the small-scale industries' products through schemes of quality marking, (iv) Establishment of sales depots and emporia at suitable places both inside and outside the State, (v) Supply of machinery to the small producers on hire-purchase system, (vi) Management of industrial estates and workshop sheds, and (vii) Management of the small-scale industries of commercial nature set-up by the State Government. In order to enable the corporation to discharge functions satisfactorily, it was proposed to make available a sum of Rs. 25 lakhs to it during the Third Plan period.

The Bihar Cottage Industries organisation which at present deals in furnishing cotton, silk and woollen fabrics and handicrafts, etc., was to be reorganised and expanded so as to function as a subsidiary of the Bihar State Small Industries Corporation.

(V) *Dispersal of Industrial Growth (Rs. 25.50 lakhs):* Wide dispersal of industrial activities was a recognised first step for the balanced economic development of the State. It was also thought essential for reducing regional disparities and for developing the depressed areas within the State. But the entrepreneur is generally diffident about the return on his investment in such areas and common experience is that in these areas capital is shy. Therefore, the Industrial Policy Resolution of 1956 provided that in suitable cases the State might also grant financial assistance to the private sector in the form of participation in equity capital. The Working Group set-up by the Government of India had suggested extension of this concept to the small-scale industries sector, and on the experience gained in Orissa where State participation in capital formation had yielded encouraging results, a sum of Rs. 25.00 lakhs was provided in the Third Plan State participation in capital formation of private enterprises. Assuming that a small-scale unit would require Rs. 1.50 lakhs from the State as equity capital, it was visualised that by this method it would possible to set-up and foster at least seventeen new small-scale units in the hitherto undeveloped pockets of the State. The Government proposed also to help the private enterprises in the above cases to raise equity capital by way of guaranteeing loss against margins required by banks for sanctioning loans. Such a provision already existed under the State Aid to Industries Act. A token provision of Rs. 0.50 lakh was made for this in the Third Plan.

(VI) *Other Services (Rs. 66.24 lakhs):* The small-scale industrial units had generally suffered in the past for want of iron and steel and other scarce raw materials. In order to cater to their requirements for these, the establishment of raw materials depots attempted during the Second Plan had been found to be useful. Accordingly, it was proposed to set-up fifteen such depots during the Third Plan so as to cover every district at an estimated cost of Rs. 3 lakhs each. Another scheme included in this category is related in the subsidy on power. This was justified on the following grounds: (i) A small-scale unit has to pay as much as three times the rate paid by the large-scale undertaking for one unit of power, (ii) the small industries have also to pay heavily for bringing power supply lines to their premises as compared to the large-scale units, and (iii) the small industrialists do not also get continuous supply of power which affects their production adversely. Appreciating all these difficulties, an outlay of Rs. 10 lakhs was made in the Third Plan.

Subsidy on rent: Rent to be charged for built-up space in the industrial estates and for workshop sheds proposed for the rural towns would range from the economic rent to just nominal rent, depending on the consideration whether these were located in the developed or the underdeveloped areas. This would mean subsidisation of rent in several cases for which a small provision of 4.74 lakhs was proposed.

Guarantee Fund (Industrial Co-operatives): A token provision of Rs. 0.50 lakh was made to guarantee repayment of loans to the artisans' co-operatives through the apex banks. The provision might be later by adjustment within the Plan depending on the progress of the scheme.

Managerial Assistance: Most of the Industrial Co-operatives formed during the Second Plan period suffered from lack of managerial assistance. Therefore, provision of managerial, secretarial and technical assistance to the industrial co-operatives was to be tackled on a substantially enlarged basis during the Third Plan. This assistance might be available to a society for a maximum period of four years only, according to the following scale:

First year	—Cent per cent
Second year	—75 per cent
Third year	—50 per cent
Fourth year	—25 per cent

From the fifth year and onward the society would be expected to maintain the above staff out of its own resources.

The Working Group of the Government of India had calculated that the annual expenditure on this account would be Rs. 3,000 for one society, roughly at the rate of Rs. 250 per month. According to this scale, Rs. 6 lakhs were provided for the grant of managerial assistance to 100 industrial co-operatives during the Third Plan period.

(VII) *Additional Staff for the Department of Industries:* The Working Group of the small-scale industries set-up by the Government of India had recommended in its report that "to cover some of the short-falls in State schemes and ensure accelerated development, the State Department of Industries should be considerably strengthened and the existing administrative machinery suitably modified to yield better results." So far as Bihar was concerned, the strengthening of the Directorate seemed justified on the following additional grounds:

(i) A few technical officers who were available in the Directorate had remained busy with the execution of the departmental schemes mostly. The developmental aspects of the small scale industries, therefore, did not receive due emphasis, (ii) In Bihar a new class of entrepreneurs had emerged. They were ex-zamindars. With the introduction of land ceiling they would need new avenues of gainful investment. They had, therefore, to be guided from scratch to finish through a well-organised contingent of technical personnel under the State Directorate of Industries, (iii) Being gifted with natural resources Bihar had been able to attract a number of industrial projects. It was expected that during the coming years a greater number of large and medium projects would be located both in the public as well as in the private sector which could be properly guided only by vigilant staff, constantly searching for new opportunities and seeking co-ordination with other developmental programmes like road construction, power project, water-supply, etc. (iv) The State Government would have invested directly during the First and the Second Plans a sum of nearly Rs. 13 crores in the industrial development of the State. Full utility of such heavy investment remained to be harvested yet, for which it was necessary to strengthen follow-up measures at all levels. The volume of increased work could be easily imagined from the scale of investment visualised during the Third Plan which, on current estimates, was going to be of the order of Rs. 1,403 lakhs out of which the small-scale industries including industrial estates alone would get a share of nearly Rs. 1,103 lakhs, (v) Experience had shown that the personnel required during the period of a particular plan had to be, if full benefits of the plan were to be realised, recruited and trained during the preceding plan period. An organisation set-up during the Third Plan would, therefore, be particularly useful for the subsequent plans.

Under the circumstances stated above, it was considered imperative to lay maximum emphasis on a well-knit and well-coordinated organisation with suitable technical personnel in the Directorte without delay. A provision of Rs. 10 lakhs was made in the Third Plan for the above staff.

Industrial Complexes in the Tribal Belts: Problems and Prospects

Many of the tribal areas have rich natural resource potential, bulk of which remains to be explored. In some areas, large scale industries and big mining complexes have been established. The pattern of development in these areas, however, has not been in the best interest of the tribal communities. In fact, most of the new industrial and mining centres are rich enclaves amidst the vast under-developed stretches. As the consciousness about the legitimate rights grows in the local community, tensions tend to build up. The industrial enterprises enjoy the advantage of moving along the current of history. Therefore, their power is incomparable to those communities who, in a way, have remained in the back-waters and are not as yet attuned to the faster pace of change, which is informing the human society universally. The result is that the simple societies, which so far have enjoyed the protection of inaccessibility, difficult terrain, strong internal social organisation, etc., and had the capacity to retaliate sporadic interventions of smaller dimensions, are now finding themselves powerless in the new situation. In an unequal contest, they seem to be destined to be over-run by the stronger systems.

As the tempo of economic development in the country becomes faster, there will be a keener search for available resources in all nooks and corners, not only to satisfy the basic needs of the average citizen but also to satisfy the greed of the small elite whose capacity to devour anything which comes its way seems to be unlimited. Since the process of change, spearheaded by the fast industrial development, has been accorded the aura of inevitability, the interplay of socio-economic forces resulting in over-running of the weaker groups is, to say the least, overlooked, if not positively helped. The result is that there is little effort to analyse the real nature of the new contact with a view to help the weak and provide a suitable direction to the entire change-process. In this book an attempt is made to understand this process intimately and provide a model which may help in humanising the process of fast change in the more backward tribal areas.

In the first instance, let us recapitulate the important characteristics of the tribal scene which is likely to be found before an industry is set-up in a backward tribal area. The tribal economy is simple, non-structured and self-contained. The community draws its sustenance from the natural environment depending on the outside world for a very small part of its requirement. The structure of local economy depends on the natural resource availability, pressure of population and the level of individual skills. On the one extreme, there may be some communities which are still at the food-gathering and hunting stage. In these cases, the natural resources are rich and the community is simply required to collect the fruits of nature or, in some cases, wrest from it the requirement for its sustenance. On the other extreme, the community may have reached the agricultural stage and may be depending on forests and other natural resources only marginally. In other words, in the latter case, pressure of population has increased and individual is required to make personal effort, in collaboration with nature, to draw his sustenance. A tribal community may be at any one of the numerous points on the spectrum defined by the above two extremes.

The economic system and the social system in a tribal area are indistinguishable. The former is really an extension of the latter. The community heavily depends on the forces of nature which it propitiates by a variety of rites and rituals performed individually or in groups or by the community as a whole.

Religion flowers spontaneously within their social and economic life and becomes an invisible thread fully integrating the whole system. The economic life of the individual, therefore, is not governed by concepts of utility and exchange, which are now common-place in the modern society. The community is more like a big family in which each may contribute according to his capacity; even the deviant may be tolerated and supported; communal enjoyment of the fruits of labour may finally settle all their mutual 'accounts'. The 'surplus' produce with an individual may have no meaning in terms of its 'storevalue'. It may be used for throwing a big feast just to gain prestige or for some other common purpose. There are limits, both lower and upper, to personal consumption and, therefore, the deprivation and affluence do not co-exist in this System. Labour has only two functions, viz., for production for one's own consumption or for helping some one else in need. Production itself has limited end-use—personal consumption or helping someone else who may be in need or social consumption. The property rights may not be recognised beyond the right to cultivate the land and right to collect the fruits. Since the community must manage its affairs as a group, individual rights are not permanent and continue to be re-adjusted in the context of emerging needs. Lending is more in the form of assistance for one who needs than an economic transaction.

The community is governed by its own social code which is influenced by its level of economic development. The role and responsibilities of women in the economic life are substantially higher than in advanced communities. Growing in a tribal community is a social phenomenon; the child acquires the necessary skills as a member of the group rather than as a member of the family. Bringing up of child, therefore, is neither a special responsibility nor particularly a burden. The woman is an equal partner in the economic life and, in fact, contributes a bigger share of labour input. Consequently, she is more free than an average Indian woman; in particular she is free to take her own decisions regarding matrimony; marriage bonds can be broken with comparative case.

The community regulates the social life by well established codes of conduct and does not depend on outside intervention to keep itself going. Social ostracism is the ultimate penalty, the severity of which is hardly appreciated by those who are used to individualistic social system where even family may not represent an essential unit of an individual's life. The less severe panel provisions are in the form of a feast to the community or minor pecuniary compensation. In a non-monetised economy, where an individual lives at the subsistance level and does not particularly care for the morrow, even small fines are 'heavy' since the individual must produce surplus in cash to pay up the fine. In fact, this means a much harder labour on the part of the individual over a long period than what he is generally used to.

There are no formalised institutions. The tentacles of administration and economic institutions, by and large, may not have reached these areas and even when they reach, their significance is hardly appreciated. Although the tradition of lightly administering the tribal areas of the pre-Independence days is not formally continued, still there is a hang-over of this concept. It is only gradually that these areas are coming within the effective purview of modern formalised institutional system. The tribal community has no comprehension of the new formal system. It largely depends on the world of mouth and tradition which is so well known to the entire society. The legal frame, which is the source of all formal authority, is a great mystery to the tribal. Let us now review the basic socio-economic structure of the new industrial complexes which are established in these areas. In the first instance, we will concentrate on typical core industry and only thereafter try to understand the formal and informal extensions of this system around the Core.

An industry comes into existence as a result of conscious decision of a group of people within a formal frame which may be defined by numerous laws, regulations and conventions. Whatever may be its form, each industry has a given objective of specific production portfolio and schedule. Therefore, its entire activity is organised with reference to achieving the production targets. Here one finds an extreme example of programming by the final objective. It must be recalled at this stage that the over concern of the industrial system, particularly in the earlier part of its history, with higher production at minimum cost has resulted in severe adverse implications for the poorer sections of the community who provided the required labour force. With the liberal concepts gaining ground, this practice become incongruous. Gradually extensive regulations were imposed on the industrial activity itself. These constraints, in due course came to be formalised either in the form of law or convention. The outstanding examples are the regulation of the labour relations, regulation of profits and regulation of standards of product. These constraints became necessary because the basic premise that economic actions of all individuals in the nation will get harmonised through the natural process of interaction between different groups and balancing forces does not hold good when some of the elements acquire greater strength because of their better organisation or when some groups acquire greater manipulative power because of their strategic position. Social intervention, therefore, becomes necessary to bring about harmony and balance, at least to the first order of approximation, which could be expected to have been otherwise achieved under normal conditions. Thus, briefly, industrial complexes are creatures of high level formal decisions. They are controlled and regulated by conventions, rules and statutes formulated in the light of experience in the more advanced areas.

A formal institution, by definition, must have all its relations formal. Each of its activity is governed by well defined rules and, in an ideal situation, there is no place for non-formal relationships. These relationships finally are translated in terms of money-exchange equations. Thus, money becomes the invisible thread permeating the entire organisational system. It may not be necessary here to go into the basis of exchange equations which get established as a result of the interplay of complex forces operating at numerous points in the economy. In this system, every thing must have money-value, and, therefore, is defined as such. The source of authority is the 'rule' which is the final form of a long process of formal deliberations at numerous levels in the system. The rule, therefore, becomes sacrosanct since any change in it would involve again a long chain of formal deliberations. The System, so long as a rule stands, abides by it; but it also abides by another rule with equal vigour once the old rule is replaced by a new one even though the new rule may be completely different. This essentially represents the mechanistic approach of the System. This approach not only extends to material objects and formal systems but tends to be applied, with equal tenacity, to human situations as well.

The above analysis of the industrial system may appear to be harsh and may represent the model in its extreme form. It is, however, necessary to understand the central argument around which the whole system is built up so that its numerous varieties and manifestations in different forms can be better understood. The above principles are central to the system itself around which the entire industrial world and its 'eco-system' moves. Unless there is a clear perception of this central theme, it will be difficult to understand the processes which are generated in the peripheries and in the hinterlands of industrial complexes.

We may now examine the social, economic and institutional systems of the industrial community which is superimposed on a simple tribal scene when an industry is established in the backward tribal area.

The economy of the industrial society is highly specialised. Each individual is assigned a position with reference to his role in the System. The central industrial activity is supported by ancillary functional services both as an extension of the industrial activity itself and as supporting services to the community which provides the manpower to be central industry and its ancillaries. These may include small service establishments, shops, cinema houses, etc. The core industrial system generally behaves as a 'closed' system. It may draw its sustenance either from the immediate hinterland or from distant centres, 'market' being the guiding force in either case. In a more backward area, there is little linkage between the core industrial society and the tribal society in the hinterland, particularly in the earlier phases.

The industrial society is an amalgam of different groups and individual drawn from a large area. The community is highly structured. In fact, the composition of different sections of the community at various levels in the hierarchy may be completely different. Higher the position in the socio-economic structure, bigger is the geographical area of possible choice for selection. Thus, members of the top management core may be drawn from anywhere in the nation or even some foreign countries. As one reaches the lower levels, the geographical area of possible choice gets narrower. Normally the local community should have substantial representation in the lower echelons. But in the tribal regions, there is a shadow zone comprising its hinterland and surrounding area, which contributes little to the central society.

Sometimes, linkage may apper to be established with the nearby villages. But it is more likely that contact points here may be provided by the migrant groups, which are not a part of the social system but are only physically located within the immediate hinterland.

Thus, the core society represents numerous regions, numerous communities, numerous skills drawn from various socio-economic strata through out the nation. They may get organised in informal groups which may be based sometimes on professional background, sometimes on language and sometimes on caste or regional considerations. Each individual or group is far away from its parent society and, therefore, has little direct outside influence on his individual or group behaviour. In this context, internalised value system is the only guide of an individual or a group. In this amalgam, individual enjoys anonymity as a member of a crowd; and here his behaviour pattern can be any thing. Since the core industry itself is organised exclusively around the goal of higher production, it provides a frame for their professional behaviour only. The informal social groupings may help in providing a peer reference frame to an individual. But it is voluntary and individual can afford to keep himself completely aloof from any of these informal constraints on his social behaviour. These small groups may also act unitedly for mutual production. They may behave as a body whenever their common accepted code is violated by one of their own members or someone else. These groups, however, may be neutral with reference to the personal and social actions of an individual if it does not strictly concern the group itself.

In brief, the core industrial society gets organised around the principle of least interference in individual affairs, so long as his behaviour pattern does not affect a section of the core community itself. It has no common accepted social code and, therefore, it cannot provide a suitable frame for behavioural pattern of each individual. The individual is free from the immediate constraint of the community of his origin and, in many cases, even from constraints of his own family. His life gets fragmented between work and social-personal activities; he himself is the sole arbiter of right or wrong in relation to his personal behaviour.

The core industrial society brings with itself the entire institutional support of the modern world like police station, law courts, etc. In fact, in a way, the core society is like an outpost of the advanced social systems in a backward region. Therefore, even institutional support system may not be established in this area for some time the community can always draw upon the support of the institutions located in the advanced areas which have formal jurisdiction over this region as well. Thus, invisible threads of authority permeate the entire geographical space. The new society takes full advantage of its knowledge of these invisible sources of power to protect itself and to advance its interests. When an institution like a police station is actually established, it is presumed to subserve the central industrial society which may have demanded for its establishment. The central industrial society, thus, draws its authority and strength from the national 'power-grid' defined by the multitude of laws implemented through the formulised administrative and institutional infrastructure.

We may now compare and contrast the quality of interaction at different points between the central society and the hinterland tribal community. In the economic sphere, the central society is a highly organised one. In a way, the hinterland tribal community has nothing much to offer. There is a functional gap between the core industrial activity and the hinterland economy. For example, the community in the hinterland may not be able to provide ordinary services or even offer agricultural and animal products required by the organised industrial society. This gap is gradually filled by the migrant communities which become a part of the central society. The industry itself begins its operations within the formal frame as may have been defined by its Articles of Association, Project Report, etc. It is a truism to say that formal system recognises only formal rights and formal obligations. Thus, the tribal community is, all of a sudden, faced with a structure which is not 'free' to negotiate. Since the formal frame has the general approval of the power structure, its blueprint begins to unfold itself with all its rigidity and ruthlessness. The tribal community is unaware of the new processes and, faced with a strong organised structure, finds itself helpless. They may be sporadic resistance, but the form of this resistance may not be within the accepted frame of the new law and can be easily brushed aside. The contradictions may come to the notice of higher decision-making centres only when resistance turns violent or when some sensitive elements in the system itself, may be, a people's representative, a civil servant or a union leader, appreciate $he inherent injustice in the new situation where the other side has not been given even a chance to be heard because they cannot speak.

In this process, the community which enjoyed command over local resources by tradition, stands completely dispossessed. It may get nominal compensation for some land over which it may have had a formal right. In relation to the forest resources, there has always been a vast conceptual difference in so far as the tribal community considers itself as the master of what it sees whereas the State thinks otherwise. The new articulate groups begin to compete even for usufruct of the natural resources which may have been providing bulk of the subsistence to the tribal community. Thus, the migrant may begin to hunt in the hinterland with more powerful weapons; he may even prove better in this art. The new supplemental economic activities like vegetable cultivation, dairying, etc., which are taken up by the secondary migrants, begin to compete for the grazing grounds around and even for more valuable land. The tribal may try to adjust for some time but may recede further into the recesses of forests abandoning every thing and, thus, relinquishing even his actual command over the resources in the periphery. This 'vacuum' gradually gets filled by secondary migration. The central industrial community begins to have a more 'satisfying' net-work of supporting services; its teething troubles, which arise because initial 'unfavourable' conditions in the hinterland, are over; it witnesses with satisfaction the extension of its own system. The new development enhances the value of lands around. The core community begins to take advantage of the unearned increment arising from the 'new opportunity matrix'. There is visible prosperity all round. The tribal community, which has been drawing its sustenance from this region, has finally withdrawn. The region presents a gratifying and beautiful picture with none to mar its scenic grandeur.

In the long drawn conflict situation discussed above, the tribal-migrant dichotomy may not be absolute. Some contact points may get established between the industrial society and the tribal communities. On the one hand, a few individual tribals may be drawn into the core industrial system for a variety of reasons.

On the other hand, the well-known spread effects may also begin to work. The first manifestation of these processes is exchange of fancy goods of the modern society with 'valuable' commodities of the traditional community. The new migrant goes about with covetous eye and surveys the scene assessing what can be taken to the best of his advantage. Thus, the valuable timber and the tribal lands may be purchased for a song; on the other hand, a fancy item like transister radio may be sold for a fortune. Whatever small surplus the tribal economy may have is gradually exchanged for spurious urban commodities which may have only fancy value. These examples have been quite common in the history of civilisation when the 'advanced' communities came in contact with the lesser developed communities; they need no elaboration. The same very process begins with greater finish in these areas when industries are set-up for the first time.

The penetration of money economy without adequate preparation continues to weaken the tribal community and provides an upper hand to the industrial society. It is well known that the 'cost of living' in the far-off industrial centres is very 'high' and liberal compensation is provided to the members of the new community as a part of the Project design itself. If the same phenomenon is viewed from the side of the tribal community, it provides a completely different picture. Here is a small 'island', where money is pouring in. In the non-monetised economy of the tribal, money is a scarce commodity and has a high value; larger sums beyond a few scores of rupees are incomprehensible. The internal equations of social and economic relationships in the tribal communities are determined without any reference to money. Monetary sanctions are the biggest deterrents. In the new contact, therefore, the 'modern man not only carries the vast authority of the System and the dazzle of higher consumption, he also enjoys the tremendous power of money which is very cheap in his system but is extremely costly in the tribal world. The new community, therefore, begins by alluring some, purchasing some others and deceiving the rest.

We may now examine the way the entire system begins to operate. The wage structure is very high in the central area. It has been designed to attract better skills from outside. In the initial stages, when the Project is in a hurry it can neither afford to wait till the tribal offers himself voluntarily to the discipline of new activity or his skills can be upgraded, even marginally to suit the conditions of the core economic activity. The easier course, therefore, is to manipulate the wage rate so as to attract persons from the more advanced areas. This migrant aristocracy of the core sector requires supporting services, some of which may be obtained from the advanced areas but a more preferable choice would be to recruit persons locally with reference to their (tribal's) money-equations. The complete disorder, which prevails just after the first confrontation when the tribal community is in the process of withdrawing, is one of the opportune moments where some of those who may have fallen behind can be 'trapped' into the new System. In the earlier stages, when money may not prove an effective instrument for this 'capture', the Core may use the services of the articulate who know the local situation better. The petty contractors may use all devices to draw the tribal in. This may include devices like giving an impression to the tribal that this is what they have been desired to do by the 'Government'. To the simple tribal, any one with 'white clothes' is a representative of the State. They may even take advantage of his weakness for liquor by offering it is an allurement. In many cases, he may be initially offered some 'unwanted' things giving him an impression that he owes something to the contractor and, thus, giving rise to an obligation to work for him.

In these transactions, conditions are always most unfavourable to the tribal and they are so manipulated that he may never be able to get out of the obligation of one who employs him. This is how they see that the tribal is 'broken in' to satisfy the need-pattern of new System. Gradually, the tribal begins to 'crawl' into the System at its bottom filling in the vacuum. The adjustment of a member of an equilitarian social system at almost the bottom of a highly structured society is most traumatic experience and needs some explanation. There is no doubt that it is a great psychological shock initially to many, who try to escape into their own world where they can breath freely. But other processes also begin to work. In many cases, the tribal has no option after losing his land and frittering away the money-compensation. Slowly, the differential in the money value, the aura of new structure and the glitter of his new possessions begin to provide him a new value orientation which enables him to face his own community with a sense of 'achievement and pride'. He fails to appreciate the implication of the new relationship. Thus, the Wheel of History moves on mercilessly.

We may now examine some of the important aspects of the social dynamics in the area. The tribal community, as an organisation, is subjected to almost a fatal blow in the new process. Since the group is not even in a position to protect it's traditional terrain, the deep seated faith of the community in its own power to guard its rights is shaken. This psychological blow is devasting. The community has had traditionally control on the life and the behaviour of all its individual members; the deviant had no choice. Even if a rebel were to run away in defiance from his own community to another area, he could not but find himself amidst a similar group where he may be required similarly to repent and behave. The new industrial centre breaks up his closed system, opens up the area and provides an escape route to a deviant member. The tendency to disregard the traditional social organisation increases as the contact of its individual members with the industrial centre increases. Individual rights get asserted; differentials begin to grow; the prestige of the community leadership gets compromised as it encounters more situations where it is helpless before the stronger intruding culture. Within a short time, the disorganisation is complete and the articulate industrial centres has at its feet an entire community which can be treated in any way it likes.

We may look at one of the well-known phenomenon constantly recurring in these areas, which is loosely, mischievously and with some amount of perversity, ascribed to human weakness and described as its universal manifestation. The tribal community, as earlier alluded, recognises a better right of the woman in contracting and dissolving marriage bonds. Marriage is a loose association between two individuals within the community. As the responsibility of child rearing in the community has not as yet devolved on the family, the socio-economic situation does not call for a strong bond to make the family an abiding unit for bringing up the next generation as is necessary for the middle classes in advanced areas. The Group, however, has a strong community bond and there is a inviolable taboo against any affair outside its own limits; any violation may be meted out with most severe consequences. The advanced communities, which have drawn in their womenfolk within the protective shell of the family, are unable to appreciate the different situation where the inviolable protective line, in the case of tribal communities, is drawn not around the family but around the big community. Therefore, they (non-tribals) are prone to describe with casualness the accepted norms of social behaviour within the tribal community about sex and martial relationship. When the tribal mores are viewed by them with reference to their own narrow family-oriented frame, which is different, they may feel free to behave as they like because they may think that their behaviour does not violate the moral code of the tribal community. They may further rationalise their behaviour by imaginary arguments having little validity in the tribal context.

The tribal woman is an equal partner in the family and in a bread-winner. In the tribal communities, she moves about freely like the gentle breeze without much restriction and ventures unwittingly into the industrial centre in mixed groups which, as already described, may be allured, purchased or cheated into the new System. She finds here a completely new world, where woman is not a bread-winner but a piece of decoration in the household. The glitter of numerous fancy goods begins to appeal to her faminine curiosity and possessiveness. There are allurements all round in this new 'hungry' world. A vague feeling begins to take possession of her inner self. The alternatives of the two systems to a young girl, as an individual, become so very striking. Her position would get completely transformed from the 'drawer of water, to a damsel in the decore'. The attraction becomes irresistible: allurements starting with petty gifts, which in money-equations cost nothing to the migrant but are coveted possession to the uninitiate, may lead her to the bed-room of the new 'aristocracy' of the central core labour, technician, petty official, trader or a *sahib*. Even offers of toffees, a washing soap, a powder-box may be sufficient to start the affair with an innocent adolescent girl. The girl used to a higher status, independent decision-making and economic freedom steps into the new System with misplaced self-confidence little realising that her community is incapable of providing the protective shield and she cannot claim the protection of the new System as she is merely an intruder and the woman is a 'weaker sex' in this world.

The articulate may see no harm or objection in this transaction and 'transformation' if it improve the condition of the woman. If she exchanges her wretehed position in the traditional society by more comfortable life, there can be protest whatsoever. This approach and argument would be irresistible if the entire scene could be viewed as a 'Operational Salvage' of members of a vanquished community where disorganisation is complete. But if it is accepted that the situation needs a rational corrective, there can be no solace in the above model.

The underlying presumption in this situation will need to be spelt out. In terms of the relationship between two groups, a situation seems to emerge in the early phases at least where the new system appears to have no use for the tribal male. He is an unskilled person who can aspire for a place only in the substratum of the new structure. The industrial core, however, can 'offer' something for the tribal woman. Can this preposition be accepted in terms of a planned group dynamics in a situation of fast change? The answer is obvious 'No'.

Let us look into some other factors in this entire chain of events. What has the tribal girl opted for ? Her world-view is that of her own society where if a man and woman are living together they are accepted as husband and wife, the formal marriage may be solemnised at any time even long after the couple begets children. There is no illegitimacy and the children are full members of the community. It may be recalled that the children are more a responsibility of the community than of the individual. In the industrial area, therefore, she falls into the new trap with a different perception about martial relationship, family responsibility, etc., since she has no other experience to go by. The utmost she would like the young man to do is to give a feast to her community which, according to her perception, would be a final seal on her relationship; even her parents and the community may feel satisfied. But in the modern frame these rituals have no value. Therefore, she inadvertently accepts the position of a 'keep' who has no right. And her relationship may last only till she is able to charm the man. The children in the new setting are responsibility of the family, the implications of this situation are beyond her comprehension. The full realisation of her real position may come only when the man disappears and she finds herself on the streets of the new centre without any support whatsoever.

The traditional social organisation, which in itself is in the new situation, proves to be helpless, notwithstanding the fact that it could exercise some option if it so wished, by forcing a confrontation. The extreme penalty, which it could earlier inflict for violating his girl, is unfortunately not available to the group; in the new setting the traditional group action of revenge against the guilty is not recognised by the law. Stray instinctive retaliation against misbehaviour or criminal assault against their women may bring full wrath of the new system against him through manipulation of the normal processes of law by the more articulate who know the tricks of the trade; the community soon comes to realise that retaliation does not pay. But in this process, the group is left with no option, particularly when its own authority has been questioned. Certain face-saving compromises like payment of compensation, therefore, may be sought from both sides. Here the community falls into a trap. Even moderate economic sanctions were to severe within their traditional frame that they were effective deterrent against any deviation. The community is tempted to impose the same financial sanctions as an alternative even in the situation. It has little realisation that once this is done, the honour of the community gets prised and can be exchanged for money which has little value in the modern society. Once the protective wall of its inviolable custom and deterrent consequence is cracked, the honour of the community can be compromised for money. The 'conquest' is complete and the morale of the local community suddenly collapses. A situation comes, when the innocent ignorant individual may feel happy if he can get any thing for the new alliance which, on the face of it, is contracted 'freely'. And the articulate takes no time to raise an accusing finger towards the 'moral deprivity'; he gets reassured about the failings of the flesh and the rationality of the behaviour of his own kind. Inability to protect the honour by the sanctions which the community could have enforced, lack of protection from the new institutional frame, non-appreciation of the worthlessness of monetary sanctions in the new situation, the element of deceit in monetary compensations, the allurements into comfortable life without any lasting obligation and the utter helplessness of the system to protect itself result in a chaotic situation which is rationalised by the articulate by ascribing it to weakness of the man and generalising it with profoundness as a universal phenomenon.

The Wheel of History begins to move faster as the wheels of

industry rotate with ever-increasing speed. Industrialisation represents a new philosophy of life in which all emotional and human bonds are squeezed out and the Human System emulates the Great Mother Machine in all detail. The tribal society must jump quite a few stages in the process of social evolution to adapt itself to the ruthless logic of the Machine Age. In the final analysis, the entire human society appears to be inexorably moving in the same direction and must finally be engulfed by the System. The aberrations from the final formal mechanistic frame can be treated only as transient.

The ultimate fate of the human society with industrialism engulfing it is any body's guess. There may be a strong reaction against this regimentation. A new amalgam, however, is bound to appear. In the long-run, the differences between man and man may not be on the basis of region, language, caste and community. But there can be no consolation in this ultimate analysis, as the problems of tribal areas are essentially the problem of transition. It is true, that any system will have a differential between the high and the low. Some groups may still be found occupying substratum in the most egalitarian systems. Perhaps, exploitation is inherent in any system, its forms may change—even new appreciation may present the same phenomenon in a different perspective. Perhaps the problem of 'high' and 'low' is inherent in a scheme of big organisation because bigness itself implies large differences, unless a big system comprises only micro-units, all of which are co-equals. It may be a Utopian dream in the new context, yet the tribal world is perhaps closest to this Model. But these small 'worlds' are being sucked by the gigantic new system. The most undesirable aspect of the tribal scene in the above analysis is that with the meeting of two systems, at a crucial points of its history, the tribal system is forced to retreat and go down. The final outcome, in the immediate context, is not equitable. A desirable possible course of development would be where the two systems may be drawn in to begin a new order and the position of their members in different strata of the society is determined according to some objective criteria and not because of a fortuitous situation in the history of one of the groups where it is unaware of new processes and is caught unwittingly in the whirl of fast change.

In the early phases of new industrial system, as the things

stand, the tribal society has no alternative but to withdraw or occupy a position in the substratum of the new system. The situation does improve gradually and, perhaps, will continue to improve with the passage of time. This time perspective, however, may be anything. The complexion of the industrial core itself may gradually change. The individuals, who are drawn into the system at the lowest rung in the beginning, may begin to appreciate the basic character of the new system and assert themself in such forms and forums as are acceptable to the System. Some of the new educated persons from the hinterland may also be gradually drawn in at comparatively higher levels in the Core Economy. The economy of the immediate hinterland continues to get diversified, although in this process the tribal may continue to withdraw deeper into the recesses of back-woods. A stage soon reaches when there are no apparent contradictions in the immediate neighbourhood of the Core. The members of the tribal community, who are drawn into this system in the substratum, become gradually, indistinguishable from the urban poor and become a part of the new economic phenomenon of 'Poverty'.

The story is repeated, with lesser severity, as the core industrial activity gradually expands. Small satellite settlements may get established deep into the hinterland. Here again the same process may begin all over again. But since the core activity in the new centres may be of smaller dimension and with the passage of time the local community acquires a comparatively better understanding, the conflict is not as severe. It has, however, to be remembered that the pace of spread effect is extremely slow in the more backward areas. The conditions may remain unchanged for a pretty long-time even within a few miles of the core industry. Consequently, industrial development in the more backward areas may essentially mean super-imposition of the new system, displacement of the traditional economy, a lower position to the local community and a more severe struggle for existence at the subsistence level in the surrounding region.

The basic question, therefore, before us is whether fast industrial development in the primitive areas, which is forced on them on national considerations, can be tamed. There are limits to adaptation on both the sides. The industrial process has its own logic and some of its basic elements must be implemented. Similarly, the primitive economy cannot change over-night.

Having recognised these two important constraints, it will be necessary to define the areas of adaptation which may help in ensuring that industrial development need not necessarily be at the cost of the local community. With the development in the area and the growth of the industrial activity, the local communities should be in a position to take benefit of the new growth. One thing is clear—in view of the extremely unequal power structure of the two systems in these areas, the process of adjustment cannot be left to the operation of free social and economic forces. Indian planning does not recognise a state of *laissez-faire* economy. But the concept of planned economy in the tribal areas cannot be limited only to well recognised boundaries evolved for the advanced areas. For defining the special features in the concept of planning necessary for these areas, we may recapitulate the process of development in the industrially developed regions and countries contrast it with the situation in tribal areas.

In the long history of industrial development, economic, social and legal institutions of now developed nation-states continually got adapted to the emerging needs of the new situation. Perhaps in all the three spheres, viz., economic, social and legal there has always been some time-lag between the level of industrial development and the desired institutional structure. In the developing countries, on the other hand, the position appears to have been somewhat different. In some of these spheres, time-lag is similar to the one experienced in the advanced industrial societies. For example, the social institutions are slow to change and, therefore, they are adjusting themselves to the emerging needs with considerable time-lag. However, the formal structures of economic institutions and legal institutions are amenable to being changed by a conscious decision of the State. Therefore, in some cases, this could be done even in anticipation of the requirements of the industrial sector. Two important cases stand out in this regard and can be good illustrations. The labour laws, which have been adopted in the developing countries in very early stages of industrial growth, are comparable to those which were accepted by the Industrial Nations at a much later stage. The other example is that of technical skills. Training of personnel, particularly in relation to higher skills, has moved far ahead of the pace of industrial growth as a result of conscious state intervention. It is, thus, clear that the growth-paths of institutional structure in developing countries has been substantially different from that in advanced industrial nations.

The tribal areas represent a sub-system with in the nation economy. The preparedness of a sub-system with reference to the level of industrial development may not be the same as that of the system as a whole. Here the basic differences between the socio-economic structures of the tribal communities and other communities in the country come to the fore. The simple socio-economic situation of the tribal regions was largely left undisturbed because of the comparative isolation and the tradition of 'lighter' administration in these areas during the pre-independence days. Consequently, their economic, social and legal institutions are undifferentiated and tend to be a unique amalgam of different elements. In the advanced areas, the legal institutions, as distinct from economic and social institutions, have now a tradition of more than a century. Economic institutions, as distinct from social institutions, are also now well established. Therefore, adaptation of the general system to the industrial system can take place in parts with different speeds. The change does not represent complete disruption for the entire system, though it has its painful imprint on the social institutional frame. Even in relation to social institutions, industrial establishments have only a limited rôle to play. The society is subjected to numerous other strains caused by forces of modernization. Therefore, there is greater resilliance in the system. The advanced areas are able to absorb the shock of new forces of industrialisation because, basically, the same social system prevails in the industrial core and its periphery. The new industrial centre does represent a new mix of diverse elements. But, if the entire industrial macrocosm is viewed as an aggregate of the numerous micro-worlds, each one still may have a close link with the social system in the hinterland or in a large comparable area. The industrial system does bring about a qualitative change but the internal forces of these micro-units play an active role in its evolution. The economic, social and legal institutions in these areas evince a continuing process of adjustment with the new situation, although the degree of adjustment may vary.

As the internal social pressures and other economic forces in the national context, are expected to balance out with some time-lag only, the concept of planning in general with reference to establishment of industries is considerably circumscribed. It extends generally to influencing their location, regulating the working condition of labour and moderating their influence on environment and ecology. In exceptional cases, pricing, use of raw material, etc., are also covered. It is presumed that if these aspects are taken care of through suitable regulations, the entire process will get balanced with the operation of numerous other forces and counter-forces at different points in the socio-economic structure in a region. The same presumption is implicit when this concept of general planning is extended to the tribal areas. It is clear that this presumption is not valid. Therefore, the very concept of planning for tribal areas will need to be extended much beyond the accepted norms for the advanced regions.

Our analysis in the preceding section shows that the economic, social and legal institutional structure of the tribal society is at the other extreme compared to the structural requirements of the industrial society. Here another important factor comes into play. The institutional frame of the tribal society does not enjoy the sanction of the law of the land except in a very limited sphere of personal law relating to marriage, inheritance, etc. The new confrontation, therefore, renders the traditional structure powerless. As it loses its life force, the new institutional frame begins to extend its tentacles in almost an 'empty' space, where individual members of the tribal society seek in vain the protection of their older system. They are sucked in or thrown out by the new system purely in terms of *their utility to the system.* It is this process which has to be tamed, humanised and converted into a force of good for the community around the Core. It is a difficult task since the industry itself has its own logic. However, one important fact has to be clearly appreciated. Under the shadow of the central figure of Industrialism, a number of other interest-groups also acquire reflected aura of inevitability. If these forces are isolated and only basic logic is accepted, the task may not be difficult in the final analysis. There is another fact of the present situation. The spurious logic of inevitability is demoralising; it gives rise to a feeling of purposelessness even to the serious planning effort and element of fatalism enters even in what is described as the highest form of rationalism.

It is, thus, clear that the concept of planning will have to be comprehensive, particularly in those tribal regions which are witnessing fast industrialisation. No specific aspect can be left out of the ambit of directed change because the missing element may be crucial to the entire process, particularly because the tribal system continues to be a non-differentiated and unstructured amalgam of all life-elements. Therefore, the dimensions and the precise area of planning in these regions should be clearly defined which should mean bringing in—

(i) a longer time perspective;
(ii) a much larger geographical area than occupied by the core industrial activity;
(iii) a broader spectrum of economic activity irrespective of the fact whether it formally belongs to the core, organised or unorganised sector; and
(iv) inclusion within the ambit of planning all social economic and legal institutional aspects of the tribal system directly affected by the new economic activity in the industrial core.

When we speak of a longer time perspective, the entire socio-economic dynamics of the region comes within the ambit of purposive planning and directed change. This is particularly so because here we will have to begin at a stage of development where even agricultural economy is not well-set. Therefore, the first task in this case would be to identify those 'weak' spots of the traditional system which make it vulnerable to the on-slaught of the new system. In the context of fast social change, which these communities will be witnessing, mere outside assistance or even a protective wall will not serve as they may give way, sooner or later, to bigger forces engendered in the core sector. It is essential that the community itself is enabled to respond to the new challenge. Mere protection makes a community weak; successful acceptance of a challenge enable it to face the growing challenges with a greater confidence making the process self-sustaining. It may be remembered here that even very small groups have been able to assert themselves against extremely high pressure under favourable circumstances.

The most important single reason for the weakness of the traditional institutional systems is their sudden irrelevance when they are pitched against systems having the support of law. It is precisely to meet such situations that certain provisions in the Fifth

Schedule to the Constitution give extensive powers to the Executive to adapt the legal frame to suit the local situations in the scheduled areas. The traditional rights of the individual and the community over the resources in the area, the traditional method of managing the social system and the traditional sanctions for dealing with the deviants will need to be honoured and, wherever necessary, provided the support of the new legal system itself. It is not necessary to consider the tribal system as immutable but, with the same token, institutional frame of the advanced areas also need not be extended to these regions as it is. A delicate compromise should be evolved with the clear objective of enabling the community to graduate successfully through the transitional period without being put to undue disadvantage simply because it had been used to a different system and cannot adapt itself to the new system without going down in the process.

The above principles are generally accepted as principles, but it appears that other forces tend to prevail actual working situations. It is, therefore, necessary that these principles are worked out in terms of concrete action-programmes for each specific situation. There is no short-cut to this detailed exercise. In this paper, however, some common elements, which appear to hold in all the tribal areas, could be brought out so as to provide suitable guidelines for preparation of detailed action programmes.

In the suggestions which follow, there are two parallel themes which have been clearly distinguished at each stage. The first element concerns itself with the 'softer' spots of the tribal socio-economic scene. Urgent protective measures needed to attend to these spots on a priority basis have been suggested. The second element comprises certain positive action programmes which will enable the community to become a partner in the new developmental processes.

In the first instance, we focus our attention on those groups which are directly affected by the establishment of an industry and its supporting services. It is essential that the rights over the resources, which these groups have been enjoying, formally or informally, are fully recognised. No narrow legalistic view should be taken in this regard; this fact should be specifically mentioned in the Project Report itself so that there are no formal objections subsequently. A direct corollary of this approach is that the loss to the displaced tribal community should not be computed purely in money-terms. The Project should take note of the fact that these are the communities which have been drawing their full sustenance from the area under their command which they will lose with the establishment of the industry. Consequently, full rehabilitation should be a part of the project itself for which adequate financial provision should be made.

The whole concept of compensation, which is purely in static terms, will also need to be reviewed in these areas. It is likely that the full rehabilitation suggested above may be worked out with reference to the 'economic' condition of the tribal when the actual displacement took place. This would be unfair since the 'economic' condition of the local community is not amenable to be computed in money-terms because their entire pattern of life is different. Such computations in terms of 'our' money-equations will always put them at a very low position in the economic hierarchy of the new system. While the value of their erstwhile property soars in money terms, they are in no position either to foresee this change or to take advantage from it. Therefore, the entire problem of their rehabilitation, etc., should be viewed in a moving time-dimension so that with the development and progress of the area, the 'displaced' community becomes a co-sharer in its prosperity. In fact, this is a well-known phenomenon in the growing urban centres where original title holders prosper with development of the city because they are articulate and can ensure that they do not lose the formal title to the property. In the case of backward tribal areas, a specified number of shares in the Industry or dividends in favour of local community could be a part of the pakage of a long-term arrangement.

The problem of directly displaced persons in the tribal areas is extremely limited compar ᵈ to the indirect influence of the industrial activity on other groups in the hinterland. Although second stage displacements and subsequent influences in the hinterland cannot be treated *at par* with the direct displacement, yet they will also need to be accorded an equally high priority. There is a qualitative difference between these two stages of displacement. Direct displacement is in accordance with certain principles, which are consciously enunciated and accepted. The administration which is expected to take care of all aspects of development, is usually a party to this arrangement. But indirect displacement is left, to varying degrees, unregulated and is generally subjected to market forces. In the context of unequal situation in these areas, these processes have to be more rigorously regulated.

The first step for providing a protective shield to this weak spot would be to create a counter force of equal strength in favour of the local community. A special organisation should be established as soon as preliminaries are started for establishment of the core Industry with the specific task of protecting the weaker groups and taming the process of change in these areas. This Organisation may have the form of a Society or a Corporation. The regulation of secondary and tertiary displacements should be under its purview. The process of second stage displacements should also be viewed in its totality as has been suggested in relation to the primary displacement. There is already a parallel to this concept as well in the metropolitan development plans though with an important difference. In metropolitan places, the entire process is looked at from the side of the metropolitan centre. The displaced are expected to adjust themselves after due compensation has been paid. In the tribal areas this concept should get completely reversed. The Organization should take care of the people while other processes should adjust themselves to the emerging needs.

This hinterland-development organisation should also have an important positive role. It should be charged with the responsibility of taking advance action with reference to the secondary and tertiary activities in the region. It should retrain the local population, as far as possible, with a view to help them to adapt to the emerging needs. It should ensure that the primary, secondary and tertiary sectors in the core and hinterland do not develop as isolates but adequate linkages are established by them with the local community.

One of the basic weaknesses of the new situation is the non-communication at various levels between the two systems. Therefore, a comprehensive educational programme will be the most important input for harmonising the relationship between the industrial and the tribal world. It will be necessary to evolve suitable programmes of formal and non-formal education and orientation programmes addressed to different groups in the area. The first element in this package should aim at enabling the simple tribal to understand and appreciate the role of the administrative system and the method to approach it, whenever necessary. A well-organised comprehensive citizen education programme may become a crucial element in providing the protective shield to the local community.

On the positive side, the educational package should comprise four elements:

(a) A programme for reorienting the senior management and the workers in the core sector and give them correct appraisal of the socio-economic situation in the tribal area;
(b) A comprehensive programme of formal education to prepare the next generation for the new tasks in the area;
(c) A programme of non-formal education to bring within the fold of education the tribal youth who may have missed the early opportunity and enable them to join the formal educational stream at advanced points; and
(d) To restructure the formal educational system itself keeping in view the requirements of the core sector and the task of enabling the local community to join the industrial society at various levels depending on their academic and professional attainment.

The source of authority of the traditional social system is its effective control of the affairs of the community and its power to deal with the deviant. In the new context, this may be termed as the sphere of informal authority. Sometimes, in some areas a formal base, like reorganising the tribal panchayats, is provided. But even when the system is formalised, the local communities are not generally trusted to adjudicate on matters in which one of the parties may be a non-tribal. This is a hangover of the colonial tradition and has a close parallel in early attempts of the British not to subject the British citizen to the jurisdiction of Indian courts. There is no reason why the traditional social organisations, which have been regulating their own community life, cannot be trusted with affairs even when a non-tribal may be involved. Their strong sense of justice and tradition of frank and free discussion are a guarantee against any partisan approach. In all fairness, the local community should have the same jurisdiction over the migrants operating and residing within their jurisdiction as they may have on the members of the tribal communities. This will give the community a sense of self-confidence in its capacity to manage the affairs of the area. This will also oblige the migrants to understand the local tradition and honour it. Thus, it will help in stimulating the process of integration. The traditional system, whenever necessary, should be brought within the ambit of law. Care, however, must be taken that it is not so much formalised that the community itself may not be able to operate it.

Traditional social organizations generally function in face-to-face situations and their jurisdiction extends to small community-groups in small geographical regions. In this context, the industrial core emerges as a big force and these small traditions, unaware even of the dimension of this force, cannot stand before its pressure. In the more backward areas, spontaneous social or community action cannot be expected because of lack of communications and non-appreciation of the position of the other side. The spontaneous retaliations in extreme situations are exceptions which have generally a very short-term impact. It is, therefore, necessary that the community is helped to appreciate the problems of the core and its hinterland in a broader context. A larger forum may be organised at the re-important problems could be remitted to this body. They could also consider problems which may have far-reaching consequences for the community as a whole and provide a direction to the smaller constituent units for regulating their relationship with the core sector. The establishment of such an organisation will help in generating a counter-veiling force within the local community of dimensions comparable to those in the modern sector.

One of the weakest spots in the new social situation is the position of women and the allurement of money and modern comforts. This weak spot will need to be covered by suitable legal and social actions. For example, employment of girls, as domestic servants and otherwise than in a group, could be prohibited by law both in the organised and non-organised sectors. The community itself could be better educated about this aspect of their new contact. They could be induced to exert social pressure so that the tendency to send out girls for employment in the core sector otherwise than in a group is checked. Special regulations could be made for the conduct of the employees, in the organised and non-organised sectors in this regard. The matters relating to misdemeanour or undesirable treatment meted out to the tribal women should be within the exclusive jurisdiction of the traditional social organisations and a special procedure should be evolved for dealing with them. Once a deviant is liable to be brought before the traditional council, the present situation of irresponsible individualism will cease to exist.

We have referred to earlier that the industrial process has its own logic which has to be honoured. Yet we have seen that what generally goes by this logic is not immutable. It will, therefore, be necessary to isolate these areas which can be influenced harmonising the central needs of the industrial process and the development and welfare of the tribal communities. The first step in this direction should be to induct tribal leaders at different levels in the industrial system in different capacities. They could be accorded a higher social position notwithstanding their formal lower levels in the organisation. This has a close parallel in the relationship of the industry with its labour-force. The local community in these areas should be an important their partner. The concept or regular employment itself should be suitably adapted. In certain areas, group employment could be recognised in place of individual employment. The leaders of these employee groups could be given a higher position although the money compensation to them may be nominal.

At the apex, there should be a meeting point for the top management and labour leaders from the industrial sector, the top leaders from the local communities and the people's representatives. The concept of workers participation in the industrial sectors has to be extended in this case to an area comprising the core and its hinterland. This forum should be responsible for guiding the direction of change for the entire region. This will engender a new sense of participation in the hinterland communities. The process of change can also be influenced in a more meaningful fashion so that the Core and its hinterland move together in unison.

Industrial Planning in the Tribal Areas

Economic development is generally characterised by diversification of economy and sustained growth of its numerous facets. In the earlier stages of economic development of a predominantly agricultural economy, a faster rate of growth in the industrial sector is desired. Experience shows that this cannot be achieved in isolation; it has to be preceded by, or at least accompanied by a steady rate of growth in the agricultural sector. It is not necessary for us to go into the theoretical aspects of a balanced or an imbalanced growth path. However, the past experience in the Indian economy brings out some essential features. The Second Five Year Plan envisaged a high rate of industrial growth; this emphasis continued in the Third Plan when a high priority was given to basic industries. The agricultural sector was not able to maintain a balanced position within the overall growth matrix in the nation. Consequently, the whole national economic structure was subjected to tremendous strain. A review of the policies was undertaken and again agriculture has been given a higher priority.

The tribal economy is even less developed compared to the general rural economy in India; it is also less diversified. Even the agricultural practices in the tribal areas are generally much less sophisticated than those adopted by an average Indian farmer. However, the entire tribal tract does not present a uniform picture. Some of the tribal regions are extremely backward and subsist at pre-agricultural level of technology while some of the more advanced areas compare favourably with the general rural scene. Many of the tribal areas have rich forest and mineral resources. The forests provide a substantial part of the subsistence in the tribal economy although their activities are limited to the collection of minor forest produce and unskilled labour in the traditional forestry operations. The tribal communities have a high level of traditional skills; but the level of literacy is low and the more sophisticated 'modern' skills are wanting. The infrastructure of roads, communications, institutions, etc., is not developed. Availability of other factors essential for setting up of industries like water, sources of energy, cheap labour, etc., are, however, plentiful in many areas.

There is no consistent picture of the industrial scene in tribal areas; in fact a special model of development of tribal economy has not been attempted. The objective of bridging the gap between the tribal areas and the more advanced areas and the desirability of the tribal communities joining as early as possible the main stream of national life are stated in general terms without indicating even broadly the possible growth paths. Therefore, it is not surprising that the growth of industrial sector in tribal areas has been ubiquitous and is influenced by other considerations rather than being a part of an overall strategy of development of these areas. The industrial process is also essentially inward looking having little concern for its impact on the tribal economy.

A number of major industries based on available raw materials have been established in the tribal areas on considerations of overall national economy. Thus, the industrial complexes of Rourkela in Orissa and Ranchi in Bihar came up in the most backward tribal areas; the Mining Complex of Kiruburu in Orissa and Bailadila in Madhya Pradesh were also started for similar considerations. In their case, once locational decisions were taken essential infra-structure like railways, roads, powerlines, etc., were developed as a part of the concerned projects. There is one important distinguishing characteristic of these big industrial and mining complexes; they are inward looking and self-sufficient having most of their linkages with more advanced areas. They do not depend on the local communities even for unskilled labour. Some other industries based on bulky raw material like timber or other forest produce, which can be processed with advantage at their source, have also been established in some areas. However, there is no systematic effort and the location of units is ubiquitous and sporadic.

As a part of various general programmes under different schemes like Community Development and Tribal Development Blocks promotion of small-scale industries, handicrafts, village industries, etc., somė steps have been taken in tribal areas. These schemes, in most cases were, however, formulated for advanced regions and have introduced, by and large, without adaptation to the specific requirements of the tribal areas. The programmes modelled on schematic patterns generally prove to be beyond the absorptive capacity of the local communities. Therefore, these efforts have not taken root in these areas. Wherever some industrial growth and diversification is visible, the growth centres are more a continuation or extension of the urban or industrial economies and do not represent real growth nucleii of the local tribal economy. The modern and the traditional fail to meet.

Impact of Industrialization on Tribal Economy

The above analysis shows that the industrial sector has so far not been consciously trained with reference to the specific requirements and potentialities of the tribal areas and people. The major industrial and mining complexes have placed some of the most modern and sophisticated socio-economic structures in juxtaposition with some of the most primitive groups in the country. There is no meeting point between the two. Therefore, the modern industrial sector, starting as small nucleii in vast underdeveloped regions, expands at the cost of the rest of the economy displacing the local communities without much benefit to them. In fact, some of the so-called 'economies' of industries in the backward areas may arise as a result of non-appreciation of the traditional rights of the local communities and their inability to assert these rights in the face of the new ȧnd stronger institutions. For example, forests provide a substantial part of the subsistence to the local community. But our concepts of compensation do not take into account this factor. Even lands in possession of the local community, which may not have been formally assigned to them, do not attract the provisions of compensation law for no fault of the tribal. The compensation is paid with reference to the pre-development state of the area. The secondary displacement is nobody's concern and the differential in the socio-economic structure works to the disadvantage of the local groups.

In the tribal areas the industries do not establish even normal linkages with their immediate hinterland. The new opportunities which arise in the form of demand for services and agricultural commodities, animal products, etc., do not benefit the hinterland. The services sector is dominated by those who come to these areas in the secondary migration waves. In the absence of any conscious effort to plan diversification of agricultural activity in the hinterland, the core sector depends for some time on distant production centres even for items like vegetables, poultry products, etc. It is the migrant group which gradually establishes small dairy and poultry units in the neighbourhood. It may also take to vegetable cultivation, etc. The skill differential between the high industrial activity and the primitive hinterland economy gets filled by the migrant groups who further displace the tribal. Thus, in the absence of a conscious effort to diversify the hinterland tribal economy, the opportunity is lost and the tribal is by-passed even in the secondary and tertiary sectors. The new migration and the second generation of the first migrants are able to meet the growing man-power demands of the new opportunities which are created as a result of the multiplier effect of the central industrial activity.

Similar is the case, though on a smaller scale, of other smaller, raw material-based industries like saw mills or processing units. These units are generally dispersed; it is possible that their benefits to the local communities are somewhat larger and their adverse effects somewhat less. However, there is another aspect. As these industries are more dispersed, they are less amenable to general administrative regulations. Therefore, the possibility of larger benefit to the local communities is also accompanied by possibility of a wider exploitative network getting established if other timely administrative regulatory measures are not taken.

We have already noted that a systematic effort has not been made in relation to village and small scale industries; thus they may not answer the needs of the area. There is hardly any efforts to build up the programmes from below. Rigid programmes may by-pass the very groups for whom they are formulated. For example, if a training programme in tailoring does not first identify the traditional groups dependents on this profession, it may help the more advanced elements making the traditional tailor even more vulnerable and susceptible to induced competition in his own area. Thus, these programmes, by and large, have not benefitted the tribal areas.

As the tribal areas are getting opened up, their last natural protective wall of inaccessibility is giving way; cheap mass produced goods are reaching deepest tribal regions. The well-known phenomenon of the early colonial period of uprooting of small artisans in the face of competition of British goods in our national economy is being repeated in these areas with greater intensity. For example, the traditional weaver is much too weak to stand the competition of mill-made cloth; hand pounding of paddy is giving way to hullors; traditional wood-workers are getting out of employment because their artifacts no longer have the same attractive market. The schematic developmental programmes have not been able to help these groups.

While industrialisation admittedly adds to the gross regional output, some basic questions arise when we consider it as an instrument of tribal development. Does the tribal community share the incremental benefits in the gross regional output ? Perhaps, before we consider this aspect, a more basic question is whether the local community is in a position to absorb the benefits of this new activity ? It is clear that the local community in the tribal areas is not ready to absorb the new benefits from a large spectrum of the industrial sector. These problems of community development cannot be tackled so long as industrialisation process continues to retain its narrow frame and establishment of a few industries by itself is considered enough for regional development. Industrialisation should not result in a dualistic economic system in the region, but it should help in diversification of the local tribal economy. The processes should be so moulded that beneficial development inpulses are generated by the new growth centres.

In the context of simple tribal situation, the next question is whether it is necessary to wait for diversification of time tribal economy in a gradual and natural sequence of events before starting an industry in a tribal area or alternatively, whether the process of diversification should be speeded up in a planned fashion. Another aspect for consideration is whether setting up of an industry by itself will be enough for diversification or whether both diversification effort and setting up of industries can be treated as two facets of the same process, provided there is adequate planning input at the micro-level. In a planned economic development effort, it is not necessary to await the result of a slow change process. Similarly, an under-developed community cannot be left just to the play of unknown forces resulting in confrontation and a dualistic economic structure. It is clear that setting up of industry cannot be accepted as an end in itself or even sufficient by itself for the development of the local community. Therefore, the concept of industrialisation will have to be somewhat broader and diversification of the tribal economy will have to be one of the important facets. Thus, assimilative capacity of the local community will be an important 'given condition' in the industrial planning of a tribal region. The levels of development of different tribal regions differ considerably. Therefore, a uniform solution or approach is not conceivable for the entire range of industrial activity or for the tribal areas as a whole. The first obvious conclusion is that industrial planning for these areas cannot be done on *ad hoc* or overall considerations; it will be necessary to add a new dimension to the micro-level planning for each of the regions so as to ensure that the new activity continuously endeavours for diversification of the local economy and aims at benefitting the tribal community.

Before we consider the policy implications of consideration of tribal development for industrial growth of a region, let us consider the problem from the industry's end. Why an industry is established in any area ? If we analyse the rationale for the industrial location, there are broadly three considerations, which can be summarised as follows:

(a) Economics;
(b) National Policy for balance regional development; and
(c) Over-riding strategic, national or regional interests.

The economic considerations may be one or more of the following:

(i) Availability of raw material, cheap factor cost;
(ii) Infrastructural development including communication net-work, availability of power;
(iii) Availability of skilled man-power;
(iv) Availability of entrepreneurial skills; and
(v) Demand for the finished products.

In case the economic factors are not favourable in a region, specific incentives may be provided to compensate for the disadvantage or even regulation making power may be used. In case to strategic installation, the cost factors may be fully ignored.

In the theories of economic development, regional development has generally been taken as synonymous with the development of the people. This may be a valid hypothesis when there are no social barriers and skill discontinuities. But it is not valid when two entirely different systems meet. This is the situation in the tribal areas where industrial culture is penetrating the traditional tribal system. The industrial locations so far, at the best, have been decided on regional considerations. Now the industrial process itself will need to be harmonised with development of the local population. It will, therefore, be necessary to accept human factor as an important element in the locational theory and suitably manipulate it for achieving optimum development of the people. In principle, human factor should be an over-riding consideration in the context of tribal development. There may be some situations, for example, establishments of strategic importance where it may be necessary to accord it a second place as a matter of conscious policy. Nevertheless, it will be useful to identify these situations so that a suitable frame for industrial development of tribal areas in general can be developed.

Industries can be classified with reference to their priority on strategic considerations or their role in the development of national, regional or local economy. Decisions for location of certain industries may have to be taken as it may be crucial to the national interest although it may not be in the local interests. The obvious examples are defence installations or a heavy steel complex in a backward region. Even here some caution may be necessary. The real priority may not be as high as may appear to be at first sight. For example, a defence installation cannot wait for any other considerations. But while planning a mining complex, the time schedule or the choice of location are not absolute. They are known to be influenced by so many considerations like financial constraints, political demand or availability of infrastructure. While these factors have to be given due weight because of the power each of them wields on decision-making, the local socio-economic constraints have been ignored so far. If the implications of their establishment to the local community are clearly spelt out and given due weight, a different priority pattern many emerge. For example, the difference in economics of an industry in an advanced area and in a primitive location may be marginal. If the local situation is accepted as a factor in decision-making, the question will arise whether it is necessary to impose the new activity in the primitive area even if it may shatter its economy. Alternatively, will it be enough if, for the time being, the second choice of location is accepted and, in the meantime, necessary steps are taken for building up human capital in the hinterland of the most favourable site. Thus, if it is clear that 'technical' considerations are not immutable and the local socio-economic situation is accepted as one of the important constraints in location of an industry, the time-phasing and location-choice can be more rationally worked out. However, this constraint should not be interpreted narrowly and in a static sense. In other words, the local socio-economic constraint is not an important consideration only at a point of locational decision-making it has to be an important initial condition of planning both for the region and the industry and will need to be constantly kept in view. It will go on changing and the equations should be continuously reviewed.

A similar logic can be extended to the projects having overriding priority for regional or local considerations. However, these considerations cannot be deemed to have the same compulsive character as in the case of projects of national priority. In their case, local socio-economic constraints should assume a greater force. Thus, there may be two location choices for an industrial complex which are neutral in the national context, but may make all the difference at the regional level. In such cases, regional 'elitist' pressure are generated. In this situation, proper appreciation of the socio-economic constraint will help in a rational choice. If there is an obvious adverse impact on the tribal economy in one region, the alternative location would be preferred. On the other hand, if one choice aids the weaker sections more effectively, that location should be accorded a higher priority.

In the above cases, certain superficial casual relationships, which are generally taken for granted, will need to be tested for their validity. For example, the statement 'a steel mill should be established for developing the economy of backward area because it has a large tribal population' makes numerous presumptions such as the industrial complex will generate employment potential, it will enable regional economy to grow at a higher pace and therefore, the tribal community will naturally take advantage of the new opportunities. The possibility of a dualistic structure with detrimental impact on the tribal economy setting in, is not recognised.

This brings us a question of appropriate strategy for industrial development for the tribal area. The very first consideration is that a prospective industry should match the 'preparedness of the tribal community'. However, both 'industry' and 'preparedness of the tribal community' cannot be treated as immutable or independent variables; both of these factors can be suitably manipulated. Let us consider first the community's preparedness. It is possible to plant consciously to appreciably raise the level of preparedness, though within certain limits, of the local community with reference to a clearly defined growth path for the region. This should make a faster pace of industrialisation possible without disrupting the local economy. But if there is no such clear focus, and the developmental effort is in general terms, it may require a much longer time for similar results.

The minimum time required for such preparatory stages of industrialisation may vary as the tribal communities may be at different levels of preparedness. Each industry may require a different time schedule for bringing the local community to a level of preparedness to absorb the benefits of comparable technological innovations. Thus, defining the initial conditions as also determining the limits for the pace of change are crucial elements in planning for these areas. The existing skill spectrum of the tribal community and that required by the new industrial activity will need to be matched with suitable adaptation on either side whatever necessary. This aspect has not claimed the attention it deserves so far.

The building up of the skill spectrum referred to in the preceding paragraph should not be interpreted too narrowly. In a backward economy, bulk of the population is agriculturist and there are only a few artisan groups. While identification of the skill spectrum in some select groups like the traditional artisans will be important but the larger community itself should not be ignored for this purpose. It possesses important skills like tool making, house building, spinning and weaving, etc., which are generally lost in the advanced cultures. The entire community should be helped to absorb the benefits of secondary and tertiary economic activity in the region. Therefore, a general diversification of the tribal economy will need to be planned which, however, should be with special reference to be specific industrial activity already started or likely to be started. Action will need to be initiated at more than one level. Educated young men may be retained for specific jobs in the industry: traditional artisans may be trained both for the primary industry or secondary and tertiary sector; special programme may be taken up for introducing simple skill of the modern sector like those of petty trader, organiser of labour force, small contract work, etc. A programme of 'citizen education' itself, aimed at giving the tribal community a better understanding of the new processes should be a part of this diversification process because it is on the foundation of this new understanding that the very first step for diversification can be taken. In this way, in the tribal situation both the concepts, viz., 'industry' and 'skill', will have to be articulated more comprehensively and moulded suitably to match each other.

Entrepreneurship

Entrepreneurship is another crucial factor in defining the industrial policy of an area. It may be remembered here that a mixed economy comprising industrial and agricultural sectors has a highly differentiated dualistic structure even in advanced areas where they share the same social background. This differential between the two sectors, which is moderate at the national level, gets accentuated in the tribal situation. In their case, on the one hand, the society has a simple structure and is unable to comprehend the new situation and, on the other hand, the modern sector is stronger and more articulate. The average tribal is not used to the competitive system; he is not familiar with the new social code where output, the touch-stone of success, justifies every other action. The tribal is not able to discard his traditional relationships; he may not be able to even manage his financial affairs. Thus, entrepreneurship necessary for the new industrial activity is likely to be a crucial missing element even when other inputs may be made available to the tribal system. This is particularly so because the modernised sector generally favours larger units requiring highly articulate entrepreneurship. In the case of the tribal even the so-called small sector is much too large for him to manage efficiently and effectively.

Another important factor in the development of entrepreneurship is the contrasting background of the tribal with a low premium on competition and a high value on group activity compared to the stark individualism and competition of the modern sector. The new activity requires operations at impersonal level requiring highest consideration for elements like inputs, output, utility, profit and loss. The individual tribal, therefore, may find his very first step as the most difficult one. Once he is able to appreciate the intricacies of the new system, perhaps, it may be so difficult for him to operate within the frame of these considerations. The younger educated group, which is under a different influence from the early age, may perhaps respond better to the new challenges. At times even this group may have difficult choice when it is torn between the pulls of the two systems. There may be some failures which are inevitable in this process. However, it may be possible that the capacity of the tribal to work as a group could be put to a better use. It will be necessary for this purpose that he is enabled to organise in a way which is not formal and which he can understand. He should be able to operate the system. The tribal may perhaps be able to take to competitive situations in a better spirit as a group because he is used to such group situations in his own setting. However, a word of caution is necessary here: the moment group association is formalised, it gets converted into an unfamiliar word to him. In fact, the cooperatives in most of the tribal areas represent to him only another form of administrative hierarchy where he is also required to participate in something which he cannot fully understand. He takes it as his duty which he is expected to perform. It is more of a direction from the administration rather than as a participative group activity arising from within. The strength of the group could be harnessed if appropriately handled.

A closer examination of the general approach in relation to entrepreneurship in the tribal context will be useful at this stage. There is a hierarchy of entrepreneurs. In a highly un-differentiated economy, the first specialisation in terms of entrepreneurship may be setting up a very small grocery shop. In fact perhaps simple lending activity may precede the small trader stage. In a traditional tribal economy no interest is charged on money advanced for consumption purposes and the period of repayment is indefinite. This system may get more sophisticated as the contact with the modern sector increases; some of the tribals may assume the role of money lender. Lending of small sums may be a comparatively simple affair. But trading activity or opening a tea shop is a much more complex phenomenon for him. The question of simple entrepreneurship has not been considered so far from the tribal-end. The approach in the planned developmental effort has been to establish cooperative for marketing and supply of consumer commodities in the tribal areas. Even very heavy overheads are borne by the exchequer for this purpose. Thus, the simplest entrepreneurial activity is institutionalised with a view to save the tribal from exploitation and provide him services at a reasonable cost.

There is considerable conceptual confusion about the role of such an institutional support: this will need to be clearly understood. What is the basic purpose of, say, a cooperative society which caters to the daily requirements of the tribal ? Is the supply of commodities through cooperatives planned as a permanent feature of the local economy, or is it designed for filling the vacuum till such time as the local community is ready to take up the relevant activity ? The cooperative movement envisages an ideal system of economic relationships where there is no exploitation and the benefit of all economic activity is fully shared by the participating community. It is, however, to be appreciated that such an ideal system cannot be established in certain pockets whereas the larger society may be proceeding on a different model. Therefore, these institutions should be treated realistically as gap-fillers rather than as an ideal institutional structure for a model socio-economic system. If this perspective is clear, the establishment of a cooperative society catering to daily requirements in a tribal area can only be the first step in the planned growth of the economy and a perspective should be clearly outlined for the next stages. Perhaps, if the general model of advanced areas is accepted, individual tribal should be prepared to shoulder this responsibility in second stage. In due-course, the temporary institutional support may not be necessary and could be withdrawn.

In the absence of such a clear policy frame for the role of cooperative institutions, this activity is not properly organised. Even if cooperative institutions are accepted as ideal institutions in a longer time frame, it has to be noted that secondary trading activity gets established with the opening up of the tribal areas and diversification of the general economy. But as there is no conscious planning for the direction and form of diversification of this economy, it is the immigrant groups which establish themselves in the comparatively higher-skill professions. Diversification of the local economy, if examined in the context of tribal development, represents really a growing dualistic structure. A cooperative society, which in the early stage of development may be the only institution in the area, becomes one of the many establishments which get established in due course. The cooperative institutional support, thus, with the passage of time may become unnecessary or uneconomical. Such an institution, even when it succeeds and plays a crucial role at a given point of time, proves to be passing phase for the local community and the normal competitive system finally overtake. But the community has not been enabled to become a partner in the diversification process. If local entrepreneur were trained with a clear and conscious policy frame to substitute the cooperative institution by local entrepreneurs at an appropriate stage, the final texture of the socio-economic structure would be different.

It is generally accepted that the opening up of an area creates conditions of severe competition for the local craftsmen and also provides an easy channel for introduction of money lender and small traders. Heavy investments are made on roads. Petty traders start with establishing small tea shops and provision stores along the road at important points. The tribals who may have owned these sites reced in the background and gradually a new trading centre gets established. This centre in due course acquires exploitative relationship with the hinterland.

A policy question arises at this stage. In the economic dynamics of the region, the road can be visualised to serve as a contact point between the tribal economy and the outside world. If this were so, selection of promising young men who could be induced and helped to establish small shops on the road side could have been taken as a part of the road construction activity itself. Whatever difficulties a tribal entrepreneur was expected to face could have been solved. Loan on easy terms or even part loan and part gram would not be a heavy outlay compared to the total capital investments involved in opening up the area. The social setting of the area would have been quite different. The new establishment would have grown and collected the more promising and innovating tribal groups around it. This centre would serve as a window of the tribal world to the modern society. It could have served as a bridge between the two and provide a foot hold for more adventurous young men to move out. This is precisely the process in the more advanced areas where there are no dividing lines between the small urban centres and their hinterlands. In the absence of such a planning frame for the tribal areas, the establishment of road communication only helps in establishing numerous centres which grow without benefiting the hinterland.

The above analysis of simple trading activity equally applies to higher industrial activity. However, it will be necessary to clearly define those areas where institutional arrangements are designed to substitute entrepreneurs on a permanent basis and those where it is contemplated as a temporary phase. The experience of some industries is quite encouraging. The bigger industries could be planned in which a cooperative or corporate institution could be assigned the entrepreneurial role on a long term basis. A cooperative perhaps could be a 'guided cooperative' in the initial stage under professional management. The control of the community on the cooperative may become gradually more effective. The professional management itself may gradually change in complexion providing a greater representation to the local entrants.

The approach could be somewhat different in the smaller industrial ventures. The plan could concentrate on the individual tribals. They could be provided necessary guidance in setting up the industry. In the initial stages a supportive institutional frame, may be a cooperative institution could be envisaged either as a protective 'umbrella' to the entrepreneurs or even as a promoter of entrepreneurship. The experience of X'vier Institute of Social Studies, Ranchi in training and guiding small entrepreneurs is encouraging and lays bare great potential in this area. The small entrepreneur established in grocery shops can, in due course, flower into bigger entrepreneurs, provided they are given opportunity and protection against competition of more advanced groups in their early period.

We have considered the socio-economic constraints in the preceding section. As matching is essentially a two-way affair, we may turn to the question of adapting the industrial process itself to the local socio-economic situation. In the first instance, industrialization should not be interpreted in a limited sense of establishing a few industries; it should be taken as a culmination of the process of diversification of the local economy and upgradation of skills all through the spectrum. Therefore, conscious linkages will need to be built up by the entire industrial sector with the local economy. In this context, no undertaking should have an idea that it can itself as an independent unit having a specific individual role free to operate in any way it likes. The local constraints of planning should be clearly defined and the process of industrialization itself should be set within those well-defined limits.

The management in industrial enterprises, particularly the larger ones, considers itself responsible for achieving the ends of the project and it is presumed that other factors would automatically get balanced. These presumptions may be valid in the more advanced areas where the socio-economic background and relative strength of different groups is not very different. But they do not hold good in the more backward areas. Therefore, it will be necessary that a sense of responsibility is instilled in the management about the implications of industrial activity to its hinterland. This point is generally appreciated only when a breaking point is reached in the relationship of the core with the surrounding areas. For each case of one breaking point, there should be numerous points of varying degrees of tension. The final result may depend on the intensity of the local feeling and the relative strength of the two groups. In most cases, the stronger industrial group has the upper hand and the local communities have two compromise for a subservient position in the new structure. This law of jungle which prevails in many areas, will need careful review. A comprehensive planning of the zones of influence of big industrial and mining complexes, therefore, is necessary for a harmonious and balanced growth.

Before we proceed to a deeper analysis, it may be noted that even in their outer form, the bigger industrial and mining complexes tend to behave as self-contained units. Thus, the social service infrastructure created by these organisations may be exclusively reserved for the members of the core industry. Thus, highly developed social services institutions may exist amidst a vast population without even elementary services. Social services can be important links between the industrial and the tribal society. In fact, medical and educational institutions have generally been the first outposts of modern civilization in the backward areas. But the very concept of labour welfare, when defined in extremely narrow frame of reference of the industry, becomes responsible for this anomalous situation. It is forgotten that the labour does not constitute the lowest strata of society in these areas; this group itself is super-imposed on the local socio-economic structure and thus, has an 'elitist' character. The tribal communities, the last group on the economic scale, therefore, cannot be ignored in any scheme of development or social services in these areas. The question of the sharing of financial burden could be separately settled. What is necessary is the realization that all organizations together should evolve a suitable strategy so that a 'non-partisan pattern' of social services can be established in the core and its zone of influence.

One more point needs to be noted here. An industry ordinarily expects the local community to adapt itself to the ways of the new culture almost instantaneously. But the working patterns of the two systems are so different that tribal cannot be expected to adjust himself immediately to the requirements of the new system. Since the industry is neutral in terms of its choice for the manpower, it prefers the migrant groups even for the lowest jobs because they answer its requirement better. This demand, therefore, simulates a secondary wave of migration to these areas.

The non-adaptation to the industrial needs, however, is not peculiar only to the tribal areas. If we persue the history of textile industry in Bombay, it faced a similar problem in relation to its labour force which was initially drawn from the North India. It took quite a long time for the two to adjust with each other. The industry then had to adjust to the prevailing phenomenon because there was no other alternative. The entire Indian labour force at that stage of our economic development was rural in character and could not afford to shake-off its social obligations. Now the situation is changing. The labour force in the advanced areas is getting used to the rigours and discipline of the organised activity. The industry, therefore, can make a choice between one group and another and afford to ignore the indigenous groups.

In view of these facts it will be necessary that the new industry in the tribal areas appreciates their distinctive socio-economic mileau. In the short-run, the industry should try to adapt itself to their requirements. Otherwise, it will be impossible to draw in the tribal. A tribal is not a lone individual, cut-off from his social obligations. He is fully integrated in his society and has to be dealt with as such. It may be possible that in the tribal setting a concept of 'group employment' may work better instead of individual employment. It could be left to the local tribal leadership as to how the group size, as required by the industry, is maintained. If such a concept is introduced, it will be possible for the industry to assume continuity and the system can afford to provide sufficient flexibility to the individual so that he can attend to his agricultural and social obligations.

It is necessary that the psychology of the individual tribal in respect of his relationship with his land and the industry is also clearly understood. The labour force coming from the more advanced areas is aware of the advantages of employment in the organised sector. He can see an assured future if he somehow is able to join the industry as a regular worker. He is conscious of the strength of the group to protect his interest on a long-term basis. However, the tribal is completely unaware of these advantages and he can have the feel of *tarre firma* only in his village and his agriculture. It is this psychological factor which explains his reluctance to join the labour force even at a much higher wage rate than what he could expect in his village. A sense of confidence in the new surroundings can grow only over a period of time.

The core-hinterland relationship has another dimension which also needs to be properly appreciated. The industrial project, working on the modern concepts of 'distance' and 'neighbourhood' may delineate a hinterland which may not have much meaning in terms of the tribals' 'world-view' living in its vicinity. The mobility of labour may be presumed by the Project over a much longer distance little realising that the spread effect in the initial stages may not be able to reach far deep in the hills and forests of the tribal regions. These anomalies arise because the perception of distance of the two groups is entirely different. Scores of miles do not matter much to those who are used to fast means of communication. The world view of the rural community in general, and the tribal community in particular, is limited to a comparatively smaller area with which it is personally familiar. Therefore, the basic equations may be wrongly defined with unpredictable results. A Project may compute its benefits to the people in the region in terms of a much wider hinterland and, in this process, may not give due regard to the aspirations and the problem of the people in the immediate neighbourhood. These people, in their turn, may have no appreciation of what is happening in the bigger area. This may lead to disharmony and tension. It is, therefore, necessary that there should be a reasonable consonance between the two views so that the mutual relationship can be better appreciated. The industrial planning may be conceived with advantage as series of micro-level plans of gradually enlarging geographical regions.

The perception of distance is essentially a social psychological problem. Another problem of group psychology is the acceptance by the local community of the industrial unit as a part of its own system. If the relationships can be so established that a community can consider an industry belonging to its own system the occasion for tensions and disharmony may not arise. The size of an industry and its location are generally determined by economic considerations and those elements which may help in establishing such harmonising relationship are scarcely taken into account. If these elements were also considered as given conditions along with other factors necessary for establishment and location of any industry the decision perhaps could be different. The social cost and the amount of benefit to local community from the establishment of an industry will depend to a large extent on its harmonious setting. If this were taken as an important factor, the choice of industry would be in the favour of a smaller unit. Effort would also be made to integrate the industry as a part of the overall production process in the area. Such a unit could be under joint ownership so that the benefits of the final production flow back to the primary producer. The cooperative sugar industry in Maharashtra is established largely on this model. It can be suitably adapted for other industries with reference to the specific local situation in the tribal areas.

The above analysis helps us in understanding the dynamics of the industrial and the tribal socio-economic system. It may now be possible to spell out the necessary elements in the industrial development plan of a tribal area. Some aspects which should attract attention of planners even at the preliminary stage of programme formulation, are discussed below.

This may include marketable agricultural surplus, the level of exploitation and potential of minor and major forest produce, minerals and other natural resources with possible range of economic value in each case, etc.

This may include: (i) density of population; (ii) distribution of hamlets; (iii) the level of literacy; (iv) occupational distribution; and (v) the extent of diversification of the social economic value in each case, etc.

The skills of the tribal population in general and higher skill of artisan groups, if any, amongst them in particular may be identified. In case of artisans it will be necessary to identify: (i) areas of their concentration, if any, and (ii) the state of their traditional crafts.

This may include the traditional consumption patterns, the new trends in demand for essential and non-essential items and the long-term change in living style leading to newer demands.

This may include existing major, medium, and small-scale industries, handicrafts, household industries, etc.

This may include the existing road, communications, electric power lines, credit institutions, etc.

Once these basic elements are clearly spelt out, it should be possible to have a suitable strategy for long-term diversification of the tribal economy. The modern industrial activity may be nonexistant in some areas while in others some industrial activity may have already appeared. It is obvious that the first step has to be to understand the relationship of the existing industrial units with the local community. In those cases, where the industrial activity is not benefitting the local community, remedial action may be urgently taken. This may involve action at a number of points like influencing the policy of the project ensuring adequate local participation, exploring the possibilities of various linkages between the industrial and the rural sector and, finally, which is the most important, strengthening the local community by suitable social service inputs.

While these steps may be necessary in relation to the established industries, the next important aspect will be to identify the industrial units having strategic, national or regional importance, which are likely to be set-up. It may be examined whether the time schedule for their establishment is fixed or is still flexible. In case it is flexible, it should be adjusted, as far as possible, in such a fashion that there is sufficient time to prepare the tribal community to enable them to take the advantage of the new opportunities. Advance training programmes, upgrading of the local skills with reference to the availability of jobs, preparing the hinterland economy for the new demands likely to be created, an intensive citizen education programme with the likely zone of influence of the new enterprises, etc. should be taken up.

It will be useful if the traditional groups, with comparatively diversified skills, are picked up for special treatment. It is they who are exposed to greater variety of situations and who can be easily moulded into suitable contact points between the modern and the traditional. Their skills, in many cases, can be upgraded easily and they can be usefully fitted in the modern industrial sector. The programmes for traditional artisans so far have been generally formulated as rehabilitational programmes and, therefore, the full potential of their likely role in the socio-economic development of the tribal areas is not appreciated. The welfare approach to such programmes has obvious limitation. If their problem is considered in isolation it cannot provide a long-term solution. The traditional artisan groups have to be built up as the possible innovator elements in the primitive social structure. They should be treated as linkages between the modern and the traditional sectors, though not the exclusive ones. If this dynamics is appreciated, the skill upgradation programmes will acquire a new dimension.

It may be mentioned at this stage that there is urgent need to plan from below. This holds good for the entire tribal economy, but particularly so, for the industrial sector. The modern industrial cultural is completely alien to the local tradition. The present position is that whatever programmes are formulated are influenced by the needs and the experiences of more advanced sectors of our economy. But, it may happen that the traditional and the modern sectors may not have developed any meeting points. Therefore, the two may be operating at different levels. In such a case, the programmes would be foredoomed to failure.

A recent study by the Industries Department of Bihar has brought to light some interesting facts about the natural spread effect of modern industries activity. Many of the local artisans around Ranchi have, of their own accord, adopted some of the newer practices; many more can benefit if only some marginal help were available. The inputs which these groups require are extremely small, may be some improved tools or a small loan as working capital. As the problems of such small groups have not been studied, there is no experience to go by with the financing institutions. Their schemes are also much bigger. Therefore, in these cases if a schematic approach were adopted, besides being costly, it may miss the essential point. Many of them may not be able to take advantage of these big schemes. If these groups can be helped in a small way, their activities will have a multiplier effect because others can emulate their example and may try to enter many other fields with greater confidence. Thus, it is necessary to plan from below on a step by step basis so that whatever programmes are taken up are within the assimilative capacity of the local groups and it is ensured that intended benefits do accrue to them. This will prepare the community for the next dose of innovative investment and upgradation process may gradually become self-sustained.

Educated youngmen comprise another potential group which needs to be tapped suitably. It may be possible to make use of this manpower through suitable training programmes. Turnkey projects may be useful for these groups. If an 'umbrella' organisation were to help these entrepreneurs initially, they may be able to venture in larger areas with great confidence. Such an organisation may be an independent organisation or it may be a subsidiary of a large or medium industry already established in these areas. We have discussed at length the role of the core industrial units in the preceding paragraphs.

The available raw material in the area is another important determinant of industrial growth. Much of the raw material from the tribal areas is exported to the more advanced areas in unprocessed form. Therefore, the net benefit of the available raw material to the regional economy is rather small. Industrial programme for a tribal area, therefore, should aim at exporting the raw material in a fully processed or semi-processed form within as short a period as may be possible. This should help in deciding the character and location of the new industry.

The other important component of industrial development is the demand. There are two aspects of demand, viz., external demand and internal demand. With the opening of these areas, the consumption needs of the tribal community are getting diversified and new demands are emerging. Many a time, the character of demand in the same product-category may be changing, for example, there is a shift from traditional designs in clothes to newer designs. Similarly, the older ornaments may be given way to cheaper mass-manufactured ornaments. In fact, there may be a conscious under-cutting in some of the important areas by bigger firms just to establish themselves in a new line of trade. These aspects will need to be carefully studied to determine the policy of diversification of the tribal economy. Where the shift in demand is qualitative, the first obvious effort should be to retrain the traditional groups as far as possible. Where the demand is in an entirely new one, it could be explored whether some of the existing skills can be utilised for meeting the new demand.

There is little appreciation of the internal demand structure which is left to the free forces of market. In fact, whenever any programme for revitalising local crafts is taken up it is linked to external demand, or in other words, the problems of marketing is considered in terms of demand outside the regions. Elaborate marketing organisations may also be established. The distant urban market, or even the export market, which are the primary focus in this approach, have obviously a limited potential in the context of the overall production potential which can be developed in the rural and the tribal areas. The longer leads are always a handicap in enabling these crafts becoming self-sustaining. It is, therefore, necessary to explore the possibility of creating demand locally for the traditional and even newer articles rather than depending primarily on distant urban centres. Here again, we find that not much attention has been paid to the aspect. There are some schemes for encouraging small or household industries but these concessions are in general terms and may not answer the specific local requirements. For example, in these backward areas, there may be no small industry to claim the concession. On the other hand, the traditional artisan may be struggling hard to find a market who may not get any benefit of these schemes. It is, therefore, necessary that local variations are attempted for helping specific groups. For example, it may immensely help the traditional groups if their arts and artifacts are used for the decoration of public buildings and other institutions of the area. Such provision can be made an integral part of the basic building designs. This would help creating an automatic linkage between the level of economic activity and demand for some of the traditional crafts.

The variables in the socio-economic situation in the tribal areas are so delicately balanced that a partial or sectoral view may easily disturb it. Therefore, a comprehensive industrial development plan peeping in view all aspects discussed above for many of these areas may be necessary. This exercise, however, cannot be taken up all at once for all such areas. Yet earlier such an exercise is taken up, more helpful it will be for achieving balanced development of these regions. The tribal areas can be grouped for the purposes of industrial planning in the categories given below:

(i) Compulsive Regions

(a) The tribal areas which already have big industrial and mining complexes;
(b) Those areas where such industrial complexes are likely to be established on national or strategic consideration; and
(c) Such other areas where some intensive economic activity in some other sector is proposed to be taken up on overall national considerations. The examples

are development of a tourist resort or intensive forestry management programmes.

(ii) Primitive Regions

There are some areas with extremely backward socio-economic situation. They could be excluded from the list of candidate areas for intensive industrial activity in the immediate future on human consideration.

(iii) Potential Regions

These regions may include: (a) population pressure areas; and (b) rich natural resources areas.

(iv) Other Regions

These areas may comprise such tribal regions which do not come under the first three categories.

We may discuss each of these groups separately.

We have already noted that urgent attention will be needed in the areas for softening the impact of sudden industrialization. Comprehensive plan, including that for industries, for these areas should be prepared on a priority basis.

These areas are those where the level of socio-economic development is very low and any large scale activity may result in uprooting the local tribal group. Some of the examples are Abujhmar region in Bastar, Madhya Pradesh, Bondo hill in Koraput, Orissa and the Paharia region in Santhal Parganas, Bihar. As a rule of thumb, all areas with less than five per cent literacy level may be considered as extremely backward. Economic development programme of those groups will have to be cautiously prepared ensuring that pace of change is not too fast. Industrialization in the near future has to be ruled out on sociological grounds unless there are some other over-riding considerations in which case a conscious policy decision should be taken at the highest level.

POPULATION PRESSURE AREAS

There are some tribal areas which are experiencing pressure of population. In these areas, agricultural and forest resources are not sufficient to support the growing numbers. In many tribal areas like those of Rajasthan and Gujarat, there is seasonal migration of tribals to the neighbouring urban industrial centres.

In such cases, the stage can be considered to be set for diversification of tribal economy in response to the local need. Such areas, therefore, could be identified and comprehensive programme could be taken up on a priority basis.

RICH NATURAL RESOURCES AREAS

Areas with specially rich natural resources should get attention for a comprehensive developmental plan on priority basis in the interest of its balanced growth. One never knows when the development of such regions may acquire a compulsive character. If such a decision is taken all of a sudden, there may be hardly any time for equiping the local population for meeting the challenges of the fast change. Therefore, it would be better if such regions are identified and a comprehensive development plan is prepared. It may be possible in that case to phase the industrial activity strictly according to the level of preparedness of the local community. Programmes aimed at human resources development may be intensified in these areas which could be gradually oriented to the possible skill-mix which may be required in future when the industries are established. Initially, these programmes may be of a general nature which could be gradually diversified and specialised as the new demands arise.

In the remaining areas, there are no immediate or likely conclusions arising from considerations of industrial development, in their case, diversification of tribal economy should be a part of the overall developmental strategy of the region. It may, however, be assigned a special position. Here again, priorities for each of the areas will have to be assigned keeping in view the resource potential, the preparedness of the people, level of literacy, etc. In these areas, industries smaller in size, dispersed and with less sophisticated technology should be preferred. Creation of an 'umbrella' organisations and preparation of 'turn-key' projects may help in industrial growth of these areas.

The quality of such special area plans can be immensely improved if they could have the benefit of a broader developmental perspective in relation to each important commodity. Therefore, different national organisations with specialisation in appropriate field could take an overall view of the potential with regard to the relevant raw material. For example, the Silk Board could assess the potential of 'Kosa' industry and prepare a blue-print for its development for the entire tribal region in the country. Within the frame so provided, individual scheme may be taken up within the integrated Tribal Development Programme of the relevant region. Similarly, the exploitation of forest resources could be viewed in the overall context of the potential in larger resource region. With such specific exercises, the overall socio-economic constraints can be assessed in larger frame and it will be possible to determine *inter-se* priorities for different areas and for different industries. Such an exercise will be difficult for a smaller area where narrow sectoral views or ignorance of what is happening in the adjoining area may influence decisions.

Beside the above generalised programmes for which planning in larger areas is necessary, smaller programmes aimed at upgrading the skills of the traditional craftsmen should get the highest priority. Even here, it will be useful if a broad over-view of different skills in tribal tracts is prepared and local programmes are evolved within that frame. Caution will, however, be necessary that in the name of evolving a strategy for larger areas no schematic or stereo-typed programmes are set. This may have the effect of super-imposition of programmes from higher levels, a process which is sought to be reversed by 'planning from below'.

The organisational structure for industrial growth in the tribal areas is an important aspect requiring special attention. It has to be accepted at the outset that there is already considerable proliferation of organisations in the tribal areas. Therefore, the idea of setting up an independent organisation for industrial development of tribal areas, if at all, will have to stand closest scrutiny. An independent organisation covering a big tribal tract will not be able to reach the deep tribal regions; it may tend to operate generally in certain important big centres which do not really from a part of the tribal economy. Therefore, many organisations may appear to be functioning in tribal areas yet may not even touch the tribal economy.

The most important element in any developmental programme is a clear understanding of the local situation by those who are responsible for planning and execution. A unified administrative structure, which is simple and within the comprehension of the people, has already been accepted as one of the essential elements for the new strategy of development. Similarly, a single credit-*cum*-marketing organization will be responsible for the credit and marketing side. This organization will be independent of, but will have a close relationship with, the administrative structure. These two organisations should be accepted as providing the basic institutional frame for the entire range of economic development of an Integrated Tribal Development Project Area. However, wherever necessary, further expertise could be built into them for attending to the industrial development aspects as well. Such an expertise will relate to planning. So far as actual implementation is concerned, the unified structure appears to be the best agency. In fact, the confidence relationship of these organisations with the tribal, which is expected to develop in their simple operations of direct relevance to him, should be the most important asset on which the new industrial programme should be built up.

In the new strategy, the credit-*cum*-marketing organisation itself will be generally responsible for collection of bulk of minor forest produce. Therefore, such an organisation should be best suited to start processing of the raw material. Since this organisation is expected to be attuned to the needs and aspirations of the tribal as a part of its normal activity, it may be reasonably expected that the decisions in relation to phasing, technology, locations, etc., for the industry and its approach will be more realistic. In particular, it will not have a bias against the more backward areas and there will be no tendency on its part to cling to the bigger places. A separate organisation, operating from a city headquarter, is likely to have such a bias.

The processing of raw materials should be nearest to the collection points. Such an arrangement will be economical to the organisation itself. This organisation can also go in for some other smaller consumer industries because it will be responsible for supply of consumer commodities as well. However, it may be useful to keep the two aspects of its operations distinct. Certain institutional safeguards can be built in, for example, the two accounts may separately be maintained.

The cases, where the industrial activity proposed to be taken up is more sophisticated and specialised, could be considered separately. The first choice should be in favour of the form of a subsidiary of the credit-*cum*-marketing organisation. Such an arrangement will have the advantage of enabling the subsidiary to have the goodwill and services of the parent body yet building up necessary expertise for handling the industrial project. In case of large industries, however, a separate organisation should be established. These situations, will be exceptional rather than a rule. However, in the neighbourhood of a big industrial complex, it will be useful if the responsibility for integrated industrial development is on that industry itself. The core industry may have a separate small cell which may provide necessary technical know-how. Suitable arrangements for coordination between this cell and the project or credit-*cum*-marketing organisation, as the case may be, can be made in each case.

Modern Industry in Tribal Belts

It is a notable coincidence that the Central India tribal belt straddling across the States of West Bengal, Bihar, Orissa, Madhya Pradesh, Andhra Pradesh has been burgeoning into a zone of intense industrial and mining activity in the recent decades. The Durgapur, Bokaro, Jamshedpur, Rourkela, Bhilai Steel plants, the Ranchi Heavy Engineering complex, a host of ancillary industries, a chain of mining complexes have made appearance in the tribal belt. A vary agro-forest traditional culture has been confronted with a modern, sophisticated industrial culture. The abrupt juxtaposition has produced deleterious results for the tribals. There has been large-scale alienation of tribal land for the public and private sector industrial and mining complexes, townships, private enterprises, etc. Having lost the basic resource, the tribals have not been able to secure alternative sources of livelihood. The first generation has found it nearly impossible to imbibe the skills and culture of the industrial age. It would appear that the shock impulses generated on account of the imposition of the modern industry have been beyond the absorption capacity of the tribal communities. In fact, for the first generation, it has been an unmitigated disaster, in as much as it has meant nearly wholesale destitution. The question whether industrialisation planned for the placid tribal areas should not contend with the human sacrifice involved, acquires significance. Should not the interests of tribal men and women be safeguarded while planning therefor?

2. We are clear, however, that we cannot keep in check the advancing tide of industrialisation. Nevertheless, we can soften the rigours of the new, alien climate. The tribals can be prepared beforehand to participate in industrialisation or, in the alternative to make gainful living notwithstanding the establishment of the new industry. But no step should be taken which is clearly foreseen to ensure in destitution of masses of innocent men and women.

3. We understand that the Ministry of Home Affairs have appointed a committee of administrators, academicians and representatives of the Ministries of Industrial Development and Education, to advise on the future lines of development in the Central Indian belt particularly in and around industrial complexes with a view to minimising adverse effects and involvement of tribals in the process of industrialisation. We have no doubt that the Government would consider the recommendations of the Committee carefully and initiate appropriate measures to ensure that tribal interests are promoted.

4. Establishment of all major and medium industries is normally preceded by feasibility studies, project reports, etc., which focus attention mostly on technical input-output factors. We suggest that no project report should be deemed complete without inclusion therein of consideration of future of the local communities based on study of all related aspects like the present socio-economic status, the cultural profile and the anthropology of the prospective developments, by inter-disciplinary teams composed of plant technologists, administrators, economists, sociologists, anthropologists, etc. The project reports should spell out: (a) the positive and the negative repercussions flowing from the establishment of the industry on the local communities, (b) steps required to be taken for their active involvement in the industry, and (c) steps for continuation of traditional avocations, culture, etc., of those members who stay out. In more concrete terms, land should be acquired or purchased from tribals only when strictly necessary; rather than cash compensation which disappears within no time, allotment of suitable land in exchange should be the general rule. Skills should be imparted in advance to enable avail of the industrial opportunities in the new

establishment; if not the first generation, some individuals belonging to the second generation might absorb the skills. The ability to face the harsh forces of the modern industrial age has to be built up in tribals through constant education. Adequate financial provision should be made for all these measures.

5. We understand that the Government of India had, a little while ago, taken a decision that the development of zones of influence of industrial and mining complexes should be prepared as a part of the project report, the idea being that investment in these areas should develop a region rather than a small localised industrial or mining complex. We are not aware of the progress in the matter. We feel that such planning exercises would be useful not only for prospective projects but also in respect of the existing industrial and mining ones. Tribal areas should become productive hinterlands. The tribal families displaced from their homes and health should be given viable rehabilitation.

6. The Working Group for Tribal Development 1978-83 had recommended that the Bureau of Public Enterprises should take up leadership role at the national level for location of industries in tribal areas and should be concerned with the public sector projects which form the bulk. The steps taken in the matter are not known to us. Since sudden intensive economic activity in the industrial regions has a detrimental effect on the economy and sociology of scheduled tribes, there should be a clear perception about activities to be taken up. Suitable regulations should be framed so that consultation at the highest level becomes a prerequisite to setting up of big industries in tribal areas.

7. It appears that licencing committees have been set-up in the concerned Ministries to scrutinise various aspects before issue of licences. To ensure that the scrutiny does not overlook the tribal angle, it would be advantageous to place a representative of the Home Ministry on these committees. In the States also, a representative or representatives of the Department of Tribal Development might be associated with similar committees or bodies.

Traditional Industries, Arts and Crafts

8. Notwithstanding the present lack of ability of a member of a scheduled tribe community to participate in a modern industry, it has to be recognised that a tribal fits in well in his own

ecosystem. He possesses the requisite and skill answering the needs of his environment. Tending to be polymorphic, usually each individual in a tribal society acquires a variety of skills each of which may not, however, be highly developed. Yet, some degree of specialisation has been observed, as in weaving, smithy, cane-work, curving, idol-making, handicrafts. The invasion of mass-produced goods has been pushing the traditional skills towards extinction.

9. The chief difficulty of the tribal artisan and craftman's is market. The traditional products find favour generally in the tribal market or international market. The non-tribal national domestic market has neither the means nor disposition to accept traditional tribal products. In so far as the tribal market is concerned, in the earlier days barter system was working satisfactorily for the artisan; the present trend of monetised economy fetches meagre returns. The market has to expand considerably to make the effort worthwhile. Execution of development plans, with consequent economic activity, should give filip to tribal markets. In fact, there have to be conscious attempts towards that. For example, a certain percentage of total building cost may be utilised for purchasing local pieces of art, use of local construction materials may help the rural artisan and worker. From the tribal craftsman to the sophisticated international market, it is a long haul with numerous links in the clain. Notwithstanding the demand in the international market and the return possible on its being tapped, the chain is plagued with missing intermediate links. The Hand-looms and Handicrafts Export Promotion Corporation should open a separate wing for tribal products for foreign sales push.

10. Tie non-tribal domestic market is today replete with mass-produced goods. An average national consumer has not the economic capacity to pay the higher price of hand-produced articles. Hence, the village artisan has the choice of either upgrading his technology or being snuffed out of this market. Some degree of upgradation is possible and steps therefor, are necessary.

11. At any rate, market study has to be a continual affair and all steps necessary in a given context should be taken to relay the benefits of expanded markets and price to the individual tribal artisan aid craftsman. A federated cooperative structure can play a useful role.

12. It has been experienced that tribal handicrafts are gradually disappearing from public view. This may not be only on account to lack of markets, but due to various other factors also. We feel it will be irretrievable loss to the nation if such valuable creative products go into oblivion. We suggest the formation of a small committee by the Ministry of Home Affairs comprised of experts and connoisseurs of tribal arts and crafts to locate them with a view to their encouragement for revival, promotion and development.

Forest-based Industries

Forest-based cottage, village and small industries have good scope. Elsewhere, we have stressed the importance of processing of minor forest produce in the tribal areas itself. The following should be considered:

(a) Honey extraction is well-known generally among all tribes and particularly among some specific tribes like the Kharia of Orissa and Bihar. Its collection and marketing should be systematised.

(b) Lac growers and collectors sell it in stick-lac-form without its conversion into even semi-manufactured form. Its processing may be taken up on cottage or village industry scale. Lacquer products are being made even now in the tribal areas and their sale should be properly organised.

(c) Bidi leaves (Kendu or Tendu or Timru) should not be allowed to be exported from tribal areas as such, but the tribals be engaged in rolling them into Bidies.

(d) Extraction of oil from Sal, Kusum, Karanj, Neem and various other non-traditional oil-bearing seeds should be taken up as an activity in the interest of tribal and national economy.

(e) Technology of tassar plantation and cocoon rearing should be upgraded in tribal areas. Higher skills for reeling and weaving of tassar should be imparted on a large scale.

(f) Tribals collecting tamarind widely in the States of Orissa, Andhra Pradesh and Madhya Pradesh should be imparted the Technology of converting the tamarind into concentrate.

(g) Since the tribal villages are usually situated near forest areas, small wood-based industries like saw-mill, furniture-making, match-making, etc., could become a sizable activity. The crafts of basket-making rope-making, etc. also may be encouraged specially in the villages that are inhabited by the primitive tribal groups.

(h) Gums collected should be refined and further processed for sale in various markets.

(i) With plenty of material for broomsticks in tribal areas, brooms should be manufactured before sending them out.

(j) Some Tribals possess the skill of carpet-making. It should be disseminated widely in favourable situations as carpet export seems to have considerable scope.

14. Among the various items, some like tassar, oil-seeds, bidi leaves have major scope. A long-term perspective for the development and marketing of all items along with clear targets for the Sixth Plan period should be spelt out. The federated co-operative structure with large-size multi-purpose co-operative societies (LAMPS) or specialised primaries or specialised regional societies, the Tribal Development Corporations, the Forest Development Corporations and other related co-operative organisations linked to each other rationally can play a substantial role in boosting the economy. The Khadi and Village Industries Commission should become responsible for certain specific items for which they should plan and provide the technical support.

Industrially Backward Areas

15. Certain districts have been recognised as industrially backward in accordance with guidelines issued by the Government sometime back. The main criterion was the then potential for industrial development within a reasonable period. The result is that most of the tribal areas, which did not have infrastructure facilities at that time, were not included in the list of backward districts. Consequently, we find an anomalous situation. Big industries, which create their own infrastructure, have got established in these regions. But smaller industries cannot reach them because certain more advanced areas get preferential treatment over them. The industrial scene in the tribal

areas is, therefore, imbalanced. This position needs an urgent review. The entire Scheduled Area, except the industrially advanced pockets, should be treated as industrially backward and all facilities should be extended to them without any further lose of time.

Industrial Training Institutes

16. The State Governments run Industrial Institutes which provide training in a number of standard trades. These trainees, however, find it difficult to get suitable jobs in the industrial enterprises in the region because their requirements may be somewhat different or they may not come upto their standards. As a consequence, one finds co-existence of unemployed trained technicians and unfilled skilled jobs. This anomaly should be urgently resolved. The Ministry of Labour, in association with the Bureau of Public Enterprises and the concerned State Government should work out an arrangement so that the industrial enterprises assume some responsibility of guidance and managing of the ITIs in their respective regions. They could also be associated in selection of trainees and reviewing their performance during the training. Special coaching classes should be held to make up for any weakness. Wherever necessary, the contents of courses could be suitably adapted to their specific requirements and some new trades should be introduced. In some cases, management of these ITIs could be entrusted to these undertakings, who have highly qualified technical staff.

Entrepreneurial Training

17. The diversification of economy in the tribal areas is throwing up numerous opportunities of self-employment like those in small trading establishments, small repair shops for cycles, radios, hand pumps, electrical fittings, etc. Self-employment requires certain entrepreneurial skills and financial support besides technical skills. A programme of entrepreneurial development has been taken up in Bihar with considerable success. The general technical training programmes do not equip the trainees for a self-employment career. It is, therefor, necessary that a substantial programme of training in entrepreneural skills, with follow-up in helping getting financial support, marketing outlets, supply of raw material, etc., is built up. This will help in diversifying the economy of the tribal.

Bibliography

I. MINISTRY OF FOOD AND AGRICULTURE

A. Directorate of Economics and Statistics:

1. *Bulletlon of Agricultural Prices* (Weekly).
2. *Agricultural Situation in India* (Monthly).
3. *Indian Agricultural Statistics*, Vols. I and II (Annual).
4. *Estimates of Area and Yield. of Principal Crops in India* (Annual).
5. *Commodities Series* (Annual).
6. *Average Yield Per Acre of Principal Crops in India* (Quinquennial).
7. *Indian Agricultural Atlas* (Decennial).
8. *Indian Live-Stock Census* (Quinquennial).
9. *Indian Live-Stock Statistics* (Annual).
10. *Indian Forest Statistics* (Annual).
11. *A Review of Forests Administration in India* (Quinquennial)
12. *Agricultural Prices in India* (Annual).
13. *Agricultural Wages in India* (Annual).
14. *Bulletin of Food Statistics* (Annual).
15. *Food Situation in India* (Annual).
16. *Indian Land Revenue Statistics* (Annual).
17. *Indian Cotton Pressing Factories Returns* (Annual).
18. *Agricultural Economics in India* (A Bibliography).
19. *Economic Survey of Indian Agriculture* (1960-61).
20. *Studies in Agricultural Economics.*
21. *Studies in Farm Managements.*

B. Directorate of Marketing and Inspection:

Report on the Marketing of Fish in the Indian Union (1951).

C. Central Forests Department:

Annual Returns of Statistics relating to Forest Administration in India (Before 1947-48).

II. MINISTRY OF COMMERCE AND INDUSTRY

A. Department of Commercial Intelligence and Statistics:

1. *Indian Trade Journal* (Weekly).
2. *Accounts Relating to the Foreign (Sea, Air and Land) Trade and Navigation of India* (Monthly).
3. *Customs and Excise Revenue Statements of the Indian Union* (Annual).
4. *Accounts Relating to Coastal Trade and Navigation of India.*
5. *Statistics of Foreign Trade of India by Countries and Currency Areas* (Monthly).
6. *Raw Cotton Trade Statistics* (Annual).

B. Office of the Economic Adviser to the Government of India:

The Economic Adviser's Index Numbers of Wholesale Prices (Weekly).

C. Directorate of Industrial Statistics:

1. *Census of India Manufactures* (1946-58).
2. *Annual Survey of Industries* (Since 1959).
3. *Sample Survey of Manufacturing Industries* (1951-58).
4. *Journal of Trade Industry* (Monthly).

D. Textile Commissioner:

Cotton and Jute Bulletins (Monthly).

E. Iron and Steel Controller:

Statistics of Iron and Steel Industry and Trade Control (Annual).

III. MINISTRY OF FINANCE

A. Department of Research and Statistics (of the Reserve Bank of India):

1. *Reserve Bank of India Bulletin* (Monthly).
2. *Report on Currency and Finance* (Annual).
3. *Statistical Tables Relating to Banks in India* (Annual).
4. *Report on the Trend and Progress of Banking in India.*
5. *Review of Co-operative Movement in India* (Annual).
6. *Statistical Tables relating to Co-operative Movement in India* (Annual).
7. *India's Balance of Payments from 1948-49 to 1955-56.*

B. Research and Statistics Section of the Department of Company Law Administration:

1. *Monthly Blue Book of Joint Stock Companies in India* (Monthly).
2. *Joint Stock Companies in India* (Annual).

C. Statistical Branch (Income-tax) of the Central Board of Revenue:

All-India Income-Tax and Returns (Annual).

IV. MINISTRY OF LABOUR AND EMPLOYMENT

A. Labour Bureau:

1. *Indian Labour Gazette* (Monthly).
2. *Indian Labour Year Book* (Annual).
3. *Statistics of Factories* (Annual).
4. *Report on the Working of Minimum Wages Act* (Annual).
5. *Report on the Working of Workmen's Compensation Act* (Annual).
6. *Report on the Working of the Indian Trade Unions Act* (Annual).

B. Statistical Unit in the Department of Mines:

1. *Annual Report of the Chief Inspector of Mines* (Annual).
2. *Indian Coal Statistics* (Annual).
3. *Monthly Coal Bulletin* (Monthly).

C. Statistical Unit of the Ministry of Labour:

1. *Report of the First Agricultural Labour Enquiry Committee* (1950-51).
2. *Report of the Second Agricultural Labour Enquiry Committee* (1955-56).

D. Statistical Section of the Directorate of Resettlement and Employment

Handbook on Training Facilities Available in the Country (Periodical).

V. MINISTRY OF HOME AFFAIRS

A. Office of the Registrar General and Census Commissioner of India:

1. *Census Report and Tables.*
2. *Census Papers*
3. *Census Survey Reports.*

VI. MINISTRY OF HEALTH

A. Statistical Bureau:

Health Atlas of India

B. Directorate of Health Services:

Health Statistical of India.

VII. MINISTRY OF BROADCASTING

A. Director General of All-India Radio:

Report on the Progress of Broadcasting in India.

VIII. MINISTRY OF RAILWAYS

A. Railway Board:

1. *Monthly Railway Statistics* (Monthly).
2. *Annual Report on the Indian Railways* (Annual).
3. *Eastern Railway Passenger and Good Revenue Statistics for Inward and Outward Traffic Stations.*

IX. MINISTRY OF TRANSPORT

A. Statistical Branch:

Basic Road Statistics in India (Annual).

X. MINISTRY OF COMMUNICATIONS

A. Directorate of Civil Aviation:

Monthly News Letter of Civil Aviation (Monthly).

B. Directorate of Posts and Telegraphs:

Annual Report of the Post and Telegraph Departments.

XI. MINISTRY OF EDUCATION

Education in States.

XII. MINISTRY OF COMMUNITY DEVELOPMENT AND CO-OPERATIQN

XII. PLANNING COMMISSION

Other Official Publications.

A. Central Statistical Organisation:

1. *Annual Statistical Abstract* (Annual).
2. *Monthly Statistics of the Production of Selected Industries in India* (Monthly).
3. *Monthly Abstract of Statistics (Including the Quarterly Review of Economic Trends in India).*
4. *Weekly Supplement to Monthly Abstract of Statistics* (Weekly).
5. *Statistical Handbook of the Indian Union* (Occasional).
6. *Basic Statistics of Indian Economy.*
7. *Selected Plan Statistics.*
8. *Statistical System in India.*
9. *Sample Survey of Current Interest.*
10. *Handbook of Statistics According to Re-organised States.*
11. *Report on the Census of Central Government Employees.*

12. *Report on the Annual Conference of Central and State Statisticians.*
13. *Key to Current Official Statistics in India.*

B. Directorate of National Sample Surrey:

Reports on the different Rounds of NSS (Including the First Report of the Eighth Round of NSS on Land Holdings).

C. Chief Inspector of Mines:

Reports of the Chief Inspector of Mines (Annual).

D. Geological Survey of India:

1. *Records of Geological Survey of India* (Annual).
2. *Indian Minerals* (Annual).
3. *Indian Minerals* (Monthly).

E. Indian Council of Agricultural Research:

Report on Cost of Production of Crops in Principal Sugarcane and Cotton Tracts of India.

F. Central Silk Board:

Annual Reports on Silk Industry.

G. Central Water and Power Commission:

1. *Public Electricity Supply: All India Statistics, General Review.*
2. *Load Survey Report.*

H. National Income Committee:

Reports.

I. National Council of Applied Economic Research:

Reports on Techno-Economic Surveys of States and other Publications.

J. Publications of the Directorate of Economics and Statistics, Bihar:

1. *Bihar Statistical Handbook.*
2. *Bihar in Figures.*

3. *Season and Corp Reports.*
4. *Tables of Agricultural Statistics.*
5. *Annual Vital Statistics.*
6. *Record of the Activities of the Directorate.*
7. *Quarterly Bulletin of Statistics.*
8. *State Income of Bihar* (1959-60).

K. Publications of the Statistical Sections of the Following Departments of the Bihar Government:

(1) *Finance:*
  (a) *Civil Budget Estimates.*
  (b) *Financial Statements.*
(2) *Agriculture.*
(3) *Labour and Social Welfare.*
(4) *Confidential Statistics Section of the Office of the Labour Commissioner.*
(5) *Rajya Transport.*
(6) *Office of the Director of Animal Husbandry.*
(7) *Housing.*
(8) *Commercial Taxes.*
(9) *Office of the Development Commissioner.*
(10) *Co-operation Department.*
(11) *Mining and Industry.*
(12) *Health and Hygeine.*
(13) *Planning.*
(14) *Education and Tribal Welfare.*
(15) *Forest and Fisheries.*
(16) *Land Revenue.*
(17) *Office of the Cane Commissioner.*
(18) *Office of the Deputy Director of Agricultural Marketing.*
(19) *Board of Evaluation and Statistics.*

L. Publications of the Bihar State Khadi and Village Industries Board.

M. Publications of the All-India Khadi and Village Industries Commission, Bombay.

N. Publications of the Small Industries Service Institute, Patna.

O. Publications of the Institute of Applied Manpower Research. Miscellaneous Official Publications:

(1) *Indian Fisheries Bulletin.*
(2) *Indian Mining Journal.*
(3) *Lokur Committee Report.*
(4) *Indian Labour Journal.*
(5) *Statistical Summary of Mineral Production.*
(6) *Report of the Committee of Direction on Co-operative Farming.*
(7) *Report of the Bihar Unemployment Committee.*
(8) *Reports of the Central Small Industries Organisation.*
(9) *Fertilizer Statistics* (The Fertilizer Corporation of India Ltd.).
(10) *Annual Reports of Department of Mines and Metals of the Ministry of Steel and Mines.*
(11) *Annual Reports of the National Industrial Development Corporation Ltd.*

Books

1. R. Balakrishna, *Regional Planning in India.*
2. R.K. Mukherjee and H.L. Dey, *Economic Problems of Modern India.*
3. J. Friedmann and W. Alonso, *Regional Development and Planning.*
4. B.G. Verghese, *Design for Tomorrow,* Bombay.
5. Gyan Chand, *Socialist Transformation of Indian Economy,* New Delhi.
6. Kedarnath Prasad, *Technological Choice Under Development Planning,* Popular Prakashan, Bombay.
7. ——, *Bihar Ke Sadhan, Krishi Aur Udyog,* Ram Narain Lal Beni Madhava, Katra Road, Allahabad.
8. Soni and Malani, *Indian Economics.*
9. V.N. Patwardhan, *Nutrition in India.*
10. K.G. Sivaswamy, *The Co-operative Movement in Bihar,* Delhi.
11. Gorakhnath Sinha, *Food Economics,* Allahabad.
12. T.W. Freeman, *Geography and Planning,* London.
13. A.O. Hirschman, *The Strategy of Economic Development.*
14. B. Ohlin, *Inter-regional and International Trade.*
15. T.R. Sharma, *Location of Industries in India.*
16. A. Beacham and L.J. Williams, *Economics of Industrial Organisation.*

17. L. Mumford, *The Culture of Cities.*
18. V.L.S. Prakash Rao, *Regional Planning.*
19. Alfred Marshall, *Principles of Economics.*
20. N.C. Chaudhuri, *The Intellectual in India.*
21. W. Isard, E.W. Schooler and T. Vietorisz, *Industrial Complex Analysis and Regional Development.*
22. F. Machlup, *International Trade and the Foreign Trade Multiplier.*
23. Sir J. Houlton, *Bihar: The Heart of India.*

Index